Our Inquiry, Our Practice

Undertaking, Supporting, and Learning from Early Childhood Teacher Research(ers)

Gail Perry,
Barbara Henderson,
and Daniel R. Meier, editors

naeyc®

National Association for
the Education of Young
Children
1313 L Street NW, Suite 500
Washington, DC 20005-4101
202-232-8777 • 800-424-2460
www.naeyc.org

NAEYC Books

Interim Editor in Chief
Derry Koralek

Director of Creative Services
Edwin C. Malstrom

Senior Editor
Holly Bohart

Design and Production
Malini Dominey

Assistant Editor
Elizabeth Wegner

Editorial Assistant
Ryan Smith

Permissions
Lacy Thompson

Permissions

Excerpt from "Teacher research," by G. Ritchie, available online
at www.teacherscount.org/topic/topic-ritchie.shtml, is used
with permission of TeachersCount.org (www.teacherscount.org).

Credits

Managing editor: Natalie Klein
Contributing editor: Leah Schoenberg Muccio

Cover photo copyright © iStockphoto

**Our Inquiry, Our Practice: Undertaking, Supporting, and
Learning from Early Childhood Teacher Research(ers)**

Library of Congress Control Number: 2011944906

ISBN: 978-1-928896-78-4

NAEYC Item # 357

Acknowledgments

First and foremost I want to recognize the teacher researchers in our field who are the standard-bearers and substance of this work. In particular are the teacher research authors in this book and Jennifer Barrett-Mynes, Susan Kraus, Stacia Stribling, and Jeffrey Wood—all who have helped us see important dimensions of teaching and learning with young children more clearly.

My appreciation goes to Barbara Henderson and Daniel Meier, the co-editors of this book and *Voices of Practitioners*, for their vision years ago and support in making a place for teacher research in our field. I am eternally grateful to the *Voices* editorial board members, Andy Stremmel, Amos Hatch, and Frances Rust, for giving generously of their time, support, and deep knowledge of teacher research and their continuing nurturing of teacher researchers.

The editorial team at NAEYC that navigated this book through to completion is amazing. This book is a reality because of Akimi Gibson, who believed in the worthiness of promoting teachers' voices and taking the "inside-out" message of teacher research seriously. Her vision and energy and encouragement are boundless. This book would not have been possible without Natalie Klein and her skill in making text flow, careful editing, and ability to think outside the box—and all of this with good nature. I thank Bry Pollack for launching the book with firm and critical guidance, and Liz Wegner for picking up from Bry without skipping a beat and calmly and competently seeing the book through to completion. I am grateful to Derry Koralek, who agreed to take a chance on a new journal—*Voices of Practitioners*—and provided wise guidance along the way. My thanks to the always hardworking Malini Dominey for her magic touch with the design and production of the book. My new editorial associate Leah Muccio hit the ground running and handled the seemingly endless details so capably it was hard to remember she had only been at NAEYC a few months.

My family has been wonderfully supportive—especially my husband and youngest daughter Cheri, who have kept the household going and tiptoed around while I was working on the book. Even Rooney (my daughter's Lab) played his part by bounding through the barrier into my office from time to time to assure me of his continued devotion in spite of my neglect of him.

—Gail Perry

Contents

Supporting Teacher Research in Communities of Practice

About This Book

Our field is awash with books that tell teachers what to believe, what to do, and how to do it. This book is about **teachers and their practice,** but the spotlight is on teachers as knowers—their questions, concerns, and interests about their own teaching approaches and children's learning. It is about teachers' beliefs and theories and their search for answers to their questions, as they interpret and make visible the educational processes that occur each day between children and teachers in their classrooms.

It is about **undertaking research.** When you think of research in early childhood, what comes to mind? For many it is a study written by a researcher on something like the long-term effects of Head Start on children from low-income families. But this book is not about outside researchers who measure and evaluate teachers and children's behaviors. It is about research carried out by teachers in their own classrooms, teachers examining their own practice through systematic inquiry. It is about the teacher research process—**our inquiry** on **our practice**.

This book is also about the **support** system that is key in helping teacher research flourish. There is a small core of early childhood teacher educators across the country, many of whom have contributed to this book, who have incorporated teacher research into their professional preparation programs for many years. This book offers a range of strategies and innovative ideas for integrating teacher research into teacher education programs; it also offers advice for mentoring teacher research groups. Our authors discuss ways to address issues that arise when introducing teacher research to university programs or early childhood settings.

Finally, this book is about what we can **learn from teacher research(ers)** and the possibilities this offers for enriching our profession. In the **Afterword**, Susan L. Lytle takes a detailed look at the current teacher research movement. She spells out the unique contribution that early childhood teacher research brings to the conversation about the best way forward for children and teachers in meeting the complex challenges of education at large.

The main goal of this book is to generate an **understanding of teacher research** and the critical role it can play in the field of early childhood education. NAEYC aims to promote the voices of early childhood teacher researchers and their contribution to our understanding of teaching and learning. We focus on extending the practice of teacher research more broadly throughout the early childhood profession by spreading the word about teacher research—what it is and how to foster its practice.

How this book came to be: From *Voices of Practitioners* to *Our Inquiry, Our Practice*

This volume grew from NAEYC's peer-reviewed, professional online journal Voices of Practitioners: Teacher Research in Early Childhood Education. Roughly half of the chapters appearing in this compilation originated in Voices of Practitioners, although a portion were significantly revised and updated for this publication.

Voices of Practitioners started with the idea of bringing a venue for teacher research, an established feature of professional development and teacher growth at the primary and secondary level, to the field of early childhood education. Originally pitched by Daniel R. Meier and Barbara Henderson to Young Children editor Derry Koralek as a feature for that publication, the journal was granted its own home at NAEYC as an online journal, with Gail Perry as its NAEYC-based coordinator. Voices of Practitioners focuses on publishing the teacher research of early childhood educators and offers informative articles on the teacher research process, summaries of a range of teacher research initiatives and inquiry communities, and articles describing creative practices and stimulating discussions for teacher educators interested in supporting teacher research. It is guided by editors Meier, Henderson, and Perry; its editorial board (J. Amos Hatch, Frances O'Connell Rust, and Andrew J. Stremmel); and its steering committee of teacher research and early childhood experts.

Voices of Practitioners is now the only peer-reviewed journal (online or print) in the country solely devoted to the publishing of teacher research by early childhood practitioners. Now early childhood teacher research—essentially a grassroots, local effort by individuals and school sites to strengthen educational practices and teacher knowledge—has its own forum for showcasing innovative educational practices and ideas. With this volume, NAEYC aims to spread the goals of Voices of Practitioners to an even larger audience. For more information on Voices of Practitioners or to submit to the journal, please visit our website at **www.naeyc.org/publications/vop**.

Using this book

This book is designed to be both thought-provoking and practical. Its readings are grouped into two main sections—**Part I: What Is Teacher Research?** and **Part II: How Can Early Childhood Professionals Support Teacher Researchers?** The chapters in Part I describe the teacher research process and include fascinating examples of actual teacher research, and practical advice for practitioners and college students embarking on their own teacher research projects. Part II offers a critical look at how teacher research can be incorporated into professional development programs on university campuses, early childhood centers, and collegial discussions in teacher research groups. We also offer lists of additional resources in our **For Further Reading** and **Online Resources** sections to spur readers' own other interests.

We envision this book will be used as a professional development resource by practicing early childhood professionals and by teacher educators with preservice and graduate students; similarly, we hope that it will stimulate rich, collaborative discussions about teaching and learning among teachers, administrators, professional development specialists, and policy makers. Most of all, we hope that all readers will be inspired by the book to focus on inquiry in their professional lives and the possibilities it offers for the advancement of teaching and learning with young children.

Introduction

Teacher Research in Early Childhood Settings: Needed Now More than Ever

—J. Amos Hatch

It has never been more important for teachers of young children to explore ways to examine and improve their own practice. The steady drumbeat from federal, state, and local education officials is to prescribe curriculum, teaching, and evaluation models for early childhood programs. This movement assumes that curriculum producers, instruction designers, and test makers know best, even though they are isolated from the day-to-day realities of teaching young children. The professional decision making of classroom teachers under this reform model is reduced significantly. Teachers are often treated as technicians whose competency is measured by how well they match expectations based on narrowly focused criteria. Teacher research is a way for teachers to systematically examine and improve *their own* practice. It is a way for members of the early childhood education community to reassert their professional autonomy.

Teacher research is sorely needed in contemporary early childhood classrooms. It provides a means by which teachers can: (1) study the special contexts in which they work, (2) make systematic improvement in their practices, and (3) lay claim to promoting educational change that makes sense in the particular circumstances of their classrooms.

One of the defining characteristics of teacher research is that it is undertaken *in context*—it is on-the-ground inquiry generating valuable information. Teacher researchers decide what elements of their practice they want to study, what questions they want to answer, and how they will collect and analyze data to find answers that make sense in their immediate surroundings. Part of being professional educators means reflectively assessing all parts of our work; this ongoing reflective practice is greatly enhanced when teacher research identifies places where improvement is needed and assesses the effectiveness of changes made. All of the processes of teacher research take place in a particular context. Therefore, the outcomes of the inquiry are directly suited to the questions teachers have about their practice. This approach is the opposite of taking findings from large-scale studies and implementing them in prescribed ways that ignore the fact that every teacher, group of children, educational setting, and community is unique. Teacher research is grounded in the contexts that frame what really happens in early childhood classrooms. Instead of assuming that teachers are incapable of shaping their own professional development, teacher research is based on the premise that teachers can figure out what they need.

As a field, we need to assert our professional independence and demonstrate that we have the means to monitor and shape our own improvement. Teacher research provides tools that support our claims that we deserve to shape our own destinies in the classroom. Part of doing high-quality teacher research is examining the professional literature that describes what others have learned about the issues we face as teachers of young children. We want to value and utilize all of the best information available as we design and implement our teacher research projects; this is vastly different from implementing a "research-based" program designed by people who have no knowledge of the particulars of our teaching settings. By utilizing the most reliable information we can gather to inform and shape our own teacher research, we can justify our claims that we are constantly improving our practices so we can provide the best experiences possible for the children we teach.

The descriptions, explanations, and examples in this book should inform and inspire current and future early childhood teacher researchers. Now more than ever we need ways to bolster our claims to autonomy and respect. Teacher research can provide an avenue for expanding our knowledge, improving our practice, and documenting our professionalism.

What Is Teacher Research?

Part I of this book is designed to give an understanding of the teacher research process. Although the meaning of teacher research is addressed throughout the book, this section provides a grounding for readers as they zoom in from broad conceptual descriptions to actual teacher research projects to the first steps of becoming a teacher researcher.

Chapter 1, "The Nature of Teacher Research," addresses the basic components and criteria that distinguish teacher research from other types of educational research. Here, the authors examine exactly what teacher research is, providing a comprehensive view of the process and rationale for engaging in it. They delve into the heart of inquiry, leading into discussions of the difference between conventional educational research and teacher research, the distinction between teacher research and action research, and an exploration of narrative inquiry. Summaries of past studies include projects such as a toddler teacher using a photo chronology to better understand children's nonverbal communication, a preschool teacher's analysis of her own childhood experiences attending parent conferences with her Tagalog-speaking parents and how she can use this understanding to improve her teaching, and a home visitor from Head Start using dialogues with parents to study the effectiveness of her emergent literacy curriculum. These illustrate a range of research designs and their use by busy teachers to address pressing classroom issues in the diverse range of early childhood settings that comprise our field.

In the second chapter, Patricia M. Cooper discusses the work of Vivian Paley, whom many view as a consummate teacher researcher, highlighting for us what her work and writing reveals about teacher research. Based on her past scholarly interpretation of Paley's work and a recent interview, Cooper's thought-provoking discussion expands and deepens our understanding of teacher research and the value to early childhood practice.

Featured in this section and indeed counted as our most important contributions to the understanding of teacher research and its relationship to early childhood teaching and learning are five full-length studies by early childhood teachers. As they pursue their own questions, interpret their carefully collected data, and use the results to inform their practice, these teacher researchers show how teachers have "learned to move with the flow of their own questions" (Paley 1997, ix). These authors/researchers take us into the complex worlds of their toddler, preschool, and primary classrooms and the role of teacher inquiry in improving teaching and learning in context. The personal educational belief systems from which their teaching decisions are made are brought to light. Perhaps most importantly, they demonstrate how teacher inquiry can and should be woven into their day-to-day work in the classroom.

This leads us naturally to the last chapter in Part I, "Getting Started and Moving into Teacher Research." Now that we understand what teacher research is, authors Barbara Henderson and Daniel R. Meier provide the tools to embark on an actual study. A wonderful resource for teachers and preservice students, the practical framework of this chapter shows how to begin and follow through on each step of a study—including asking a researchable question, designing a study, collecting and analyzing data, writing, getting feedback from colleagues, and more.

All in all, these chapters give the reader a solid foundation in what teacher research is and what it looks like in practice in the early childhood field.

© Anna Golden

The Nature of Teacher Research

Barbara Henderson, Daniel R. Meier, Gail Perry, and Andrew J. Stremmel

Teacher research is intentional and systematic inquiry done by teachers with the goals of gaining insights into teaching and learning, becoming more reflective practitioners, effecting changes in the classroom or school, and improving the lives of children (Cochran-Smith & Lytle 1993; 1999). Teacher research stems from teachers' own questions about and reflections on their everyday classroom practice. They seek practical solutions to issues and problems in their professional lives (Corey 1953; Stringer 2007). The major components of teacher research are: conceptualization, in which teachers identify a significant problem or interest and determine relevant research questions; implementation, in which teachers collect and analyze data; and interpretation, in which teachers examine findings for meaning and take appropriate actions (McLean 1995). Teacher research is systematic in that teachers follow specific procedures and carefully document each step of the process—from formation of a question, through data collection and analysis, to conclusions and outcomes.

Teacher research takes many forms and serves a range of purposes, but it is conducted by teachers, individually or collaboratively, with the primary aim of **understanding teaching and learning in context and from the perspectives of those who live and interact daily in the classroom** (Meier & Henderson 2007; Zeichner 1999). These studies thus provide unique insider perspectives on meaningful issues in early care and education settings. A preschool or primary grade teacher, an infant/toddler caregiver, a family child care provider, or a home visitor begins an inquiry by asking a genuine question about the work in which she or he is engaged with children and families. Research questions can begin simply enough: "Should we allow pretend gunplay in any circumstances?" "How can I use storytelling to build literacy among bilingual preschoolers?" "What is it about me or my caregiving that helps me build securely attached relationships with toddlers?" Teacher researchers learn about themselves as teachers as they try to understand children's learning.

Let's take a more detailed look at the teacher research process. After defining the problem or interest, a teacher may draw upon a combination of theory and intuition, experience and knowledge of children, observation and reflection, and perhaps the experiences of valued colleagues to develop relevant questions and assumptions (hypotheses). These questions develop gradually after careful observation and deliberation about why certain things happen in the classroom. Questions are not formed with the goal of quick-fix solutions, but rather involve the desire to understand teaching or children's learning in profound ways. Information (data) is collected through multiple means, which might include doing formal and informal observation, conducting interviews, collecting artifacts, or keeping a journal, to name a few. Assumptions may be reformed or reconstructed by gathering and analyzing evidence. Ultimately, discoveries are used to further reflect on and address the original problem, and the cycle of inquiry continues as the teacher lives out the process in the classroom. This process, often more messy and disorderly than may be implied here, is nonetheless a process of reflective inquiry as shown in "The Cycle of Inquiry."

Because the word *research* is often associated with the use of rigorous scientific methods, the term *inquiry* often has been preferred. However the distinction between teacher research and conventional outsider research about teaching is less about methodology and more about the very nature of educational practice (Anderson & Herr 1999). According to Dewey ([1933] 1985), education is best practiced as inquiry, and teacher research employs the "scientific approach" to inquiry. While some teachers

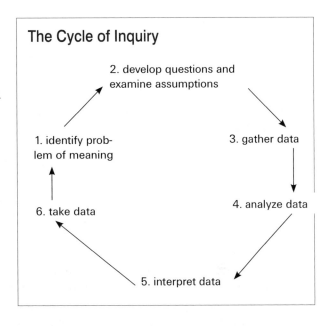

The Cycle of Inquiry

2. develop questions and examine assumptions

1. identify problem of meaning

3. gather data

6. take data

4. analyze data

5. interpret data

regard inquiry as a natural part of their everyday work in the classroom (e.g., Paley 1981), some teachers collaborate with university researchers while teaching full time in their classroom or center, contributing insights to the questions under investigation (e.g., Booth & Williams 1998; Charlesworth & DeBoer 2000; Miller 1990; Nicholls & Hazzard 1993; Stremmel & Hill 1999). Whether reflecting on experiences in the classroom or systematically studying an issue, teachers are often in the best position to ask and answer questions about children and learning.

Children are at the forefront of teacher research. The studies are usually designed to help teachers gain new ways of seeing children, develop deeper understandings of children's feelings and growth, and become more responsive to children. Children's voices are heard through their own words and gestures, photos, drawings, and any other ways by which they are best portrayed. As teachers begin to observe closely, they see children's development played out in their own unique classroom contexts, always influenced by the potentially overlapping cultures of home and school lives. Unlike with conventional educational research, children and families are not *just* the subjects of research; they are participants and often co-researchers. In this way teacher research is participatory, inclusive of differences, and democratic in nature.

Teachers who research their classrooms are systematic and deliberate in their use of observation and reflection to make sense of what they see and experience. Reflection involves a teacher's deliberate scrutiny of his or her own interpretive point of view, which is rooted in personal and formal theories, culturally learned ways of seeing, and personal core values. What distinguishes teacher research from teaching reflectively is the commitment to a disciplined method for gathering and analyzing data, and that the research can be publicly shared (Borko et al. 2007).

Although the questions and reflections teacher researchers explore are specific to their own classrooms, they enable teachers to relate particular issues to theories of teaching and learning via documentation and analysis; hence, teacher research links theory with practice (Bullough & Gitlin 2001). Teacher researchers attempt to create new knowledge (or what may be called *local knowledge*) about teaching and learning that will contribute to improving classroom practice.

Teacher research and *action research* are often used interchangeably in the literature, the latter being the preferred term in Britain (Cochran-Smith & Lytle 1993). Action research is broadly defined as a reflective process of progressive problem solving undertaken by individuals working with others as part of a community of practice to improve the way they address issues and solve problems. It is employed in many disciplines and organizations outside of education, such as by scientists or business leaders. As Meier and Henderson note (2007), not all teacher research is action research, although teacher research frequently shares the goal of some type of action to improve practice. As is evidenced in Part II of this book, teacher research also flourishes when it is lodged within a supportive network of colleagues and mentors and becomes a collaborative activity.

Teacher research examples

The following brief examples illustrate the range of formats, teacher questions, and methodologies that might be used in early childhood teacher research. For more examples of and information about teacher research, see NAEYC's online *Voices of Practitioners* journal, at www.naeyc.org/publications/vop.

Example 1

Friendships: A critical incident study of two children

A teacher of toddlers presents a photo chronology of two children's social interactions as they use the classroom environment to promote their friendship. Six photos taken over two months show critical incidents in the children's budding friendship.

The teacher adds anecdotes to accompany the photos. She also includes her analysis of how this research has increased her understanding of how the toddlers' nonverbal communication within the environment impacts their relationship.

Example 2

Improving environments with voices and images of families

A Spanish/English bilingual teacher at a state-subsidized center serving a Latino population finds ways to make her center more homelike and comfortable for children and their families. She writes vignettes of her mother's history as a teacher in rural Mexico and offers a narrative of how this relates to her own personal growth as a preschool teacher.

These family memoirs help her understand and explore the kinds of changes she wants to make in the classroom environment and why. She documents the impact of the changes by recording conversations with families about their feelings on the environment's redesign and with photos of the children and their families as they interact in the new environment.

Example 3

Understanding teaching through memories

A Filipina American teacher reflects on her English language learning as a first-grader and what it was like to attend parent conferences with her Tagalog-speaking parents. In both English and Tagalog, she tells a story of childhood shame and pride as her mother and teacher talked together. She uses her writing to consider how she supports English learners and their families in her own classroom.

Example 4

Seeing links through a home-based program

A home-based visitor from Early Head Start records and transcribes dialogues between a few parents and children with whom she works to evaluate an emergent literacy curriculum she has created. These transcripts allow her to document the effects of her intervention.

She sees results in parenting skills built through positive, low-stress opportunities for parent and child to interact over books and writing. Using these experiences, she argues that home-based programs offer families a powerful way to bridge home and school, as literacy practices become part of normal home life and parents see themselves as their child's first teachers.

Example 5

Children's behavior prompts a valuable metaphor

A veteran preschool teacher working in an inclusive classroom for transitional kindergartners finds a group of boys having persistent trouble concentrating during circle time. She begins taking field notes on the children's behavior and writes vignettes, which she shares with her colleagues. From these comes a metaphor of the Rolodex card file (as in "OK, how do I respond to this challenge? Let's see . . ." [*flip, flip, flip*]).

Using this metaphor allows her to shift her relationship with one capable child as she sees her own unintended rigidity. Instead of acting on how she thinks he should behave ("He can do this!"), she attends to his actual needs, which shifts his behavior and lets him build self-regulatory skills.

Narrative inquiry

Narrative inquiry, an important form of teacher research, is a process of studying and understanding experience through storytelling or narrative writing. Information is gathered for research through stories. The researcher then writes a narrative of the experience. "Humans are storytelling organisms who, individually and collectively, lead storied lives. Thus the study of the narrative is the study of the ways humans experience the world" (Connelly & Clandinin 1990, 2). Those engaged in narrative inquiry seek ways to enrich and transform lived experiences for themselves and others. The process of story living and telling, and reliving and retelling, are central themes in narrative inquiry. Stories are a powerful way to sharpen our inquiry skills, bringing us closer to moments and incidents of learning both for children and for ourselves. Teachers make a conscious and deliberate effort to embed stories into daily observations of children at work and play and to use stories as a way to reflect and change their teaching. In the process, they can experience shifts and changes in their identities, shifts that create changes in the way they see themselves as teachers or see children as learners.

In inquiry, teacher researchers use field notes, interviews, journals, letters, oral stories, and autobiographical memories when collecting and representing their data. Two good examples are "Understanding teaching through memories" in this chapter and Chapter 6, "Exploring the Forest: Wild Places in Childhood." In the latter study, Anna Golden incorporates memories of her own childhood and work as an artist with stories of the children's and teachers' explorations and understanding of the importance of natural places to young children.

There are connections between narrative inquiry and action research primarily in that both are focused on change and action (Connelly & Clandinin 2006; Pushor & Clandinin 2009). For example, both narrative inquiry and action research can bring to light practitioner knowledge gained through the inquiry process. In particular, narrative inquiry enables practitioner researchers to tell the stories of how they have taken action to improve their situations by improving their own learning (McNiff 2007). Through telling their stories, they gain insights into what they are doing and why they are doing it. The process provides critical "points of contact" for deepening the curriculum, improving the quality of adult-child interactions, expanding opportunities for play, and seeing more effective ways to observe children and use these reflections for increasing teacher knowledge.

Perhaps nothing is more important than keeping track of the stories of who we are and who has influenced us along the way. As Connelly and Clandinin (1990) note, narrative inquiry produces a mutually constructed story out of the lives of both researcher and participants. It is through our shared stories that we become fully known to ourselves and others, and see new possibilities for educational change.

How do teachers benefit from doing teacher research?

Through teacher research, teachers have an opportunity to shape their professional development and to validate, affirm, and improve their practice. In every teacher research project, the voice or perspective of the teacher is as important as that of the children. Giving voice to an idea is taking ownership. As Ritchie states:

> Investigating their own questions, rather than waiting for someone to tell them what to do, empowers teachers to generate their own knowledge about "what works" in teaching and learning. Teachers who conduct research are engaging in ongoing, professional learning embedded in the workplace. It encourages them to be reflective and adopt a questioning stance toward teaching and learning—what Bob Fecho calls critical inquiry pedagogy. Teachers who improve classroom teaching/learning through their inquiries become more accomplished practitioners. And, accomplished practitioners have a positive impact on student learning. In addition, the knowledge generated from classroom-based research can inform local policy decisions, by providing the evidence to back up teachers' claims about best practices. (2011)

As this book explores in Part II, teacher research benefits teachers, other professionals, and the field of early childhood education as a whole by providing an inside view of the diversity of teaching and learning in early education settings. When teachers undertake research, they deepen and improve their teaching relationships with children and with one another as professionals. The process offers an innovative approach to strengthening the professional development of early childhood professionals.

References

Anderson, G., & K. Herr. 1999. The new paradigm wars: Is there room for rigorous practitioner knowledge in schools and universities? *Educational Researcher* 28 (5): 12–21.

Booth, C., & K.C. Williams. 1998. Research partners: A new look at faculty and classroom teachers. *Journal of Early Childhood Teacher Education* 19 (3): 285–92.

Borko, H., D. Liston & J.Whitcomb. 2007. Genres of empirical research in teacher education. *Journal of Teacher Education* 58 (1): 3–11.

Bullough, R.V., & A.D. Gitlin. 2001. *Becoming a student of teaching: Linking knowledge production and practice.* 2d ed. New York: Routledge Falmer.

Charlesworth, R., & B.B. DeBoer. 2000. An early childhood teacher moves from DIP to DAP: Self-Study as a useful research method for teacher researcher and university professor collaboration. *Journal of Early Childhood Teacher Education* 21 (2): 149–54.

Cochran-Smith, M., & S. Lytle. 1993. *Inside/outside: Teacher research and knowledge.* New York: Teachers College Press.

Cochran-Smith, M., & S.L. Lytle. 1999. The teacher research movement: A decade later. *Educational Researcher* 28 (7): 15–25.

Connelly, F.M., & D.J. Clandinin. 1990. Stories of experience and narrative inquiry. *Educational Researcher 19* (5): 2-14.

Connelly, F.M., & D.J. Clandinin. 2006. Narrative inquiry. In *Handbook of complementary methods in education research*, 3d ed., eds. J.L. Green, G. Camilli & P. Elmore, 477–87. Mahwah, NJ: Erlbaum.

Corey, S.M. 1953. *Action research to improve school practices.* New York: Teachers College Bureau of Publications, Columbia University.

Dewey, J. [1933] 1985. *How we think, a restatement of the relation of reflective thinking to the educative process.* Boston: Heath.

Fecho, B. 2004. *Is this English? Race, language, and culture in the classroom.* New York: Teachers College Press.

Hankins, K.H. 1998. Cacophony to symphony: Memoirs in teacher research. *Harvard Educational Review* 68 (1): 80–95.

McLean, J. 1995. *Improving education through action research: A guide for administrators and teachers.* The Practicing Administrator's Leadership Series: Roadmaps to Success. Thousand Oaks, CA: Corwin.

McNiff, J. 2007. My story is a living educational theory. In *Handbook of narrative inquiry: Mapping a methodology,* ed. D.J. Clandinin, 308–29. Thousand Oaks, CA: Sage.

Meier, D.R., & B. Henderson. 2007. *Learning from young children in the classroom: The art and science of teacher research.* New York: Teachers College Press.

Miller, J. 1990. *Creating spaces and finding voices: Teachers collaborating for empowerment.* Albany, NY: State University of New York Press.

Nicholls, J.G., & S.P. Hazzard. 1993. *Education as adventure: Lessons from the second grade.* New York: Teachers College Press.

Paley, V.G. 1981. *Wally's stories.* Cambridge, MA: Harvard University Press.

Pushor, D., & D.J. Clandinin. 2009. The interconnections between narrative inquiry and action research. In *The Sage handbook of educational action research*, eds. S. Noffke & B. Somekh, 290–300. Thousand Oaks, CA: Sage.

Ritchie, G. *Teacher research.* Accessed October 12, 2011. www.teacherscount.org/topic/topic-ritchie.shtml.

Stremmel, A.J., & L.T. Hill. 1999. Towards multicultural understanding: A reflective journey. In *Affirming diversity through democratic conversations*, eds. V.R. Fu & A.J. Stremmel, 141–55. Upper Saddle River, NJ: Prentice Hall.

Stringer, E.T. 2007. *Action research.* 3d ed. Thousand Oaks, CA: Sage.

Zeichner, K. 1999. The new scholarship in teacher education. *Educational Researcher* 28 (9): 4–15.

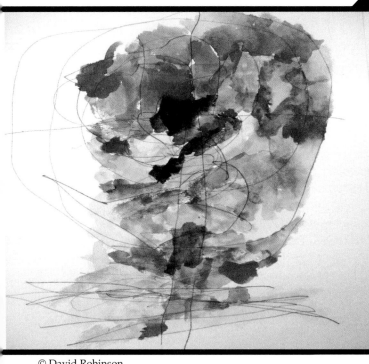

Chapter

02

Understanding Vivian Paley as a Teacher Researcher

Patricia M. Cooper

When I had been teaching about four years or so, I agreed to participate in a research project investigating the impact of the dictation and dramatization activities Vivian Paley introduced in Wally's Stories: Conversations in the Kindergarten *(1981) on young children's narrative development. I had not yet read the book, and wouldn't until the study was over. My role was to implement the activities regularly in my kindergarten classroom. Separate from the study or the results (see McNamee et al. 1985) was the impact of the process on my identity as a teacher of young children. The effect was, quite literally, immediate. Gone was my concern over the mundane in teaching. Gone was my worry about an understimulating curriculum. Dictation and dramatization—or what Paley calls storytelling and story acting—not only made me a teacher of stories, it made me a student of child development. Suddenly, there was so much I needed to understand about young children's thinking. Why, for example, did so many of my children's stories end when the main character fell in a hole, or why did some children tell stories but not act in them (at least initially), or why was Darth Vader so very, very important to 5-year-olds? Later I would come to see how much of my reaction mimicked Paley's own. This makes sense, given the riches storytelling and story acting reveal about young children's thinking. The only thing I knew at the time was that the feeling was thrilling.*

Eventually, I moved from the classroom to the director's office and, ultimately, to teacher education. Along the way, Paley supplied me with a steady stream of things to think about, teach, and research. I have written elsewhere on storytelling and story acting as curriculum, as well as its impact on early literacy development (see Cooper 1993; 2005; Cooper et al. 2007). I also conducted an analysis of Paley's body of work to uncover what I call her pedagogies of meaning and fairness (Cooper 2009).

Over time, I have had the pleasure of getting to know Paley, who agreed to be interviewed for this book. She has not previously spoken on the subject for print.

Vivian Paley has been identified with the teacher research movement since the 1980s. It's also fair to say that her 13 books and stack of articles on young children's development in school have had a major impact on teacher research. In their popular book on teacher research, Cochran-Smith and Lytle (1993) describe Paley as a conceptual researcher. Clandinin and Connelly (2000) and Lyons and LaBoskey (2002) look to her as a narrative inquirer. More recently, Meier and Stremmel (2010) describe her as the "consummate teacher researcher" of narrative inquiry. Related narrative-dominated research traditions, such as autoethnography, literary documentary, and hermeneutics, also include Paley in their ranks (see Burdell & Swadener 1999; Carter 1993; Clift & Albert 1998; Göncü & Becker 2000; Preskill 1998; Reifel 2007).

Paley's books and articles have been continuously employed in teacher education for over three decades to bridge the distance between theory and practice for preservice teachers, a service all good teacher research provides. She is self-conscious in addressing this stubborn disconnect between research on teaching and what it means to be in a classroom when she writes, "the way life in the classroom reinterprets the research" (Paley 1990, 19). Paley is referring here, of course, to traditional education research in which the teacher is not the investigator and generalizability is the desired outcome of the findings. Teacher research, on the other hand, is conducted by the teacher; the desired outcome is *authenticity.*

Paley's own views

Ironically, Paley has long rejected the mantle of teacher researcher. Similarly, she prefers the title of storyteller over theory-maker, especially when it refers to relations with children "who do not assume expected roles" (Paley 1990, 32). Her true priority is to remain open to discovery. As Philip Jackson writes in the Introduction to her *Boys and Girls: Superheroes in the Doll Corner* (1984), Paley aims not to advance any other agenda but what she has learned on the ground about children and being a teacher of children. When asked directly if she is a teacher or a researcher, Paley says there is no question. She is a teacher, albeit "a teacher who writes books" (Paley 2011). To borrow from Paley herself, her themes are: "What does it feel like to be a teacher?" and "What does it feel like to be a child?" ([1979] 2000, xvii). Indeed, what categorizes Paley's teaching is the element of surprise. That is, not proof of a hypothesis, but the unanticipated evidence against it; not a method of investigation, but an individual child who changes its direction (Paley [1979] 2000). The embodiment of Dewey's master teacher, Paley does not trade in the *doing* of research and theory; she trades in *translating* it, or as noted above, "reinterpreting it" into real life.

That said, Paley is willing to indulge the obvious. "Good teaching at any level," she postulates, "involves teacher research" (2011). Lest we be confused, however, this should not be misconstrued as a concession on Paley's part as to her self-identity. "I cannot be given a label by anyone that I do not choose to give myself," she insists.

Interestingly, the label Paley chooses is "anecdotist" (2011). She reveals her decision in the epigraph for her latest book, *The Boy on the Beach: Building Community through Play* (2010):

DEAR YU-CHING:

I have a name for us. We are anecdotists. The dictionary says this is someone who collects and tells little stories. Of course, our stories are all about young children, but I think the name fits.

DEAR VIVIAN:

Do anecdotists ask why? If so, then I agree to be called an anecdotist.
—Letters to and from Taiwan

Do anecdotists ask why? Clearly, Paley means us to believe they do. But so do many teacher researchers. Thus, despite our respect for Paley's right to choose her own label, we persist in bestowing upon her at least honorary status as a teacher researcher because evidence and analysis suggests we have cause. Having taken this liberty, however, it behooves us to remember that for the most part we have reasoned backward about Paley's work in this regard. That is, we have drawn assumptions about her research based on our assumptions about teacher research, without truly understanding the process by which she conducts her investigations. The problem is this not only ignores her resistance to the label of teacher researcher, it underestimates the complexity of her research accomplishment.

The question for teachers, teacher educators, and teacher researchers is: What can we learn from Paley about teacher research despite, and perhaps because of, the way in which she views her own investigations?

Paley as a teacher researcher

Operating within the qualitative tradition, teacher research has been defined as a systematic, intentional inquiry by a teacher designed to explain a phenomenon or answer a question. Methodologies vary, but analysis is typically circumscribed on all levels by its relevance inside the teacher's classroom. The primary measure of validity is increased teacher knowledge and improved instruction at the local level (Cochran-Smith & Lytle 1993). At the same time, the possibility of universal themes breaking through is not precluded. Arguably, this is the source of its deep appeal to its many advocates and readers.

Paley as a conceptual teacher researcher

In their delimitation of categories and types of teacher research, Cochran-Smith and Lytle describe what they mean when casting Paley as a conceptual teacher researcher, or a scribe of the full-length essay:

> In conceptual research, teachers recollect and reflect on their experiences to construct an argument about teaching, learning, and schooling. Drawing on students' work and classroom observations, for which there may or may not be complete written records, teachers write essays to convince others about particular ways to teach and understand the processes of teaching and learning. They also theorize about children's learning and development, the school as workplace, professional growth across contexts, and sources of knowledge. (1993, 35)

Summing up this effort at "making meaning," the authors borrow from Erikson ([1950] 1985), to conclude that conceptual researchers choose "examples [from the data] that provide for a more public audience a kind of 'evidentiary warrant' for the general assertions" (Cochran-Smith & Lytle 1993, 35). Also, the authors contrast conceptual teacher research with its sister category, empirical research. The latter more closely resembles traditional qualitative research in that it requires the collection, analysis, and interpretation of data, albeit modified by the teacher's impact on it. The three types of teacher research in this category are journals, oral inquiries, and studies.

The impact of conceptual research can be powerful, often making its mark on classrooms well beyond the boundaries of traditional education research. Cochran-Smith and Lytle (1993) remind us of Sylvia Ashton-Warner's groundbreaking *Teacher* (1963), as well as Herbert Kohl's *36 Children* (1967), which has been credited with starting the post-war campaign to reform urban schools (Freedman 1998). Paley's own *White Teacher* ([1979] 2000) is viewed by some as the model, albeit at times a controversial one, for the many books by white teachers of children of color that followed its publication (Willis & Harris 2004).

On one level, all of Paley's books fit Cochran-Smith and Lytle's above description of conceptual research quite neatly. Each employs recollection, reflection, and argument. Each aims to theorize and persuade, to change the conversation. In *Wally's Stories*, Paley intends to "search for the child's point of view with which I can help him take a step further" (1981, 213). By the book's end, however, the reader is poised, like Paley, to accept that the magical thinking and fantasy play that characterize the kindergarten year does not need interference or interruption, but extension.

Paley and narrative inquiry

Although valuable for its emphasis on the pragmatic, a problem with the categorization of Paley as a conceptual researcher is that it does not adequately reflect her methods or the way in which her findings expand and mature. In fact, of her 13 books, only *A Child's Work: The Importance of Fantasy Play* (2004) can truly be described as a full-length essay; in this book Paley takes on the wrongheadedness of the academic kindergarten. All of her other work has far more in common with the short narrative or "literary tale," a term Paley uses to describe *The Girl with the Brown Crayon* (1997). The well-known "characters" of her tales include Wally, Mollie, Jason, Ayana, Reeny, Teddy, and the boy on the beach. Then there are the boys and girls in the doll corner, the bad guys without birthdays, and those who can't play. Grown-ups include Mrs. Tully and, of course, Paley. As in all good tales, these characters become better known to us as the tales progress. However, what happens to them only reaches significance for the reader, as it does for Paley, when she interprets earlier stories in light of later developments, and thus creates new stories altogether.

This recursive nature of Paley's work is precisely what moves it out of conceptual research and into narrative inquiry. According to Clandinin and Connelly, the way to think about narrative inquiry is as "both the phenomena under study and as a method of study," or a way to both "represent and understand experience" (2000, 4). In story terms, as it is often discussed, they see it as "stories lived and stories told" (2000, 20). Meier and Stremmel refer to narrative inquiry as "reliving and retelling" stories that "enrich and transform" the lives of researcher and participants (2010, 1). Lyons and LaBoskey also defend the role of storytelling in narrative inquiry, but sum up the task simply as a methodology to ask why humans do what they do (2002, 163). Like anecdotists—like Paley.

Paley's Methodology

Questioning

A paradox of Paley's resistance to being labeled a teacher researcher of any sort is her expert use of its tools in general, narrative inquiry in particular. Her research always emanates from an experience that needs explaining or a question that needs answering, to which she invariably adds the additional undercurrent of *why*. Hundreds of whys. For example, in the preface to *White Teacher*, Paley reveals her original question: Is this classroom in which I live a fair place for every child who enters? But that's a clinical question. Soon, the whys follow: Why does she talk so much about black children? Why would a black child fear her? And why does she favor Ayana over the other black children? In *The Boy Who Would Be a Helicopter: Uses of Storytelling in the Classroom* (1990), she invites us to wonder what makes Jason the "quintessential outsider" and the key to the moral landscape of school. However, her search cannot be disassociated from her need to understand why a child is not happy at school. And her effort to understand the purpose of children's storytelling in *Wally's Stories* (1981) soon leads her to ask why all superhero stories are the same.

In other words, for Paley a research question is never set in stone; nor is it in teacher research, as discussed elsewhere in this volume. It's always metamorphosing based on new revelations, from the beginning of each study until its end. And, at the risk of exhausting us, Paley often doesn't stop at that. Many of her studies resume explorations from earlier works when subsequent experiences intrude on her consciousness; in doing so, she revisits all or portions of the original text. This is especially characteristic of her three books that center on race, through which she moves from the teacher's perspective, to the community's, to the child's. Unfortunately, her first is the most visible—*White Teacher* is often viewed in a stand-alone context, undermining Paley's fuller perspective on race in the classroom.

The overt attempt to re-see her own work is also evident in *Wally's Stories*. She revisits its concluding remarks—"Our contract reads more like this: if you will keep trying to explain yourselves I will keep showing you how to think about the problems you need to solve"—close to 10 years later in *The Boy Who Would Be a Helicopter*. As she tells the reader,

> After a few years the contract needed to be rewritten. . . . Let me study your play and figure out how play helps you solve your problems. Play contains your questions, and I must know what questions you are asking before mine will be useful. (1990, 18)

Collecting and analyzing data

In terms of data collection methods, Paley's classroom studies always involve use of the tape recorder. It is a well-regarded tool of narrative inquiry, according to Clandinin and Connelly, because "if stories are the target, we need to get them right" (2000, 79). Paley's assessment verifies this. The tape recorder, she writes,

> . . . has become an essential tool for capturing the sudden insight, the misunderstood concept, the puzzling juxtaposition of words and ideas. I began to tape several years ago in an effort to determine why some discussions zoomed ahead in an easy flow of ideas and others plodded to a halt, and I was continually surprised by what I was missing in all discussions. (1981, 217)

My recent interview with Paley sheds even more light on her use of the tape recorder, transcription, and control for anonymity. First, she is adamant that the only valid data on the tape comes from what children say in her presence. Voices recorded when the teacher is not there, she says, are without context and amount to no more than eavesdropping. Children, she insisted, must not be tricked into saying what is private. The wisdom in this method is clear, however deeply nuanced, reflecting Paley's beliefs about teaching and research. It is the world children are willing to share with us, not their private lives, that can be known and influenced. All else must be left alone.

When transcribing the tapes, Paley eliminates all the natural disruptions in young children's speech, such as backtracking, repeated phrases, unintentional misspeak, and sounds like "um" or "uh." (This also accounts for why the children's conversations in her books often appear so fluent to the reader.) She refers to this as "transcribing for meaning" (Paley 2011). Again, it gets her closer to the "phenomena of experience" (Clandinin & Connelly 2000), even as it becomes one of the methods by which she tells the story.

Paley's data analysis extends this effort and also adheres to recognized standards for narrative inquiry with regard to uncovering meaning. As to what by now should be expected, she says it comes down to: "What's the story in this?" Like Anton Chekhov, one of Paley's literary heroes, she is interested not in the merely representative when searching for meaning in the data, but in what she calls "the extreme moments of humanity" (2011). We might think of them as the super-representative. But, this is only the first layer of meaning. In *The Boy on the Beach*, she also calls upon Virginia Woolf in referring to moments of discovery in the story in which "life stand still here" long enough for both children and observers "to watch the ways chaos finds a sensible shape" (2010, 13).

However, if Paley maintains a set of literary references to frame her approach to research, she also resists the concept of story as metaphor, individually or collectively, as it generates the assumption that the stories are somehow less than real or meaningful in and of themselves. For Paley, as for narrative inquirers in general, "My stories always boil down to [the fact that] *they are true*" (2011, emphasis hers).

Another standard method of teacher research that is explicitly tested in narrative inquiry is the use of anonymity, especially when children are involved. Because story is the unit of analysis, and reconstruction of the stories creates the findings, the question of whose story is being told raises special concerns. To guarantee anonymity, Paley naturally changes names, titles, and so on. Where gender and ethnicity are not vital to the meaning of an event, she changes these, too. (One exception is the story of the child Paley called Jason, the boy who would be a helicopter, whose family gave permission for her to reveal his gender and other telling details about his story.)

When writing about her own classroom in the somewhat insular community of Hyde Park, where she also lives, Paley collapses two years' worth of data into one, so as to belie any outsider's effort to identify a particular cohort of children. While as much as two years' worth of data undoubtedly complicates Paley's presentation, it also allows her to demonstrate her skills as a storyteller. This is akin to what she believes is the best thing about her teaching—her "habit of drawing invisible lines between the children's images" that, in effect, stitch stories together for greater meaning (Paley 1990, xi).

The drawing of invisible lines for the reader is also captured in Clandinin and Connelly's (2000) three-dimensional model of data analysis in narrative inquiry. According to the authors, all data is simultaneously comprised of the temporal, the personal and social, and the place (2000, 54). There can be no doubt that Paley's interpretations of data rests on her control of all three. Listen to how she opens *Mollie Is Three: Growing Up in School*: "On the first day, Mollie sits quietly at the playdough table watching Frederick. She is waiting to find out what happens in school, and he is someone who makes things happen" (1986, 1).

This introduces what we might call a fourth dimension of narrative inquiry: positioning findings for the intended audience (Clandinin & Connelly 2000, 167). As a storyteller, Paley prefers to think in dramatic terms. "The point was this: Just as I transcribed from the tape recorder for meaning, I transcribed the community for classroom theater." It is, she insists, "the primary way we get to know the children in our classroom" (2011).

Conclusion

Because Paley does not willingly accept her role as a teacher researcher, I conclude with letting her "storytelling methodology" stand on its own. The following excerpt from the last few pages of *The Boy Who Would Be a Helicopter* provides the evidence. Up to this point Paley has been watching, recording, and reflecting on Jason's broken and repaired helicopter stories and events for the better part of the school year. Though Jason has autistic-like symptoms, Paley warns us in the preface that she refuses to "attach a label to him" (as she refuses to label herself). He is to be known, she advises, only through the unfolding of his story.

Yet, despite Paley's masterly efforts to know and integrate both Jason and his broken helicopter story into the larger classroom narrative, she is not able to figure out its true meaning for most of the book. She grows somewhat despondent. Then, late in the spring, Jason invents a scenario in which he uses a "three-seater"—functioning—helicopter to "pick someone up at school. Because not anyone will come to pick them up and bring them home. They're going to hold everyone's hand," he tells Samantha, a fellow classmate. "One kid's going to hold the other kid's hand" (1990, 146). Paley suddenly realizes this is the story Jason has been trying to tell her and the children. She writes:

> Jason may be revealing the biggest piece of the story. In his fantasy play no one has arrived to take the schoolchildren home; *the child is lost at school.* Jason's helicopter will be the agent of rescue from school to home. The ultimate fear and loss, Jason tells us, is separation. (1990, 147. Emphasis in the original.)

Then, accessing the privilege of a good teacher (or narrative inquirer), Paley goes further to identify being alone as a concern for all young children in school, despite this being an unusually dark take on early childhood education. Paley uses Jason's story, then, to write a new one for her and other teachers. "If [Jason] is right," she informs us,

> aside from all else we try to accomplish, we have an awesome responsibility. We must become aware of the essential loneliness of each child. Our classrooms, at all levels, must look more like happy families and secure homes, the kind in which all family members can tell their private stories, knowing they will be listened to with affection and respect. (1990, 147)

Paley says she ends the year with more questions than answers, "as always." The book's epilogue is called "New Questions."

It seems clear that the teacher research community has not erred in associating Paley with its pursuit of authentic representations of classroom life. Method and mission indeed appear to overlap in significant ways. Yet, it also seems clear that Paley's resistance to accepting the label of teacher researcher is not only her prerogative, but a message to the teacher research community that must not be taken lightly. A hallmark of teacher research has always been the latitude it grants practitioners in terms of how they position themselves in relation to their work and their audience. Surely this extends to Paley, however inconvenient or confusing for the teacher research community it may sometimes prove. The more important truth is that it does not matter what we label Vivian Paley in the end if our goal is authenticity. It only matters that we disseminate her work to the next generation of early childhood teachers, so that they, too, may tame the classroom chaos to find and study where life stands still.

References

Ashton-Warner, S. 1963. *Teacher.* New York: Simon and Schuster.

Burdell, P., & B.B. Swadener. 1999. Critical personal narrative and autoethnography in education: Reflections on a genre. *Educational Researcher* 28 (6): 21–26.

Carter, K. 1993. The place of story in the study of teaching and teacher education. *Educational Researcher* 13 (1): 5–12.

Clandinin, D.J., & F.M. Connelly. 2000. *Narrative inquiry: Experience and story in qualitative research.* San Francisco: Jossey-Bass.

Clift, R.T., & L.R. Albert. 1998. Early learning and continued development for teachers: Teachers as researchers. In *Issues in early childhood educational research,* eds. B. Spodek, O.N. Saracho & A.D. Pellegrini, 139–55. New York: Teachers College Press.

Cochran-Smith, M., & S.E. Lytle. 1993. *Inside/outside: Teacher research and knowledge.* New York: Teachers College Press.

Cooper, P.M. 1993. *When stories come to school: Telling, writing, and performing stories in the early childhood classroom.* New York: Teachers & Writers Collaborative.

Cooper, P.M. 2005. Literacy learning and pedagogical purpose in Vivian Paley's 'Storytelling Curriculum.' *Journal of Early Childhood Literacy* 5 (3): 229–51.

Cooper, P.M. 2009. *The classrooms all young children need: Lessons in teaching from Vivian Paley.* Chicago: University of Chicago Press.

Cooper, P.M., K. Capo, B. Mathes & L. Grey. 2007. One authentic early literacy practice and three standardized tests: Can a storytelling curriculum measure up? *Journal of Early Childhood Teacher Education* 28 (3): 25–75.

Erikson, E. [1950] 1985. *Childhood and society.* New York: Norton.

Freedman, S.G. 1998. A century of art on a blackboard canvas. *New York Times,* May 17, 1998.

Göncü, A., & J. Becker. 2000. The problematic relation between developmental research and educational practice. *Human Development* 43 (4/5): 266–72.

Kohl, H. 1967. *36 children.* New York: New American Library.

Lyons, N., & V.K. LaBoskey. 2002. *Narrative inquiry in practice: Advancing the knowledge of teaching.* New York: Teachers College Press.

McNamee, G.D., J. McLane, P.M. Cooper & S.M. Kerwin. 1985. Cognition and affect in early literacy development. *Early Child Development and Care* 20: 229–44.

Meier, D., & A.J. Stremmel. 2010. Narrative inquiry and stories—The value for early childhood teacher research. *Voices of Practitioners: Teacher Research in Early Childhood Teacher Education* 5 (4): 1–4. Online: www.naeyc.org/files/naeyc/file/vop/VOP_MeierStremmel.pdf.

Paley, V.G. 1981. *Wally's stories: Conversations in the kindergarten.* Cambridge, MA: Harvard University Press.

Paley, V.G. 1984. *Boys and girls: Superheroes in the doll corner.* Chicago: University of Chicago Press.

Paley, V.G. 1986. *Mollie is three: Growing up in school.* Chicago: University of Chicago Press.

Paley, V.G. 1990. *The boy who would be a helicopter: The uses of storytelling in the classroom.* Cambridge, MA: Harvard University Press.

Paley, V.G. 1997. *The girl with the brown crayon.* Cambridge, MA: Harvard University Press.

Paley, V.G. [1979] 2000. *White teacher.* Cambridge, MA: Harvard University Press.

Paley, V.G. 2004. *A child's work: The importance of fantasy play.* Chicago: University of Chicago Press.

Paley, V.G. 2010. *The boy on the beach: Building community through play.* Chicago: University of Chicago Press.

Paley, V.G. Interview by author. September 20, 2011, New York.

Preskill, S. 1998. Narratives of teaching and the quest for the second self. *Journal of Teacher Education* 49 (5): 344–45.

Reifel, S. 2007. Hermeneutic Text Analysis of Play. In *Early Childhood Qualitative Research,* ed. J.A. Hatch, 25–43. New York: Routledge.

Willis, A., & V.J. Harris. 2004. Afterword. In *Multicultural issues in literacy research and practice,* eds. A. Willis, G.E. Garcia, R. Barrera & V.J. Harris, 290–96. Mahwah, NJ: Lawrence Erlbaum.

Two's Company, Three's a Crowd:

Peer Interactions in a Preschool Social Triangle

Christopher Taaffe

Even long-time teachers like **Christopher Taaffe** often struggle to deal productively with children's social conflict. This study explores how even very young children form intense social bonds with peers, and how complex their social interactions can be. A real strength of this study is how it reveals the social competence of children who have just turned 3—competence attained far earlier than traditional developmental theories would suggest. Taaffe becomes increasingly aware of the reason and need behind the children's behavior, and uses his insider status as their teacher to make changes to the curriculum to serve them and the class as a whole.

The study's findings are strongly linked with the broader literature, demonstrating how teacher research can add significantly to the educational knowledge base. In fact, there are few naturalistic studies of triad relationships with children this young. Taaffe has a sharp eye for observing children in their element. His observations capture the girls as they talk amongst themselves and in their interactions with teachers. Peer-to-peer conversations are some of the most telling evidence showing how much of what looks like simple social aggression is actually a workshop for children's thinking about how to get along.

—Barbara Henderson

Lisa is the last of three girls bobbing across the yard, playing follow the leader on yellow Hoppity-Hops. "Wait for me, guys! Play with me, guys!" she begs. Ellen and Gretchen don't stop or look back. Other children peer up anxiously as Lisa, in tears, wails plaintively, "You guys have to play with me. Play with me, guys." The other two bounce on, ignoring her. Lisa notices me watching and cries out, "I want them to play with me and they won't. They won't!" My answer is naïve, unaware: "But you are—you're hopping right with them!" Her face is a mask of misery and panic. "No, they won't play with me!" But a short while later it is Gretchen who is hurtling herself face down onto the sand, tears streaming, wailing that Lisa won't play with her. Lisa is now running happily with Ellen.

A few days later . . . Gretchen and Ellen are in the block area happily using tools. As Ellen watches, Lisa moves in and tries to grab a toy shovel from Gretchen, who resists and pulls back. Lisa retorts, "Let's go play somewhere else, Ellen!" Ellen replies brightly, "Yes! Let's go play in the playhouse," [dramatic play area] and they leave. Gretchen is bereft, sobbing.

Ellen, Gretchen, and Lisa, not yet 3, were locked for many weeks in a social triangle, wrenched by escalating clashes over who got to play with whom at any given time. Like other young preschool girls, each one strongly preferred to play in a dyad (Benenson 1993). As all three initially refused to play with any other children, one of the girls was always left out. The excluded child would invariably throw a tantrum, screaming at and sometimes even physically attacking the other two. Even more upsetting, the trio rearranged their pairings several times an hour. Each shift would result in tears, shouts, frustration, and anger. This deeply stressed the girls, interrupted their play time, and sharply disturbed the other children's activities. As scenes such as those unfolded, I asked myself: What micro-events, what confluence of factors, causes these abrupt re-pairings? If I could answer that, I might be able to help ease them past their conflicts less painfully.

As a veteran early childhood educator, I don't expect a conflict-free classroom. But these were not the typical toddler disputes. They were similar to the pitched emotional battles over friendships and play partners often seen in older children (Underwood 2003.) Oddly, too, this was the second year in a row my class included a very contentious play triangle. The previous time it had been three boys, so gender didn't seem to be a factor. The children's harsh strife, deep anguish at being excluded, and disruption of other children's play all greatly troubled me. This led me to the questions at the heart of my teacher research: How could my coteachers and I figure out what was going on in the girls' interactions? **What could we do to help these children manage their relationships?** My initial impulse was to somehow understand the source of these painful incidents mainly so we might anticipate and prevent them.

Review of literature

A large body of literature describes typical child development and the evolving cognitive and affective capabilities that underlie young children's growing social competence. Much research describes the typical maturation of emotion, empathy, thinking, and language involved in play among 2s and 3s (Brownell & Kopp 2007). However, practical help for educators regarding classroom management strategies, and teachers' roles in scaffolding positive peer interactions with older toddlers, is limited within early childhood research. Its inquiries usually focus on correlates and effects of behavior. A few studies describe teacher strategies to help less-skilled children enter play with available partners (Bullock 1988; Fox & Lentini 2006; Gillespie & Hunter 2010; Hazen & Black 1984), although this wasn't quite the situation we faced. The same was true of other studies that examine how children interact in short-lived three-way child encounters in the laboratory (Ishikawa & Hay 2006; McLloyd et al. 1984). However, I could find no naturalistic or clinical research about young preschoolers involved in exclusive, persistent and highly conflicting groups of three.

Peer-culture studies helped me better understand the trio's tumultuous encounters (Corsaro 2003; Kantor et al. 1993; Neimark 2012). As I read this work I began to see that children's exclusions and rejections were not necessarily cruel or even artless. The central tenet of such studies is that children are social agents, shaping their relational networks and seeking to control their social worlds outside of adult agendas. The peer culture literature reminds teachers to focus on the child's point of view, on how any given behavior is meant to serve her goals of creating knowledge or connection (Avgitidou 2001). In this view, when children hoard certain toys, dominate certain spaces at school, invent private language or rituals, speak harshly to each other, or exclude each other (all behavior that Ellen, Lisa, and Gretchen used regularly), these interactions serve as little workshops in which they gradually forge satisfying processes of play and companionship.

Older toddlers, more aware of the delights of shared play and gradually moving into more collaborative play, are just learning the complicated skills of keeping these play connections going. Their play with other children may feel so fragile and precarious to them (Corsaro 2003) that they act to protect it with exclusionary behavior or verbal aggression. Such acts may not be the evidence of selfishness, defiance, or even antisocial impulses that many adults tend to assume. As I started this study, the intensity of the triad's conflicts, and their appearance so early in preschool, tended to make me wonder if the girls' hurtful behavior resulted from emotional disequilibrium or even aggressive traits.

The constructivist view of child development says that children actively assemble knowledge and meaning, rather than just imitating others or passively receiving understandings. Piaget (1966) saw this process of cognitive growth as a mainly internal, solitary process, with only peripheral attention to the role of play with others. Vygotsky (1978), in contrast, described such learning as occurring mainly in social contexts, during moments of close collaboration in shared activities. The notion that children develop an ability to see that other people have feelings or understandings different than their own is called the "theory of mind." This ability is key to collaborative learning. How were the three girls learning from each other's reactions in these situations, and what were they learning?

The sociocultural perspective of Rogoff and others provides another frame for this teacher research. The customary practices, values, and language of a society shape its children's encounters with each other. Children's behavior mirrors cultural norms of emotional expression, friendship, community, status, conflict, and property (Rogoff 2003). Culture and economic class also mold the teaching methods and child behavior that early childhood teachers consider appropriate (Tobin et al. 2011). For instance, in Japanese culture, preschool teachers permit other children to tease or exclude certain girls so as to evoke their *amae,* or culturally-valuable feeling of loneliness, and *sudan shugi,* or social mindedness (Hayashi & Tobin 2009). My own culture model led me to suppress conflicts and "negative" feelings.

My frame of reference

My upbringing provided another frame, teaching me to see the exclusion of others, or the refusal to share, as selfish and egoistic. To nurture children and better our society, I'd always taught children to treat each other gently and avoid excluding others as part of building their sense of community. Prior to this study, in my role as a teacher I uncritically endorsed the "you can't say you can't play" guidelines (Harrist & Bradley 2003; Paley 1992), automatically insisting in each situation that children include all others who wish to join in.

My own teacher training also affected my thinking about conflict between children. Echoing Piaget's theories, it taught me that young children are egoistic thinkers, and therefore, empathetic behavior couldn't develop until later in childhood (Piaget 1966). I learned from this that young children require adult instruction to form positive social attitudes, and that children's clashes were to be minimized as antisocial.

My initial research on the sources of the girls' painful interactions challenged prior assumptions. Looking closely into the causation of the girls' sudden regroupings, exploring what insight they gained and how they gleaned social knowledge, all changed my perspective. I had wanted to see how my colleagues and I could lessen classroom discord and help children manage their relationships. What I didn't know beforehand was that my study would greatly shift how I understood the functions of conflict, which in turn influenced how the children related with each other.

Design of the study

The participants and the setting

My teacher research project included three children and three teachers in the oldest toddler class of a private preschool. I started collecting data halfway through the school year. Lisa, who was sturdy, lively, passionate, and opinionated, was most likely to express negative feelings about the others' behavior, and often tried to direct their play. Ellen, verbal and impish, often negotiated her way back into a dyad by using skills of planning and persuasion. Gretchen was the most outwardly emotional one, most upset by exclusions or frustrations. She needed the most help from teachers to regain her equilibrium. All three loved dancing, chasing, trying new materials at the art table, and playing under the climbing structure or in the dramatic play area.

The children came from intact, two-parent, middle-class families. All were Caucasian, like 76 percent of my students. The 17 children in the class ranged in age from 24 to 34 months when they started in the fall.

My school is a private nonprofit in a university town with a full-day, play-based program using an emergent curriculum approach and emphasizing social-emotional learning. Our class, housed in a modest-sized room, has many learning materials available on open shelves and an inviting dramatic play area in a roomy alcove three steps up from the main room. We have our own yard, surfaced with sand and lined by foliage, with a redwood tree in the corner, a playhouse, a climbing structure, and a dome. The teachers were Martha, Annie, and myself. Martha and Annie each had more than three years teaching experience; I have taught for more than 30 years.

Research plan, data collection, and analysis

As the study began, I avoided intervening in the girls' conflicts because I intended to study how they dealt with each other free of my interference. However, I watched to make sure they weren't harming each other, stepping in to guide them only when they became too overwrought to cope. Yet at the same time, from my own experience I knew that very young children also need extra help in relating. As one teacher researcher wrote, "I realize more strongly now the importance of building and guiding friendships for toddlers. I need[ed] to learn the different cues that toddlers use to [communicate to understand when and what kind of intervention might] promote friendship" (Fickle, in Meier & Henderson 2007, 104). As the study progressed, therefore, our teaching team decided to offer more active assistance.

Data collection. In order to answer my questions, over a period of five months I documented the children's interactions with each other throughout the day, recording my interpretations and those of the teachers and parents. I began my research by creating various time charts, to log the girls' interactions by the minute and get a clearer view of their social dynamics. This proved unworkable because I had little chance to write many notes, and because encounters didn't fit into neat five-minute time slots. I then created a simpler, split-page chart on which I could record the social "moves" that accompanied their re-pairings. My data included transcripts of the girls' conversations, reflections in my journal, a few photos, and the field notes about their interactions. I also used my coteachers' observations, checking my field notes and analyses with them to strengthen accuracy. I spoke about the children's behavior at home with their parents, who described the usual sibling conflicts and the mostly typical behavior of 3-year-olds. I separately interviewed each girl (once in February, once in April) about her likes and dislikes, her playmate preferences, and her feelings about the others.

Analysis methodology. I analyzed my field notes and transcripts and identified anecdotes that illustrated key social behavior and teacher intervention methods. I coded them by date, type of interaction, participants, emotional tone, the resulting dyad after conflict (or cooperation), and the language of inclusion and exclusion they used. I looked for patterns, beginning with the order of the three girls' arrival at school each morning as they arranged their initial dyad formation. I also considered how personality and temperament might be shaping their interactions.

Findings and analysis

This study helped me construct a more detailed understanding of how children learn about social connections and dynamics through their experiments with exclusion, pairing-off, verbal exchanges, and hurt feelings. I was able to see some effects of this new understanding on the children, and on my classroom practice.

My first finding was that **conflict among children is not always negative, requiring adult intervention**. This called my previous beliefs into question. The data I collected about these highly interactive conflicts challenged the widely held conclusion that young children are chiefly egoistic, inherently insensitive to each other, and lacking in empathy or social awareness. The three children's conflicts were real, and often hurtful, which is why initially I saw them primarily from a disapproving adult perspective.

My data reinforced the finding that peer cultures among preschoolers involve a resistive stance toward adult expectations and rules that teachers often mistake as defiant or headstrong (Corsaro 2003). But children creating peer cultures bend adult rules more out of a desire for self-identity and creativity, to mark them as the *children's* inventions, slightly outside of adult control. The triad's whole pattern of noisy conflict fit this feature of peer cultures. The girls' frequent re-pairings gave each one many chances to violate teacher expectations in a variety of roles.

Through analyzing the data, I came to see that deficit-based thinking about children's behavior during conflict only obscures useful insights about such behavior, and thus undermines effective teaching. Instead, I began to understand that these girls exhibited much more sophisticated social skills at this early age than I had thought possible. I was often jolted by the girls' persuasive abilities and their maneuvers to shape their world of play relationships, as in this excerpt:

From Field Notes, February 5:
Ellen and Gretchen are sitting on the toilets together. Gretchen had needed to use the bathroom, and Ellen quickly volunteered to go along. They conversed:

> Ellen (at once asking and insisting): "We're just gonna play together, Gretchen."*(Gretchen replies inaudibly)*
>
> Ellen (persisting): "I'm just gonna play with you, right Gretchen? Not Lisa."
>
> **Gretchen** (evasively): "I'm not playing with Lisa, I'm going to the potty!"
>
> Ellen (wheedling): "You're not Lisa's friend, right?"
>
> **Gretchen** (slightly challenging): "Are *you* Lisa's friend?"

Ellen: "No, I'm just your friend!" (She changes the subject.) "Is your brother *your* friend?"

The children's display of interpersonal awareness and planning surprised and impressed me with its intricacy and intentionality. I felt that Ellen arranged this chance to be alone with Gretchen (a captive audience) to monopolize her loyalty and seek Gretchen's vow not to play with Lisa. Gretchen at first seemed to evade the issue, but wound up fishing for Ellen's statement of commitment to her ("Are *you* Lisa's friend?") Ellen pressed on, telling Gretchen that she was *her* preferred playmate. Moment by moment, both girls seemed to be assessing the other's words and intonations, intuiting each other's intentions, seeking to modify each other's stance, and adjusting their maneuvers as they engaged in purposeful planning to exclude the third girl.

In looking at the patterns across my data, I found that **each girl was aware of her own emotional states, and grew more aware of the feelings of the other two**. Each deeply felt the pain of exclusion or the triumph of being "chosen." However, even though each girl seemed aware of the grief of being the "odd man out," she nevertheless *always* chose the privilege to play as a dyad when it was offered—or when she could arrange to get it.

Another finding suggested by the data was that **the girls were perceptive observers**. Their jockeying for dyad connection showed how they paid attention to each other, a cognitive as well as affective advance. They derived interpersonal knowledge from facial expressions and postures. They seemed able to predict each other's behavior, plan future action, intuit each other's states of mind, and act to influence, delay gratification, and even assess each other's play potential (Corsaro 2003; Neimark 2011). Each girl created tactics to get herself "in good with" the desired partner, using knowledge of her play preferences or family ties. For example, in the vignette above, Ellen shifted the awkward conversation by mentioning the older brother whom Gretchen adored.

The girls also appeared to monitor their own efforts to influence others' actions and adjusted their strategies as needed—another example of their increased skills of self-regulation. For example, on April 15, as Lisa and Gretchen lay giggling beneath the favorite quilt on the play bed, Ellen playfully leaped on top of them and begged Lisa to come with her. Lisa told her to go away. Using her awareness that Lisa loved baby care, Ellen switched tactics. She snatched up a doll and crooned temptingly: "Here's your baby, Lisa, here's your baby! C'mon!" Considering Lisa's feelings enabled Ellen to choose an other-centered strategy—though in the end Lisa didn't go off with her as she had hoped!

Teacher approaches

As the study progressed, my approach to the children was modified by my enhanced understanding of their exchanges. I came to see that tussling over their alignments allowed them to explore interpersonal power and negotiate social mazes. My early response to the triad conflicts had been automatic rather than thoughtful. Initially, when conflicts occurred I found that my efforts to lecture or to suppress the conflict didn't work, as this incident shows:

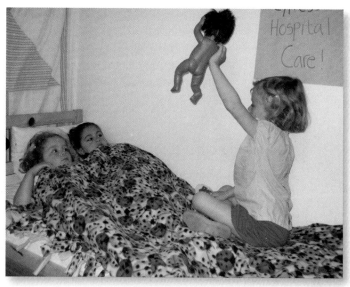

From Field Notes, March 4:

> Gretchen is playing with Mita (an unusual combo!) in the book area. Lisa runs up, taunting "You can't be our fre-end" in a singsong way, and then scoots away. Gretchen's face dissolved in a flood of tears and sobs. Annoyed, I stepped in, leading Lisa back over to Gretchen. "Look at Gretchen's face, Lisa." I scolded. "When you say that to her, it hurts her. That's why she's crying. It's not OK to hurt our friends. What could you say to Gretchen that might help her feel a bit better?" Lisa's face crumpled, as she began to sob.

We teachers conferred privately to find more effective responses. As adults we couldn't "make over" their play arrangements, much less guarantee their tranquility. Instead, to model gentler language and sociable behavior, we set out to role-play some different ways to interact. On four occasions my coteacher Martha staged short plays for all the children at story time (using puppets) in which the characters excluded each other and acted upset. Then she asked the class to suggest other ways the characters could speak to each other. She helped the children develop some new responses, such as "You can play with us later!" instead of "You can't play with us!" Martha then re-enacted the scene using these new phrases, which yielded happier outcomes for the puppets.

From Field Notes, March 18:

> Ten days after the second similar "puppet show," I overheard new dialogue: Lisa and Ellen approached Gretchen at the art table, chanting: "You have to be the monster, Gretchen!" "I'm not the monster!" she said, refusing to play. I expected Lisa to argue, but she replied cheerfully: "OK. We'll play with you later." The next day

Lisa was loudly excluding a tearful Ellen. To end this, I began to call Lisa's name. I hadn't made more than the initial 'Lee-' sound when she turned on a dime, as if expecting this. In a singsong voice, eyeing me, she chirped, "You can play with me later, Ellen!"

At the moment, I was surprised at how quickly the adult modeling from our puppet roleplay had influenced her. On reflection, I wondered if the interaction had been her bid for adult attention rather than a measure of our modeling success.

Suggesting other playmates

By February 20, we'd seen the girls occasionally try playing with girls outside of the triad. A few days later, I noted first Gretchen, then Lisa, become engaged with Natasha. After spring break we teachers started a new strategy. One day when the other two noisily excluded Gretchen, I waited a bit, and then murmured to her that Charlene might like to play. They clicked! I was surprised, since the trio had seemed so ingrown and the newer playmates were developmentally younger. I noticed, however, that the alternate playmates got abandoned in a flash whenever a triad member became available for play. These ventures into wider play choices prompted us to urge the girls' parents to set up playdates with various children outside the triad.

Broadening choices with "friendly" speech

Despite the play with new friends, the three girls kept up their taunting language toward each other. So in mid-March, we teachers invented a game called "Friendly Words" to foster kindness in social speech (Doescher & Sugarawa 1992). Since tone conveys meaning, the teachers took turns uttering common phrases in a variety of tones, then asking, "Are those words 'friendly' or 'unfriendly'?" We varied the order of the choices to avoid cuing the children, and we implied no right or wrong answers. We didn't say "nice"/"not nice" because these loaded phrases are commonly used by adults to evaluate children *themselves*. We might, for example, say "I don't want to play right now. Maybe later," in a pleasant tone. Some children called that "unfriendly," others "friendly." Some could even explain why they "voted" as they did, revealing their skills in perception, causation, and language. In following days, we also asked children at random moments to rate classroom exchanges that we overheard as friendly or unfriendly. Soon I heard more new snippets of conversation:

From Field Notes, March 30:
Lisa urged, "C'mon, Gretchen, give me a hug," and turned to the teacher: "Hey Martha, I'm *friendly* at her!"

Later that day I remarked to Lisa how considerate she had been earlier. She replied happily, "'Yes, I'm a *friendly* girl!"

From Field Notes, April 2:

> When Lisa muttered, "Hey, Ellen, let's not play with Gretchen, OK?" I cut in: "Hey, is that unfriendly or friendly?"
>
> Ellen said, "Unfriendly."
>
> "Friendly," Lisa replied impishly, grinning.

Lisa's answer itself might have been in part a performance, another form of the rule-breaking peer culture that expresses children's independence of adult expectations.

Here's an example of how the three girls began to develop more nuanced social skills:

From Field Notes, April 9:

> **Ellen** (arriving at school): "Hey Lisa, do you want to go play?"
>
> **Lisa** (coloring with Charlene): "After I play with Charlene, I'll play with you, Ellen."
>
> **Lisa** (a minute later): "Hey Ellen . . ."
>
> **Ellen** (archly, annoyed): "I'm going to play with you later."
>
> **Lisa**: "Do you have to, Ellen?"
>
> **Ellen**: "You hurt my feelings."
>
> **Lisa** (Two minutes later, yells across the room from the Dramatic Play center): "Hey Ellen, you want to take your rain boots off? Get dressed up?"
> *(After a pause, Ellen agrees.)*

In this anecdote the three girls diversified their choices of social discourse. Their exchanges back in January had often seemed angrier, reactive, revealing little ability to wait for the favored playmate or to refocus their attention when disappointed. Earlier in the year, Lisa would never have ignored Ellen to keep playing with Charlene, and Lisa and Ellen wouldn't have discussed their divergent plans so calmly. In this anecdote Ellen may have felt angry with Lisa ("I'm going to play with you later"), but her answer to Lisa's regretful protest "Do you have to, Ellen?" sounded poignant, not angry: "You hurt my feelings." Lisa's response feels like a gentle attempt to reconcile with Ellen. The growing frequency of their consideration and negotiation were not just due to our coaching, of course, but were based also in new choices they were making about relating.

My notes show that talk between the three girls always accompanied (or sharpened) their conflicts, unlike with younger toddlers who clash using fewer words. Their language of inclusion and exclusion was so ritualized that I learned to abbreviate their phrases as letter strings (for example, YCBMYF was "You can't be my friend"). Over time they began to echo the teachers' models of social language ("I'll play with you later" and "You hurt my feelings") and to develop their own versions ("Will you play with me when we go outside?"). Also, they learned to connect more successfully by using language to fit into the existing dynamics of the play or to suggest a new game ("Want to take your boots off? Get dressed up?").

My field notes showed that by mid-April, intense conflicts decreased in frequency as the girls chose gentler interactions. The girls sometimes played with "outsiders," used more friendly tones, and joined in play as a trio for brief periods. Also, I saw times when the "out" girl approached the dyad and the other two would gently *redirect* her to other play, instead of just taunting or baldly rejecting her.

Another possible finding for the changed behavior is that **each of the three grew to care more deeply for the other two**. Data from late in the study showed the girls striving at times to meet each other's needs and to avoid mutual harm. On April 7 Gretchen went to sit with Ellen, Lisa, and teacher Martha at the picnic table, but began crying that they hadn't left room. Ellen swiftly scooted over to allow her to sit *beside her*. Their mutual caring may have come to seem as valuable to each one as the temporary pleasure of having the dyad partner all to herself.

Conclusions and implications

Through my study, I came to understand how my preconceptions about children's conflicts had diminished my teaching success; formerly, I wasn't able to see that my assumptions often obstructed my insight into the girls' actions and motivations.

Each aspect of the girls' increasingly sophisticated social behavior relied on the development of cognitive and affective abilities. The ability to recognize and react to others' feelings rested on growing awareness that others have similar emotions that can be influenced. This growth allowed them to be more compassionate. The awareness of others as distinct from oneself, each with a subjective mental state, made persuasion and negotiation more practicable. Greater language skills enabled them to influence others, and let their play become more complex. Maturing abilities in self-monitoring and self-regulation allowed them to better control their impulsive, hurtful behavior, and to adjust it when they found changed circumstances. It's likely that their conflicted sparring helped them develop these capabilities.

Although less frequent and intense as the spring wore on, the trio's emotional struggles with each other persisted. Children act to achieve goals, even if not consciously. The three of them achieved something by enacting these painful conflicts. Since children learn about themselves by encountering others, the skirmishes likely served to build crucial interpersonal knowledge—revealing how each girl felt, paired off, recombined, and made up. Conflicts are also chances to assert individuality, measure the strength of individual wishes, and compare divergent interests. The girls' dramas of exclusion, abandonment, and ecstatic re-inclusion may have served as a kind of risky ritual that served to define their social network, control its territory, and test its durability.

There are three ways this study contributes to the broader field of early childhood. First, it illustrates how early childhood teacher research can illuminate our work with children (Meier & Henderson 2007). What began as a practical matter of dealing with intense conflict evolved into a purposeful, detailed study of the children's behavior, practitioner methods, and the influence of conflict on the classroom. My "insider" status as their teacher enabled me to closely observe the girls' behavior and the effects of our interventions on a day-to-day basis, something that an outside researcher could not do. The teacher research tools of systematic observation, thoughtful description derived from patterns of behavior, practitioner reflection, and cross-validation with colleagues enabled me to construct a deeper understanding of child behavior to inform my teaching, and to offer to other teachers in similar situations.

Second, close examination of the girls' interpersonal dynamics throughout the study also challenged my assumptions by helping reveal children's surprising early competence in social interactions. It highlighted the intricacy of their thinking and planning about friendship, play, and belonging. It shed light on the purposes and social operations of networking and peer cultures among young children. These were revealed as fields of action for enhancing self-knowledge by experiencing the lives of other children; for building social skills; for establishing independence and autonomy from adults; and for extending learning through peer collaboration, as Vygotsky described the process. This all created changes in my teaching, and therefore in the girls' interactions.

Third, by tracing how we helped the girls outline the social choreography of their small community and enhance their relational skills, this teacher research suggests strategies that other practitioners can try—and pitfalls to avoid—as they encourage children to manage conflict and choose from a broader range of prosocial approaches to classmates.

This study had the main effect of changing my thinking about peer interactions of all kinds, which improved both my thinking and my practice. My early response to the triad's conflict focused on prevention; it was formulaic rather than thoughtful. With good intent, I sought to ease conflict by pressing for my adult notion of prosocial play—"enforced togetherness." Like many teachers, I had assumed that conflict arises mainly from deficit: immaturity, or worse, anti-social impulses. Admonishing the girls to meet adult standards of behavior didn't work. However, when I studied the intricate and intentional ways they interacted, I learned to see their actions as experimental efforts to carry out social and emotional goals.

We teachers began to provide more positive choices of prosocial action. We modeled examples of more engaging language. Via discussions about other children's experiences and mental states, we equipped children to better perceive and identify each other's feelings. Throughout, we respected children as architects of their own relationships: "Allowing children more space to develop their own authentic ways to interact can be more effective in strengthening collaborative play and building their social competence with peers" (see Neimark, in this volume, 64). When we reinforced and supported the capabilities underlying prosocial relations, the girls could better *choose* to adjust their own behavior to the benefit of all three.

Play-based programs with a social-development emphasis could benefit from trying similar strategies, as could any other kind of early childhood program. Other early childhood practitioners may experience conflict and injury far more challenging than our conflicted play triangle. Conflict is part of life. We must find ways to teach within and from conflict instead of just suppressing it. We should capitalize on children's innate empathy and sensitivity, instead of acceding to the basically antisocial notion that humans are controlled by self-centered impulses. If we give children opportunities to build their strengths, we can reinforce their ability to get along with others throughout their schooling and lives, and make a contribution to a more just and humane society in the process.

Photos courtesy of the author.

References

Avgitidou, S. 2001. Peer culture and friendship relationships as contexts for the development of children's prosocial behavior. *International Journal of Early Years Education* 9 (2): 145–52.

Benenson, J. 1993. Greater preference among females than males for dyadic interaction in early childhood. *Child Development* 64 (2): 544–55.

Brownell, C., & C. Kopp, eds. 2007. *Socioemotional development in the toddler years.* New York: Guilford Press.

Bullock, J.R. 1988. Encouraging the development of social competence in young children. *Early Childhood Development and Care* 37: 47–54.

Corsaro, W. 2003. *We're friends, right? Inside kids' culture.* Washington, DC: Joseph Henry Press.

Crick, N., J. las Casas & B. Mosher. 1995. Relational and overt aggression in preschool. *Developmental Psychology* 33 (4): 579–97.

de Haan, D., E. & Singer. 2003. 'Use your words': A sociocultural approach to the teacher's role in the transition from physical to verbal strategies of resolving peer conflicts among toddlers. *Journal of Early Child Research* 1 (1): 95–109.

Doescher, S., & A. Sugarawa. 1992. Impact of prosocial home- and school-based interventions in preschool children's cooperative behavior. *Family Relations* 41 (2): 200–04.

Fox, L., & R.H. Lentini. 2006. "You got it!" Teaching social and emotional skills. *Young Children* 61 (6): 36–42.

Gillespie, L.G., & A. Hunter. 2010. Rocking and rolling: Supporting infants, toddlers, and their families. Believe, watch, act! Promoting prosocial behavior in infants and toddlers. *Young Children* 65 (1): 42–43.

Harrist, A.W., & K.D. Bradley. 2003. "You can't say you can't play": Intervening in the process of social exclusion in the kindergarten classroom. *Early Childhood Research Quarterly* 18 (2): 185–205.

Hayashi, M.K., & J. Tobin. 2009. The Japanese preschool's pedagogy of feeling: Cultural strategies for supporting young children's emotional development. *Ethos* 37 (1): 32–49.

Hazen, N., & B. Black. 1984. Peer acceptance: Strategies children use and how teachers can help them learn them. *Young Children* 39 (6): 26–60.

Ishikawa, F., & D.F. Hay. 2006. Triadic interactions among newly acquainted two-year-olds. *Social Development* 15 (1): 145–68.

Kantor, R., P. Elgas & D. Fernie. 1993. Cultural knowledge and social competence within a preschool peer culture group. *Early Childhood Research Quarterly* 8 (2): 125–47.

McLoyd, V., & E. Thomas & D. Warren. 1984. The short-term dynamics of social organization in preschool triads. *Child Development* 55 (3): 1051–70.

Meier, D.R, & B. Henderson. 2007. *Learning from young children in the classroom: The art and science of teacher research.* New York: Teachers College Press.

Neimark, A. 2012. Do you want to see something goofy? Peer culture in the preschool yard. In *Our inquiry, our practice: Undertaking, supporting, and learning from early childhood teacher research(ers),* eds. G. Perry, B. Henderson & D.R. Meier, 53–64. Washington, DC: NAEYC.

Paley, V.G. 1992. *You can't say you can't play.* Cambridge, MA: Harvard University Press.

Piaget, J. 1966. *The construction of reality in the child.* New York: Ballantine Books.

Rogoff, B. 2003. *The cultural nature of human development.* New York: Oxford University Press.

Tobin, J., Y. Hsueh & M. Karasawa. 2011. *Preschool in three cultures revisited: China, Japan, and the United States.* Chicago: University of Chicago Press.

Underwood, M. 2003. *Social aggression among girls.* London: Guilford Press.

Vygotsky, L. 1978. *Mind in society: The development of higher psychological processes.* Cambridge, MA: Harvard University Press.

Chapter

04

Encounters with Sunlight and a Mirror Ball

Diane M. Spahn with
commentary by Barry
Kluger-Bell and Ellen Hall

In this study, **Diane M. Spahn** embarks on a project involving light and reflection inspired by professional development work with Dr. Barry Kluger-Bell, a physicist. Using photographs, video, and reflective journals in a unique way, Spahn captures those telling moments of discovery, of uncertainty, and of trial-and-error as young children try to make sense of their engagement with light-related phenomena.

Spahn provides a wonderful example of a teacher's artful use of key teacher research tools to enrich and deepen teaching. She shows how her own expanded knowledge about the properties of light enabled her to approach the children's learning in a new way. Careful documentation not only of the children's words and actions but of her own interpretations of their thinking helped her see possibilities for the children's explorations. Ecologist Amy Seidl explains that there is the phenomena of change and there is the perception of the changes. This is what Spahn has done so well—using teacher research tools and modes of representation to help us see how children experience the phenomena of light and how they perceive themselves in relation to changes in light and the environment.

—Daniel R. Meier

This teacher research study depicts the intertwined stories of a professional development workshop and its impact on the investigations of an early childhood educator and of three preschool-aged children. The study highlights the children's encounters with sunlight and a mirror ball, and reflects the lasting influence that professional development can have on teaching. Two related questions are the focus of this teacher research: How do young children experience and understand a complex concept like the properties of light? How do my own expanded understandings of light and shadow translate into my practice and subsequent ability to support children's explorations and construction of knowledge? It is written from my perspective as a member of the faculty at Boulder Journey School, and includes commentary on the science content and children's comprehension of scientific concepts by physicist Dr. Barry Kluger-Bell of Hawkins Centers of Learning.

Boulder Journey School, located in Boulder, Colorado, is a private school with a community of over 200 children ages 6 weeks to 6 years, their families, and a faculty of 50. We view the school as a place in which learning, for both children and adults, is invited and nurtured through relationships. Relationships with one another, with those in our community, with the environment, and with materials are realized daily. We take inspiration from our relationships with educators in the world-renowned schools for young children in Reggio Emilia, Italy; Reggio-inspired educators from around the world; and most recently, educators participating in the Hawkins Centers of Learning project. These relationships have strengthened Boulder Journey School's longstanding commitment to professional development.

Boulder, Colorado, is known for its beautiful mountain views and sunny skies. We happily welcome an average of 300 days of sunshine annually. Our many days of sunny skies have had an impact on the culture of the school and have naturally developed into an ongoing schoolwide study of light and its properties. To support this work, in the spring of 2008 we created an environment within the school's large theater space, the Theater of Light and Shadow, in which children and adults encounter light as a material that can be used to co-construct, represent, and express their ideas about the physical world. As the theater teacher, my role is to facilitate the children's experiences in both the Theater and Theater of Light and Shadow.

The primary focus of our work in these spaces is using our bodies in combination with other materials. Our large Theater houses traditional materials (such as puppets, musical instruments, and costumes) as well as nontraditional materials (such as pool noodles, bubble wrap, cardboard tubes, and wooden cubes). One area features a climbing wall and gymnasium mats for gross motor work and play. Children and adults use the space to dance, sing, climb, run, and act out original stories, plays, ballets, and impromptu play scripts.

Our smaller Theater of Light and Shadow is more specialized, featuring smaller, open-ended materials, an overhead projector, light box, and fabric panels. This is the only space within the school that can be made completely dark. Blank walls provide the backdrop for children's explorations of the interactions between beams of light (from flashlights, light sticks, and other sources) and their bodies and/or other objects.

This research is comprised of several stories: the encounters several children had with sunlight and a mirror ball, my observations and reflections as a theater teacher on the children's work and my practice, and a commentary by Dr. Kluger-Bell presented alongside the main text, reinforcing and clarifying the possible scientific explanations contained in the children's ideas. I chose to present this story in as close to its original form as possible; the narrative lens includes journal entries featuring observations of children, my reflections about the children's developing understandings, other reflective writing, video clips and photographs, transcripts featuring children's conversations with their teacher and peers, and children's drawings of their thinking about light. Along with my colleagues, I analyzed the data by reviewing my recorded observations, journal entries, videos, and video transcripts, uncovering patterns of children's thinking about light. I also consulted with Dr. Kluger-Bell regarding my interpretation of the children's potential developing understandings to determine the accuracy of my interpretations. This data represents authentic evidence of the far-reaching effects of relevant professional development.

The story began in the beginning of the school year, when the faculty of Boulder Journey School invited Dr. Kluger-Bell to lead a professional development workshop on the properties of light. We wished to deepen our understanding of these properties, play with light, and explore some of the relationships light has with shadow, form, and reflection. The following section relates Dr. Kluger-Bell's story of that workshop.

The professional development story

In the fall of 2008, I led a professional development workshop on light and images for educators at Boulder Journey School. I had the opportunity to visit this remarkable school several times prior to the workshop and had been impressed by their version of a Reggio-inspired infant/toddler program and preschool. Working with this school also gave me a chance to reconnect with my own early experience in education. I began my work in education by working alongside David and Frances Hawkins at the Mountain View Center for Environmental Education (Kellogg 2010) in Colorado. The founder and executive director of Boulder Journey School, Ellen Hall, also had formative educational experiences with these seminal educators. The Hawkins helped shape both of our thinking about learning.

I came to the Boulder Journey School workshop with background experience as a professional physicist; I also have more than 20 years of experience in professional development for teachers at the Exploratorium's Institute for Inquiry. Although most of my experience had been working with elementary school teachers, I spent some of my early career working with Frances Hawkins in preschools, where I developed some understanding of preschool teaching.

At Boulder Journey School, I observed a great deal of work with light and shadow in classrooms. Light and shadow explorations were a major focus of my inquiry-based work at the Exploratorium, so I felt that this was an area where I could contribute to their work.

My goals for the professional development workshop at Boulder Journey School were twofold. First, I wanted to help teachers learn about light, experience new and unfamiliar phenomena, and develop new ways of thinking about light. Second, I wanted to model and have the teachers reflect upon the pedagogy underlying the inquiry approach of this teaching.

Helping teachers learn more about light prepares them to take greater advantage of potential opportunities in the work they already do with children. With greater knowledge and confidence in their understanding of the underlying science, they can better recognize opportunities for further learning that might arise; realize the value of certain experiences that they may have missed before; and utilize new "tools" for going on to further explorations.

The pedagogical modeling of the inquiry model included providing engaging "provocations," drawing questions from the learner, and providing materials and sensitive guidance to help the learner find her own path to understanding.

The teachers' reactions to the workshop, as reported in written reflections, indicated both an increased understanding of light and a positive reaction to the pedagogy. For instance, one teacher wrote, "I had never really considered how light can be used to create 'pictures and shapes' based on the light bulb you use." This was experienced within the workshop when viewing pinhole images. Another teacher wrote, "Our work . . . has caused me to think about work not just with light but also with other materials in many new ways." This generalization of the pedagogy was just what I had hoped for.

But even more impressive was the dramatic development of this work in classrooms. In one of the phenomena experienced by teachers in the workshop, light passing through a pinhole produced an image of the light source. For instance, if the filament of a clear light bulb were in the shape of a C, light from that filament passing through a pinhole would create a C-shaped light image. Teachers saw that even a square hole would produce that image. And finally, teachers saw that if they placed a small square mirror in the place of the hole, it would redirect the light and that light still formed an image of the light source. If that light source happened to be the sun, the image would be round.

As theater teacher Diane Spahn reflects, that experience "would prove not only to excite the faculty, but would have lasting appeal for the children of Boulder Journey School as well." Her documentation and reflections, which follow, on her remarkable interactions with young children around mirrors and light illustrate how a receptive teacher can take ideas and methods from professional development, combine them with knowledge about young children, and create high-level classroom learning experiences.

Unfolding stories of sunlight and a mirror ball

The following accounts and personal reflections are taken directly from my journal, which I use as one tool for curriculum development and planning. I find the process of revisiting my notes, photographs, and video also helps me to slow down and take a breath. It is in that space of breathing that I find I am thorough and more thoughtful about how to best support the children's work.

09/25/08 **Journal Entry**—This morning I noticed a ray of sunshine cast upon the shadow screen and reflected in the large wall mirror. Since our work with Dr. Kluger-Bell, I have been noticing light, natural and otherwise, in new ways. I'm simply more aware of its complexities than I had been prior to his visit.

Several preschool children requested a space to "race around in cars." I left the shadow screen in the position by the window. This proved to be a key element of a new provocation. It should be noted that the mirror ball is kept on the end of the frame of the shadow screen. While the children were engaged in their car race around the theater, time passed, and as if by magic, rays of sunlight struck the mirror ball. The space was filled with round dots of light.

The children's movements caused the mirror ball to sway slightly. The dots of light danced about the walls, floor, and ceiling. All of the children stopped what they were doing and excitedly discussed what was taking place.

In this moment I was thrilled to have a video camera hung about my neck with which I could document the children's investigation of this phenomenon. While I was setting up the camera, Maddy, who was close to age 5, explained her theories. She pointed out that as the mirror ball moved "up and down" the reflections (dots of light) also moved up and down. Maddy's initial theory may have been that the mirror ball is the light source, and it is producing the dots. Challenging Maddy and her peers, I posed the question of how the mirror ball was making the dots.

Eric, who was also close to 5, answered, "alien ships." Zen Rose, age 4, incorporated both Eric's alien ship idea and Maddy's observation of the movement of the dots into her own short narrative: "They're alien ships that shine light bright. And down and up and down and up and down and up." This suggested that Zen Rose was co-constructing knowledge within her peer group, incorporating everyone's ideas, including her own. Building on Zen Rose's use of the word, "bright," Eric stated that as the lights got near, they got "really bright." Perhaps Eric was making a correlation between distance and intensity.

Justin, age 4½, took a different approach. He pointed out that the sun was shining through the window, onto the individual squares of the mirror ball, and then onto the surfaces of the room. Justin used words, as one would a pencil, to draw a map of the path on which the light traveled. In his explanation, Justin included the detail of the individual square mirror tiles on the surface of the mirror ball. He speculated that the **squares** were "shining **dots** from the sun." Having known Justin since infancy has given me insight about how well he receives critique and inquiry. I pointed out the semantics of squares being square and dots being round and asked how that could be so. This stopped Justin briefly, and he and his peers went back to riding around in the space for several minutes before returning to the mirror ball. Had I not experienced the recent workshop with Dr. Kluger-Bell, I cannot be certain if I would have asked that particular question.

Commentary by Barry Kluger-Bell

Eric's correlation between distance and intensity seems to be based on prior experience. Applying prior experience to explain new phenomena is an example of the hypothesizing skill.

Justin's thinking in terms of the path that the light is taking is a sophisticated way of looking at light. Early understanding of light, even for some adults, pictures light more as a medium (like air) in which we are immersed. I imagine that the school-wide ongoing study of light and its properties helped the children develop the idea of light having a source and traveling out from the source.

Video transcription #1—September 25, 2008

Teacher: How is it making it?

Maddy: Look it's going up and down. And that thing, (indicates mirror ball), going up.

Teacher: I still don't understand. How is that thing (pointing off camera to the mirror ball) making these dots everywhere?

Zen Rose: I know! I know!

Eric: Alien ships.

Zen Rose: 'Cuz they, they're alien ships that shine light bright. And down and up and down and up and down and up.

Teacher: Alien ships definitely can shine light. It's all over the place.

Eric: Once they get near you they're really bright.

Teacher: They're really bright?

Eric: Yeah, once they get near you I mean.

Maddy: I'll see you later Diane, I'm going to work.

Teacher: Okay, Maddy, I'll see you later, too. Thanks for your ideas about these beautiful light dots, whatever they are.

Justin: They're um. I know why. I know why they're, they're like high 'cuz the shuh, the sun is shining on there (indicates mirror ball) and then, and then, and then and then those squares are. Then the sun is shining on the squares, then the, then the squares are shining on the, the squares are shining, shining dots from the sun.

Teacher: Okay, but the squares are square and the dots are round.

After about five minutes Justin and Maddy returned to the mirror ball and agreed that, because the sun was round, the light dots reflected in the theater were also round.

Justin: Maybe the sun tries to make them round.

Maddy: Yeah, because the sun's round.

The children happily returned to their work of racing, and no further mention was made of the light dots or mirror ball.

Video transcription #2—September 25, 2008

Justin: The sun is, um, doing it (makes circular gestures). And the sun is shining on that (indicates mirror ball). Maybe the sun tries to make them round.

Teacher: The sun tries to make these dots round.

Justin: Yeah.

Maddy: Yeah, because the sun's round.

Justin: Yeah, and it doesn't have these pointy things.

Teacher: What pointy things?

Justin: These pointy things that are sticking out.

Teacher: Oh. You mean like in drawings of the sun.

Justin: Yeah.

Teacher: Mm hmm.

I noted the following possible next steps: revisit the video clips with the children; encourage the children to draw, critique, and discuss one another's ideas; invite the children to compose one drawing consisting of the components they agreed upon from their individual drawings or to build a model of their idea based on a collaborative drawing.

11/14/08 Journal Entry—A new group of preschool children experienced something similar to the phenomenon of September 25, when sunlight hit the mirror ball and the room was filled with light dots. Clara, almost 5, explained this by drawing her theory.

I asked Clara to describe what she was drawing. "That's the sun," said Clara as she pointed to a circular symbol near the top of the page. She continued explaining that the "hotness" (emanating from the sun) passed through the window and touched the "glow ball" (the mirror ball). This was very similar to Justin's theory. I wondered how many preschool children had similar theories but hadn't communicated them,

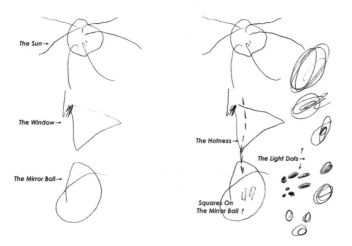

The Sun →
The Window →
The Mirror Ball →
The Hotness →
The Light Dots →
Squares On The Mirror Ball ↑

Commentary by Barry Kluger-Bell

When I first heard Justin and Maddy's discussion in the video I was stunned. I have worked with this phenomenon with many adults, and they struggle to figure out why the patches of light are round when the mirrors are square. The children came to the conclusion that the light was the shape of the source (i.e., the sun) much more rapidly than most of my adult students.

Commentary by Barry Kluger-Bell

Clara's use of the term "hotness" and her drawings of the flow of the hotness seem to be an early form of the concept of energy and energy flow. She recognized that the sun produced more than just visible light. I would translate her idea to include radiant heat (infrared radiation) as well as light in her vision of what was coming through the window.

or had, but they had gone unobserved by an adult. At some point these children gained an understanding that light can pass through objects. Both Clara and Justin mentioned light coming through the window. What other similarities would we uncover?

I asked Clara how the sun made the mirror ball work, and she replied that she didn't know. Her drawing would seem to indicate otherwise; she had an idea of how this could work as she explained that "hotness" traveled from the sun, passed through the window, and hit the individual square mirrors, which made round light dots of varying sizes appear on the wall. I noted the following possible next steps: invite Clara to work with Justin and see what might occur when their similar ideas were explored within a small learning group, and to revisit with Clara the video of Justin where he refers to images of the sun usually having "pointy things" (i.e., rays of light) emanating from it.

11/17/08 Journal Entry—Following the initial work of investigating the cause of the mirror ball reflections (light dots) in the theater, classroom teachers identified three children who remained interested in continuing the work. They were from two different classrooms and had not worked together in a small group to date. Clara, Sami, and Justin, who were all approaching age 5, were invited to revisit one another's work concerning the mirror ball. I set up the theater so that the mirror ball reflected many light dots on the walls. I also brought in an easel, anticipating and hoping that the children might want to explain their ideas with the aid of drawings.

We began by watching the video clips of Justin, Maddy, Zen Rose, and Eric from September 25. We also looked at Clara's drawing. I invited the children to make one collaborative drawing that would explain how the mirror ball worked. They immediately and individually set to work without much discussion. I asked, "What are each of you working on, what parts?" hoping to signal that this was a collaboration and that the drawing belonged to the group. The children did not reply verbally, but instead began working in earnest. They sketched quickly. Sami drew a large object in the center of the board. I pointed this out to the other two children.

Both Clara and Justin glanced over to look at Sami's portion of the drawing, and then moved away from the easel. Clara announced, "I'm all done, already." Obviously, to the children, a shared drawing was not important or yet warranted. Justin and Clara moved toward the shadow screen. The light dots on the walls began to move slightly and appeared to wiggle. This could be attributed to the children's movements across the floor, which caused the shadow screen, and subsequently the mirror ball, to tremble. The children did not seem to make this correlation. At some point we could embark on an investigation of vibrations and/or movements, but at this point, I felt it would be too leading and might cause the investigation to end prematurely.

Justin noticed the movement of the light dots and asked aloud, "Why are these dots moving?" Clara repeated his question. Justin inspected the mirror ball and de-

clared that it was indeed wiggling. The children did **not** actually say the dots moved **because** the mirror ball was moving, but Justin implied this by way of stating his observation.

Justin rushed over to the easel and began to sketch a spider-like object, with many lines protruding from its edge. He explained that it was a drawing of the power inside the "glow ball." This process of drawing, explaining the drawing, and adding to the drawing appeared to be growing comfortable for the children. After some time at the easel, Justin declared, "I'm gonna **make** the glow ball instead of just drawing it." Our colleagues in the schools of Reggio Emilia often mention shifts of contexts and/or materials, a strategy children choose to further explore their ideas. In this case, scale and the move from two dimensions to three proved to be vital.

Video transcription #3—September 25, 2008

> **Justin**: I'm trying to make the, I'm gonna make the glow ball instead of just drawing it.
>
> **Teacher**: You wanna make the glow ball. I'm not, I don't understand what you mean.
>
> **Justin**: So first of all I'm gonna use, (looking around) let's see, two noodles and I'm going to use ahh, ahh, one of those, those blocks that Malissa (Marissa) is next to for the, for the dots.
>
> **Teacher**: You're gonna use other materials to make a symbol of what the glow ball looks like?
>
> **Justin**: Yep.
>
> **Teacher**: Go right ahead. You've got this whole room to build your symbol. And you have these friends to help you Justin.

Justin places two noodles ends touching on the floor. They are naturally arc shaped.

> **Justin**: See? See how it makes a circle? (Off camera to Sami.) I'm doing it my way.

Clara and Sami, off camera, carry on brief dialogue.

Teacher: Justin, is there anything that Clara and Sami can do to help build this symbol?

Justin: Well, yeah. Well um, I'm trying put these around the glow ball and make this symbol.

Teacher: Well it looks like you're just, you have all the ideas but maybe if you would speak to them about some of the ideas they could help.

Justin: You guys can help me make the glow ball. There, now we have to put some on top.

Clara: Why?

Justin: So there's more. So there's a lot of, a lot of, a lot of dots. We gotta put a lot of them on there.

Clara: Oh, now. Hey Sami.

Justin: Are you stacking them up to put them on the glow ball?

Sami: No.

Justin: Oh, oh brother. Okay, now and now we need to put the tubes on.

Teacher: And what are the tubes for?

Justin: The tubes are the dots. Well, I'm—ah. The tubes are to make some more dots. Since she gots (refers to Sami) she says she's not gonna put those blocks on the thing, on the glow ball. We're making these to make some more dots. (Cube falls)

Clara: Oh well.

Justin: Let me connect this. There we go.

Justin looked around as he described the materials that would comprise his physical representation, and then Clara joined him in the work of constructing the model/symbol. Sami opted to construct a separate structure, working nearby, but not directly with Clara and Justin. Two white swimming pool noodles were placed with ends touching on the floor, representing the circular shape of the mirror ball. By moving the representation into a new context, Justin not only demonstrated his vision in three dimensions, but also could accept help from his peers without giving up the integrity of his idea. Work on this scale was large enough to require many hands. Several wooden cubes were chosen

Commentary by Barry Kluger-Bell

The various forms of modeling what was going on in the children's work (i.e., verbal description, drawing, and three-dimensional modeling) parallels scientists' use of multiple models to obtain more complete understandings of phenomena. Each form of modeling has its own strengths, which add to the individual's understanding. In addition, the actual act of modeling is a sophisticated abstraction from the concrete phenomena. The fact that these children initiate or readily take on making models to explain what is happening shows a remarkable ability for early abstraction.

to represent the individual mirror squares. At one point, Justin explained to Clara that a lot of cubes were needed because there were a lot of dots. He appeared to be working on one-to-one correspondence. Was Justin again theorizing that each square mirror tile makes a light dot? Perhaps his theory was: groups of dots are made by groups of mirror squares.

The work in the theater continued for almost an hour after Justin initiated the construction of the large-scale mirror ball representation. He and Clara, and at times Sami, worked cooperatively to build their glow ball. The structure naturally became a setting for dramatic play, moving the work into yet another form. The children added materials, edited their choices, and paused the action of their play script to debate the functions of various glow ball parts. Although the natural light coming into the theater changed throughout the morning and the light dots faded away from the walls, the children remained steadfast in their important roles as the operators of the glow ball, traveling through the sky, shining light dots on the world.

Later, when the children were individually asked if they would like to return to the Theater to revisit their work, their answers spoke volumes. Justin, eyebrows furrowed, replied, "Well that would be silly. We already did that work." Clara said, "Um, what about making something new?" Sami declined. Clearly, for these children, this work had ended. Certainly, I wanted the investigation to continue, and indeed it will at some future time—possibly with the same children, more probably with new players. So this entry ends with the words of Patricia Ryan Madson, a professor at Stanford University who writes in her book, *Improv Wisdom*, "Substitute attention to what is happening for attention to what might happen" (2005, 38).

Over time, many children have experienced the wonder of the light dots dancing about the theater. One further area of study, which I have enthusiastically embraced, is how a younger peer group of 1-year-old children experience the reflected light of the mirror ball, and what their theories might be.

A final reflection

As my background is in professional film and theater, I am always looking for the ways in which these disciplines inform my teaching and learning with young children. I spent 11 years honing the skills inherent in team improvisation, and have found that two consistent principles stem from that experience: one, that you always keep the scene **between the players**, and two, that you use the **tools you find around you** to build the scene. For the children, Justin and Clara in particular, the "glow ball" model grew in complexity and form as they utilized the available tools and materials **found** around them. As their work moved from individual ideas to a shared experience, it grew **between** them. In my own practice I can apply those same principles. The work of collaboration is between myself, my colleagues, and the children, and by employing the tools I have at hand—our questions, reflections, and findings—I am better able to recognize, co-construct, and take part in the many opportunities for all of us to learn.

It is my hope that, in sharing this work, the striking effects of collaboration among colleagues of all ages will become evident. All of the players involved—children, theater teacher, and physicist—worked in harmony and relied on one another for inspiration, provocation, and reflection. All were seen as experts, and the contributions of all were valued. The traces of Dr. Kluger-Bell's dynamic and relevant in-service workshop for educators at Boulder Journey School, my reflections as a theater teacher, and the amazing findings of Justin, Clara, Sami, and their peers continue to be examined, revisited, and made visible to children and adults. Investigations around light, shadow, reflection, and the mirror ball surface regularly and are met with enthusiasm and a view toward new understandings.

Reflections on the Mirror Ball Investigation

Ellen Hall

The mirror ball investigation explored in this study can be viewed as a microcosm of the experiences that are regularly initiated and developed at Boulder Journey School. Teachers create environments that are designed to encourage children's natural curiosities and build on their competencies. Observation and documentation of the children's interactions with their physical and social environment become the basis of teachers' research. Multiple perspectives on the documentation from both children and adults are invited, adding breadth and depth to the ensuing analyses. Initial research questions are refined, and the environment evolves.

Interpretations are enriched through ongoing study of classic and contemporary child development, learning, and motivational theories. In a parallel process, teachers' research surrounding children's learning processes prompts adult interactions with materials. The visibility of the work initiates discussions, debates, and decisions. The school is seen as a place of knowledge co-construction for all members of the learning community.

Professional development is highly valued in this system. Several aspects of professional development at Boulder Journey School are worthy of note. First, professional development is developed from the "inside out." Using the mirror ball investigation as one example, the children's interest in light and the absence of light (or shadow) led to teachers' curiosities surrounding this material. The school supported this interest through work with Dr. Kluger-Bell, culminating in a day-long workshop. Investigations of light and shadow in infant, toddler, preschool and prekindergarten classrooms continue. Second, professional development includes making the work of the school public. The mirror ball investigation has been the focus of many presentations, a catalyst for new experiences, and is now the basis of a study in this volume.

References

Harlan, W. 2005. *Teaching, learning and assessing science 5-12.* 4th ed. Thousand Oaks, CA: Sage Publications.

Kellog, B. 2010. *David Hawkins and the Pond Study.* Bloomington, IN: Xlibris.

Madson, P.R. 2005. *Improv wisdom: Don't prepare, just show up.* New York: Random House.

Chapter

05

"Do You Want to See Something Goofy?"

Peer Culture in the Preschool Yard

Aaron Neimark

This study is a wonderful example of a teacher researcher looking carefully at the sometimes hard-to-see foundations and benefits of young children's play. At a play-based preschool, **Aaron Neimark** collected data on children's invented games and looked closely at how the formation and playing out of the games reinforced the children's sense of a social peer group. Over the course of three months, Aaron collected data on whom the children played with, their choice of games, and the manner and kind of materials and props they used. He was influenced by particular studies and ideas from the research literature on children's play groups.

If, in early childhood education, we are to return to seeing and valuing play as a true hallmark of excellent teaching, then we will need more teacher research studies like this one. Through the efforts of teacher researchers like Aaron, we can reclaim play as a foundation for children's growth and learning during their earliest school years.

—Daniel R. Meier

Greg and Jamal are tossing their hats in the air, trying to get them stuck in the trees and on top of the climbing structure. Edgar, who is also wearing a hat, joins in by throwing his hat up the slide. This activity goes on for about fifteen minutes, with the children commenting humorously about what their hats can do and frequently calling out, "Look at my hat!"

In the play-based preschool where I taught in San Francisco, one priority is fostering children's social development through play activities. It is never an easy task for young children to play cooperatively without teachers' assistance, but what kind of support should teachers offer?

Looking back on my six years of teaching preschool and three years of teaching kindergarten in a public school, I reflected on how teachers can help children play together. My thoughts and questions led me to explore how children attempt to enter peer group play. Experience told me that the strategies a child uses to gain access to a group of children playing together can affect the dynamics of the play and determine whether the child is accepted or rejected by the group.

This study is based on a teacher research project I conducted at the preschool in spring 2005 to examine the relationship between the peer culture in a preschool class and the children's ability to gain access to the collaborative play of other children in the school yard. At the same time, I wanted to learn something new about my teaching. As part of the teacher research project, I examined how my teaching methods changed as I took into account the children's peer culture. Thus, this study was also an action research project—a project involving teachers making changes in their practice based on what they discover through inquiry (Hatch 2002).

I addressed three questions in the study:

- How do children attempt to gain access to collaborative play activities in the play yard on their own, without teacher assistance?
- How does a child's understanding of the peer culture help him gain access to other children's play?
- How can teachers intervene more effectively by learning about the children's peer culture?

Peer culture knowledge and using a sociocultural perspective

In my inquiry I used William Corsaro's concept of peer culture to examine how children interact while playing outside in the yard (1985; 2003). Corsaro sees children as active agents in making social meaning from their play. Through their play activities, children construct their own peer culture, which he defines as "a stable set of activities or routines, artifacts, values, and concerns that kids produce and share in interaction with one another" (Corsaro 2003, 37).

The research of Rebecca Kantor and her colleagues also influenced my approaches and my research questions (Fernie et al. 1995; Kantor et al. 1993; Kantor & Fernie 2003). In their study of a preschool peer group, they found that peer culture was established by the children at the whole classroom level and in "several distinct, stable and enduring friendship groups . . . each with its locally constructed peer culture patterns" (Kantor et al. 1993, 127).

I used a sociocultural perspective to learn more about children's peer cultures. Kantor and colleagues explain that "sociocultural researchers seek to understand different types of contexts . . . but distinctly define contexts as cultures; consequently, social interactions are viewed as having cultural meanings and, in turn, the group culture is seen as framing ongoing interactions" (1993, 129). This approach is relevant to teachers as they help children improve their ability to join collaborative play and connect with one another during self-directed play.

Methods

Participants and data collection

My main source of data was the children engaged in social play in the play yard and those attempting to join in others' play activities. The study involved 30 children ranging in age from 3 years and 3 months to 5 years and 2 months. Most were from middle-class families, with 33 percent receiving some form of financial assistance. Their ethnicities included European American, Latino, African American, German/Peruvian American, Asian American, and Indian/Pakistani American.

The majority of the data was observations of the children's interactions with each other, collected during outdoor play after lunch. The play yard has two climbing structures: one is a jungle gym and the other is a large wooden structure with stairs, a slide, and a steering wheel. Toward the back of the yard, two tire swings are partially covered by vegetation encroaching from a neighbor's yard. There are also monkey bars, a small basketball hoop, and areas of sand. When the children are outside in the yard, they may play in any part of the yard as long as they stay in observable areas. There are general rules for safety and to guide interactions, such as no hitting and asking others before touching something they are using.

© Aaron Neimark

Data were collected through

1. Observations in the outdoor play yard

2. Reflective teaching journal

3. Research memos of noteworthy events

Over 10 weeks, I observed three times a week during the afternoons, after my work shift ended. Following the approaches of Corsaro and of Kantor and her colleagues, I noted not only the cultural processes affecting individual children's behavior, but also those influencing interactions between the children and the setting. I watched closely to see what activities the children were creating on their own, without teachers' assistance. I wanted to understand the group dynamics and what rules they followed. For example, I learned about the important role the children's object use played.

In addition to my formal observations of the outdoor play sessions, I also wrote down insights and informal observations while I was teaching in the morning. I kept my observational journal handy to quickly jot down what I had seen. I also recorded my thoughts and questions in a reflective teaching journal. This helped me recognize how my research question changed as the study progressed. I wrote research memos adapted from my reflective journal. The memos included events that I thought to be noteworthy from my observations, such as how one child appealed to other children by placing a plastic cone on his head in the same way they were doing. During the time I was conducting my research, I was also a graduate student at San Francisco State University. Colleagues in my university seminar and I frequently shared our research memos to gain other perspectives and to help clarify our own views.

Data analysis

At the conclusion of the study, I had conducted 31 observations of play sessions. I read each observation shortly after collection and sorted them into categories based on the strategies children used when attempting to join a play group. As the study progressed I indexed my data to reveal the instances in which a child who was attempting to enter a play group demonstrated that she understood the way that particular peer group played and interacted. Children did this in different ways; one such way was by using objects according to the roles assigned by the group.

In analyzing the data, I looked for all of the incidences of object use and indexed them according to which play sessions they were from and under what circumstances the objects were used. I sometimes asked other teachers for their interpretations of the data I had collected. I found this to be of the utmost importance, as they sometimes offered different perspectives on the same raw data. These voices proved helpful in my own understandings, and the teachers I consulted felt invested in the project as collaborators.

I received some validation of my data analyses from discussions with other staff at the preschool and my colleagues at San Francisco State University. Because of the interpretive nature of the study, I found their input useful in helping me clarify my perspectives and offer them in more realistic and insightful ways. When examples occurred that did not seem to fit my theoretical framework, discussion with others was extremely helpful in shedding light on some aspects of play.

© Buen Dia Family School

Findings and discussion

Two general findings stood out in the data. First, I learned that the ways that children used objects in the yard was an important element in the peer culture of some of the play groups. In many instances, the children used the objects in "goofy" ways—creative and imaginative ways rather than the objects' typical or expected uses. My findings about a locally constructed "goofy culture" became essential to my study of peer culture in the yard.

Second, it seemed to be more difficult for some children to find ways to enter peer group play activities in the yard than in the classroom. Outdoor play can send ambiguous messages to children about what they are expected to do (Perry 2001). There are not always clear areas outdoors that define for children what or how they may play, unlike the art area, block area, or dress-up corner, which are usually found indoors. This is partly why many children in the preschool created such interesting and inventive games.

I offer below brief descriptions of seven of the 14 activities the children created that highlight peer culture play patterns. Then, I analyze three episodes from a peer culture perspective. The third episode includes my own intervention as a teacher. As I learned more about the social significance of the children's unique activities, I began to interact and intervene differently. The seven activities include the following:

Jewels—Children used colored juice tops as "jewels" and barred other children from their activity.

Power Girl—A "power girl" chased around boys, who expressed both fear and excitement.

Goofy Brooms—A child joined two other children in hanging toy brooms on the basketball hoop (using the toy brooms in unusual ways that defied the teachers' intended uses).

Conehead—A child attempted to gain acceptance from a group of children by banging a plastic cone on his head to show an understanding of the group's humor.

Instant Monster—Children spontaneously took up roles of monster and runners to collectively share both excitement and fear (as in a power girl chase).

Basketball Babies—Children pretended that basketballs were babies and placed them in a double stroller.

Rings—Children used plastic rings, intended for ring toss, in other ways, such as rolling them down ramps. Another child hid them to entice others to join his game.

I discuss here only the play episodes I feel are the clearest examples of the vibrant and unique peer culture in the preschool yard. For a further discussion of some of these episodes, see Meier and Henderson (2007, 66–73).

Jewels: Children Protect Their Interactive Space

Sara and Molly are playing with "jewels" (colored juice tops from the art area) on the top of the climbing structure. After a few minutes, another child, Cathy, starts to climb the structure to join the two girls. Molly shouts, "No, you can't come up here! We're playing here!" As Cathy begins her descent, another child climbs up and is also barred from entry.

Most early childhood educators will recognize this scenario and would intervene in different ways and with positive intentions. Certainly the children's behavior can be seen by adults as uncooperative or selfish, raising concerns about the effects of exclusion on children (see Katch 2004; Paley 1993). Before I conducted this research, I would have aggressively intervened, finding ways to "make" Molly and Sara allow Cathy and other children to join their activity. However, something socially significant is happening here, beyond two children excluding another child. In the past I did not always pay close attention to the games children were playing, how well they related to one another, or the development of fledgling friendships. Through my observations in conducting this field study, however, I began to see children's behavior during free play differently. I thought about all the times children showed this kind of protection of their play from others. Corsaro (1997) contends that "this tendency is directly related to the fragility of peer interaction, the multiple possibilities of disruption in most preschool settings, and the children's desire to maintain control over shared activities" (p. 140).

On the one hand, I came to view this aspect of peer culture—children excluding others from their play—as crucial in deepening the social connections of the children engaged in play, as they try to control their communal activities. In the Jewels episode, the creativity of using an art material in a different way perhaps helps Molly and Sara bond. They may feel that their play—and maybe even their friendship—must be protected from others, which may be why they feel the need to exclude other children. On the other hand, this behavior presents challenges to the children who attempt to gain access, as the above example with Cathy illustrates.

At times, these activities provided a way for children to join in who otherwise might have had difficulty doing so. Goofy Brooms is an example of an activity established by two children in which another child—a child who often had difficulty socializing—was able to participate:

Goofy Brooms: Children Resist School Rules and Change Objects' Meanings

Greg and Juan take turns hanging child-size brooms on the basketball hoop. They laugh, and then Juan purposely falls on his bottom, exclaiming, "Ow, my butt!" He promptly receives laughing approval from Greg.

Allen sits on a nearby bench watching, perhaps aware that he is not a usual member of the group. Juan makes a joke about Allen's sunglasses but soon follows with the inquiry, "Do you wanna see something goofy?" Before Allen can answer, Juan quickly knocks over a small chair and sits on the back of it. All three children laugh.

Allen then prances over to the basketball hoop and hangs a broom. He finds a soccer ball and another broom and uses them as a hockey stick and puck. The three boys continue these goofy performances for the next few minutes.

Goofy Brooms was a spontaneous play episode evolving from previous play sessions in the yard. The particular goofiness had been established over many months. Children set unwritten rules requiring a type of unique physical humor that other children had to learn in order to be accepted. The appeal of Goofy Brooms is partly based on the resistant nature of the play, the way the children do the *wrong* thing with the objects (brooms, basketball hoop, soccer ball, chair). Corsaro (1985; 2003) found that through such resistant peer culture play, children show their awareness of the adult world's restrictiveness as compared to their own imaginative and creative worlds. They are merely finding an avenue for expression of such awareness as they also find their own ways to socially connect.

As I observed children's outdoor play, focusing on how children try to gain access, I found that children frequently use objects to try to connect with one another. Fernie and colleagues (1995) discuss how objects in a preschool classroom can serve an affiliation purpose and be "entry vehicles" for children attempting to gain access. The children in Goofy Brooms reinterpreted the meaning of objects in ways that made sense to them. They may have first considered sweeping sand off the pavement with the brooms or sitting on the seat of the chair, but this would possibly be less socially significant to their peers. It also might not have provided an entry point for Allen to join.

As I reflected on this episode and others like it, I thought about the ways I had tried to help Allen socialize with others, with varying degrees of success. Allen was very interested in adult discussions with teachers and had a harder time playing with children. In joining goofy brooms play, Allen showed social competence by knowing what to do to be accepted by Juan and Greg. He had learned about the goofy culture of the group and showed his peer culture knowledge by abiding by the group's goofiness. Allen did not use the typical teacher-promoted query, "Can I play?" to try to get in. From my teaching experience and observations, asking is not a guaranteed method of joining others who are already playing, especially if they are feeling protective, as in the Jewels episode.

I concluded that there was something very important about allowing peer culture play in the yard. The fact that the children believed they were resisting the rules was a significant part. I began to talk to other staff about my new perspective. The more I observed yard play, the more I began to understand how to be more effective in my interventions (besides just recognizing the importance of this kind of child-directed play).

The next example again illustrates peer culture play with objects. A child who attempts entry in an intelligent way is ignored, and I find a way to intervene within the context of the play.

Rings: An "Outsider" Uses Objects to Join Others

Matthew and Jay are playing with plastic rings (from a ring toss game), creating their own game by rolling them down the slide. Although there is a general rule about not rolling things down the slide, I want them to continue their peer culture routine. I suggest that they build ramps with plastic blocks and roll the rings down the ramps. They agree and begin the play. Another child, Ray, apparently finds this game appealing and easily joins in.

On the other side of the yard, Marc is also using rings. He puts them in trees (maybe because of a past activity where children put hats in trees) and buries them in the sand. After a few minutes, Marc approaches Matthew, Jay, and Ray and asks in a soft, high-pitched voice, "Who wants to do a scavenger hunt?" He is completely ignored, perhaps because the three boys are protecting their new ring routine or maybe because he annoys them. Whatever the reason, Marc has just expressed interest in joining the play, and I want to help him gain access.

Early childhood teachers can be effective interpreters to help children connect with one another and gain more social competence (Kemple & Jalongo 2004.) Adult intervention is especially important in the play yard, because this is a place where children are often left to their own devices. I was becoming increasingly aware of how some children need teachers to help them connect with others. I believed that Marc was trying to connect in his own way, and if the others knew about his creativity with rings, they would be interested in playing with him.

I explain to Jay, Matthew, and Ray in the simplest terms what I think Marc is asking them: "It sounds like Marc is asking if you want to look for rings that he is hiding." Matthew looks at Jay, and they drop their rings. Ray follows as they run over to other side of the yard, where Marc has hidden several rings. I ask a teacher in that area if he will help with the logistics of the scavenger hunt, and the hunt begins.

Later, as I wrote in my notebook about what had transpired, I thought about the way goofy peer culture had been transmitted through the children's use of rings. My

© Aaron Neimark

intervention helped Marc communicate his intentions and his understanding of the group's peer culture. I asked the other teacher how the scavenger hunt had gone, and he said that the children enjoyed the game and Marc liked taking a leadership role by hiding the rings.

I did not believe that this activity would instantly transform Marc into a completely socially competent child, able to join any group of children. However, he showed an awareness of other children's play that I had not noticed before. My new perspective on children's play and on intervening had helped bring Marc's social awareness to my attention and ultimately caused me to intervene.

Implications and reflections

The three play episodes in this study showed me that there was a real-life basis for the peer culture theories of Corsaro, Kantor and her colleagues, and others. I learned how valuable a new perspective could be for me as a teacher. As I continued to observe children playing, my understanding of their perspectives developed further and I became better able to communicate my findings to other staff and parents.

The value of using a peer culture lens

I believe that when teachers are mindful of children's peer cultures, they will be more effective. Hubbard and Power (2003) suggest that when teachers conduct their own research, they gain power over their practice. For me, this power involved bringing the theory of peer culture perspectives into the classroom and changing my methods of intervening to recognize the importance of peer-established routines, values, and beliefs when supporting children's social interactions. Introducing these ideas to other teachers at my school made me feel that I had truly made a connection between theory and practice. My research had inspired me to change how I taught, and I felt empowered as I discussed these ideas with my colleagues. Ultimately, I presented my findings at education conferences, and I continue to do this type of classroom inquiry today.

Teachers in various school settings can look more closely at their own practice and learn more about it by learning about the peer cultures of their students. They can examine the ways the children's peer cultures are recognized and given space in the context of the classroom culture. When teachers know more about the ways the children naturally relate to one another and the ways they establish their own routines, teachers can make wiser decisions about how to negotiate the presence of peer culture within the classroom and the school.

The following example shows how a teacher negotiated with the children to make space for a strong peer culture addition to the traditional celebration of children's birthdays:

> On days when we celebrate a child's birthday, the class bakes a cake. At group time, before we display the cake and sing "Happy Birthday," a teacher asks who helped make the cake and which ingredients they added. After a few children state that they put in eggs, flour, or baking powder, children begin to excitedly shout things like, "I put in the whole school!" or "I put in Michelle's [a teacher] head!" or "I put in the whole Aaron [me]!" The children and the teachers then share a laugh, abiding by the peer culture.

Sometimes it seems like the children's creative remarks go on long enough for the birthday candles to completely melt. However, the humorous peer culture practice of making silly comments about the cake has become part of the circle time routine at children's birthday celebrations. The teachers accepted this variation initiated by the children, and they negotiated a space for it in the birthday routine, even though they expected the children to name the actual ingredients they put in the

© Buen Dia Family School

cake. The children became more invested in participating in group time on days like this, something all teachers desire.

Many of the examples I discussed in this chapter are typical in early childhood settings. My particular interventions may not be applicable to other situations, but teachers can benefit from considering children's play behaviors in new ways. Teachers can reflect on approaches they use that may be less effective than they had thought them to be, such as the way they approach exclusion.

Conclusion

Do our imposed solutions when facilitating social interactions really foster peer competence in children? Allowing children more space to develop their own authentic ways to interact can be more effective in strengthening collaborative play and building their social competence with peers. Teachers should use children's peer culture to teach social skills more effectively and to help create a more harmonious balance between school culture and peer culture.

Updated from *Voices of Practitioners: Teacher Research in Early Childhood Education* 3 (1). Copyright © 2008 NAEYC.

References

Corsaro, W. 1985. *Friendship and peer culture in the early years*. Language and Learning for Human Service Professions monograph. Norwood, NJ: Ablex.

Corsaro, W. 1997. *The sociology of childhood*. Thousand Oaks, CA: Pine Forge Press.

Corsaro, W. 2003. *We're friends, right? Inside kids' culture*. Washington, DC: Joseph Henry Press.

Fernie, D., R. Kantor & K. Whaley. 1995. Learning from classroom ethnographies: Same places, different times. In *Qualitative research in early childhood settings*, ed. J.A. Hatch. Westport, CT: Praeger.

Hatch, J.A. 2002. *Doing qualitative research in education settings*. Albany: State University of New York Press.

Hubbard, R., & B. Power. 2003. *The art of classroom inquiry: A handbook for teacher researchers*. Portsmouth, NH: Heinemann.

Kantor, R., P. Elgas & D. Fernie. 1993. Cultural knowledge and social competence within a preschool peer culture group. *Early Childhood Research Quarterly* 8 (2): 125–47.

Kantor, R., & D. Fernie. 2003. What we have learned through an ethnographic lens. In *Early childhood classroom processes*, eds. R. Kantor & D. Fernie. Cresskill, NJ: Hampton Press.

Katch, J. 2004. *They don't like me: Lessons on bullying and teasing from a preschool classroom*. Boston, MA: Beacon Press.

Kemple, K., & M.R. Jalongo. 2004. *Let's be friends: Peer competence and social inclusion in early childhood programs*. New York: Teachers College Press.

Meier, D.R., & B. Henderson. 2007. *Learning from young children in the classroom: The art and science of teacher research*. New York: Teachers College Press.

Neimark, A. 2005. *Do you wanna see something goofy? Peer culture in the preschool yard*. Master's field study, San Francisco State University.

Paley, V.G. 1993. *You can't say you can't play*. Cambridge, MA: Harvard University Press.

Perry, J. 2001. *Outdoor play: Teaching strategies with young children*. New York: Teachers College Press.

Chapter

06

Exploring the Forest:

Wild Places in Childhood

Anna Golden

Anna Golden uses a narrative format to tell the story of her preschoolers' explorations of and relationships to the natural world. Using the narrative lenses of written stories, photographs, and selected literature, she brings us along an artistic walk through elements of a story arc in the children's experiences with nature. Anna's piece stands out by integrating memoir and her own artwork as sources of data to help her understand the children's special connections to the forest. We see the power of teacher research to go back in time as she revisits her own childhood memories of experiencing a sense of place in nature.

The voices of the children and her own passionate voice as a daughter, an artist, and a teacher all come together to help us understand the critical role of play in untamed natural spaces for young children.

—Barbara Henderson and Daniel R. Meier

The preschoolers leave the school building and wait, pressing up against the playground gate. When I open the gate, they take off like horses let out of a stable where they have been shut in too long. I follow behind them, trying to keep up in the bumpy and overgrown forest. I have my usual tools, a clipboard and pen, and the children each have the same. At times I bend down to pick up a clipboard that has been tossed aside in an effort to cover ground more quickly. They yell back over their shoulders so that I can record what they discover as they fan out over the land.

*Alec brakes at the creek bank. "There's a beach! There's a beach! There's a cute little beach!" Scrambling down, Evan shouts back to alert his friends: "A toadstool! A toadstool! If you see poison, **scream**!" Then, before inhabiting his rocky beach, Evan turns and warns again: "Guys, if you see poison, scream more!" Alec and Ryan, walking alongside a fallen pine, spy the creek. "A river!" They both sprint. "Ryan, I'm right on your tail," Alec yells.*

Henry, kneeling over his clipboard, shouts, "Hey, I found a berry. I drawed it!" Jack comes over and picks up an orange shell encasing a round pink berry. "Oh. Those are cute," he says. "It's like a pumpkin disguise." But Henry is already off. "Leafs! Leafs!" he hollers back. "I need to draw leafs!"

This is the story of a teacher/researcher/artist/daughter who, with her group of 4- and 5-year-old children, explores the untamed woods outside a school. This teacher research study encompasses the experiences I had with the children, my reading on the importance of wild places for children, and my personal reflections on sense of place in my childhood.

What draws children to build forts, seek and create hideouts, and make out-of-the-way places to play? These common behaviors create a *sense of place* for children that extends beyond the simple act of building. Inside all of us are memories associated with place. They touch the core of who we are and inspire us beyond childhood, into adulthood. That childhood sense of place often has a huge influence on adult ideas. For children, the physical and sensory experiences of place imprint themselves on memory. I saw the children in my preschool class make magical connections to place in their excursions beyond the playground fence.

I am a teacher and the *atelierista,* or studio teacher, at Sabot School, a progressive preschool in Richmond, Virginia, that is influenced by the philosophy of the schools in Reggio Emilia, Italy. An *atelierista* is an art specialist who helps young children express their ideas through drawing, building, and other media, and helps teachers with ideas about art media, ways to extend and deepen children's inquiry, and documentation. I am inspired by the work of the teachers in Reggio Emilia. Learning and teaching in this way is a process that doesn't end. There is always more to learn and new areas of inquiry to explore with children.

The piazza question

This teacher research project began with a staff discussion about the Italian tradition of the *piazza.* In Italy, towns are built around a central square—a piazza. This is where people socialize, conduct business in open-air markets, hold festivals and celebrations, and gather for quiet talks in the evening. The noise of a hundred conversations fills the piazza. It is the heart of the community. The preschools of Reggio Emilia are built around a central piazza for similar reasons. In this common area, children of different ages play and learn, families interact, and daily school meetings take place (Malaguzzi 1993).

For American teachers interested in adapting Reggio Emilia ideas, there is no piazza tradition to build on. In Richmond, the closest thing to a piazza is the beloved James River and the municipal park that runs along its banks. It seems that every Richmond resident has experienced this natural place, our own urban wilderness. But the park is too far away to serve as a meeting place for our school community. At Sabot, we wondered, What is *our* piazza? We craved a place that we could share with the children and families, a place that would bring us together.

Because Sabot's families are from the city, suburbs, and outlying rural areas, the school grounds seemed to be the only place that we all had in common. When we realized this, we thought of the woods beyond the school grounds.

Sabot School, which shares its building with a church, sits next to a large undeveloped lot, a wooded area just outside the playground fence. There are tall pines and many trees downed by Hurricane Isabel, the strongest, most damaging hurricane in the 2003 season. We thought the children could use the fallen trees as bridges and the large roots as mountains to climb. The lot has a long, thin, shallow, drainage ditch with steep banks and a rocky bottom for exploring. The children called it "the creek" and referred to the wooded area as "the forest."

As we thought more about the woods, many questions came to mind. How could we use the forest as a space for young children? What could the school community gain from moving out into this space? Would families use the space? Could expanding into the woods bring our school community together? Could the forest become the Sabot School's piazza?

The staff decided that we would explore the forest with the children. We weren't sure what that would entail, but we were committed to taking the children outside the playground fence to see what would happen. We began reading *The Geography of Childhood* (Nabhan & Trimble 1994), a book about the benefits of a relationship with nature. We read one chapter at a time and discussed it in staff meetings.

The staff talked about potential dangers and possible accidents in the woods. Adults sometimes let fear stop them—and children—from interacting with nature (Nabhan & Trimble 1994). If we teachers let worry rule us, we would never take children beyond the playground. As a group, we decided to focus on the endless benefits of the experience rather than worry about what might go wrong.

What would the children learn from being out there? Would they investigate the area and make it their own? Could children of different ages and grade levels work together to inquire about and solve problems? Would the shared experience build community, leading to greater collaboration between children, families, and teachers? The teachers decided to document the children's introduction to the woods and bring the documentation to Monday staff meetings for discussion and planning.

Meanwhile, I was inspired to read more about children and their relationship to nature. The more I read, the more I recognized how my personal connection to the outdoors had evolved through my childhood experiences.

Nature in my own childhood

During the time we were debating about our American-style piazza, my father became ill and moved in with my family and me. My father and I had always been close, and when he moved in, I was happy for his company. My dad had worked as an accountant, but he was also an artist and photographer who loved wilderness. Curious and studious, he read the journals of American pioneers and ancient explorers. After my brother and I had left home, he moved to a rural Virginia county to fulfill his dream of living close to the land. When I was thinking about taking the children at Sabot School into the woods, I thought about my dad when he was healthy and exploring the things he loved.

When my dad died, I missed him. His books and belongings filled every room in my house. Opening his boxes of photographs, negatives, and slides flooded me with memories. There were street photographs from Washington marches, portraits of family and friends, and nature photography that he had sold at the Audubon Society store in Alexandria. My father's photographs represented spaces and places burned into my subconscious. They have always influenced me artistically as a painter and sculptor.

Thinking about the secret spaces of my childhood yielded quick impressions, rich with feeling and sensory memories—like flashbacks in a movie, only more real. Our neighborhood in Arlington, Virginia, was close to military bases, and I remember climbing chain-link fences, sliding down the banks of Four-Mile Run, poking around in muddy water for crayfish, and scrambling up fast when somebody yelled, "Snake!"

I remember the communal nature of this play, the feeling that we children were doing something important together. I remember the joy of being away from adults and the exciting feeling of being on the lookout for any intruders in our secret place. I also recall the private nature of the play, because sometimes, even in a group, my imaginary world was mine alone.

My favorite spot in the creek was another world to me. It was a place apart from my life at school and home, a place where I felt all kinds of magical things could happen. When we kids heard taps over the military base's loudspeakers, it was time to go home. The real world flooded back in, and I would suddenly remember that I had homework and chores and that I was hungry.

In going through my father's things, I looked for one photograph in particular. I found it in a box labeled Misc. It was a photo of a dilapidated barn in North Carolina, my brother and me barely visible in two of its large windows. I was about 7, thrilled to be exploring the old barn with my brother and two family friends. The photograph triggered a wave of feelings and memories.

Childhood experience of place fuses with daydream and then changes into memory (Bachelard [1958] 1994). Childhood daydreams are experienced again in adulthood through creative thought. For me, the old barn photo brought back the nuances of memories of that barn—the sound of laughter, the smell of the lofts, the scary creaks and groans of the old wood in the wind, the itch of hay on sweaty skin, and my strong connection to my dad. I began a new series of paintings, working out my feelings of loss, reliving my childhood experiences, and riding the powerful wave of creativity that rushed through me.

© Allyn Walters

Exploring the forest

With the staff committed to the investigation of the forest with the children, we began the exploration of the woods. Each day the children would ask, "When are we going into the forest?" We would go into the forest after planning time, usually for 45 minutes or more. I would bring a notebook and pen for myself, a digital camera, and maybe a tape recorder to document the children's experiences.

When the forest exploration project was first proposed, we teachers had hypothesized about what the children would consider important when they got outside the playground fence. We assumed they would be interested in collecting and identifying natural treasures, like rocks, ferns, and flowers. We pictured the children with their clipboards, studiously drawing the things they observed, just as they did inside the classrooms and playground.

During those early investigations, I thought I would point out wild roses or a sleeping salamander; however, once the gate was opened, we found that the children were most interested in physical and sensory exploration. They didn't want to draw yet or even talk; they needed to climb up a tree root or down into the creek. They were in motion: running, crawling, jumping, scrambling. Our early trips were truly exploratory, with the children and me climbing into the densest, most overgrown sections of the forest. The children were determined to physically go over every inch of the place.

They dragged around large branches, used sticks to dig holes, found footholds to climb up a bank, and discovered bouncy spots among the fallen leaves and debris on the forest floor. The confident children moved more quickly and took on more challenges while I walked more slowly with the less-confident children. This tested my teacher's tolerance. I wanted everyone to stay together, but the children's different skill levels made that impractical. The other teachers and I observed, allowing the children to show us what was important to them about this learning experience.

Moore says that "children possess their environment by making places; by the way those places offer the twofold gifts of adventure and sensory identity" (2003, 61). Young children cannot help but be immersed in the environment because they are physically so close to the ground, their bodies in direct contact with nature—getting wet in streams, climbing trees, or rolling down hills (Chawla 2002). There is a real, elemental, sensory connection to place; this type of connection and physical contact with a special place is a way we first identify with the world around us. The act of being in a natural or wild place—the sounds, the smells, and the strain of muscle against an obstacle—is what defines this connection. Such relationships with natural spaces may be crucial to human development.

> Children come to know themselves through their transactions with both the physical and social worlds. Unlike people, the physical world does not change in response to a child's actions but simply reflects his manipulations, so it offers a particularly valuable domain for developing his (or her) sense of competence. (Hart et al. 1983, 67)

In other words, children create their understanding of place first by experiencing its physical and sensory characteristics. These sensations help in developing understandings about personal limitations and potential. So children build their concepts of who they are and what they can do through physical contact with the world around them.

Later, after the children had explored every forest nook and cranny, I observed them slowing down and investigating more closely. They began comparing their findings with each other and forming groups to explore things more thoroughly. The groups that initially went out to explore became more mixed in age as the year went on. The children began forming groups based on common interests. They were creating, drawing pictures of each other and maps of the forest and wondering about the red-tailed hawk and its nest and about the origins of the water in the creek. They collected some treasures to take back the classroom, but mostly the children left things where they were and drew pictures of the objects to bring inside. Drawing became a way of cataloguing the objects the children found in the forest. Their maps and drawings took on two meanings: they were signs of both a very private connection to place and of the communal nature of play in wild places. Remarkably, even children like Henry, who rarely chose seat work in the classroom, felt compelled to draw what he was seeing in the forest. Was he trying to keep what he saw by drawing symbols of these natural objects?

When you listen to children in wild places, you find so much happening. As illustrated in the opening vignette, children made analogies ("It's like a pumpkin disguise"), references to popular culture ("I'm right on your tail," from *Star Wars*), and strategies for dealing with danger ("If you see poison, scream").

The children soon began creating imaginative scenarios. One day I watched a group of 4- and 5-year-old girls find a large puddle at the base of an upturned tree. They quickly gathered long sticks and began fishing. One girl exclaimed, "I caught a fish!" and another asked, "Is it real?" A third shouted, "A whale!" and all the girls began swishing their sticks through the water to find whales. The magic of that experience lasted a long time, and for months afterward the girls talked about the day Layla caught a whale in the forest.

Another aspect of the children's explorations involved dramatic play that empowered them to face imagined fears or dangers. I observed children pretending to be lost baby birds trapped in tall trees, searching for their mothers. Their play often revolved around survival—"We're lost and no one can find us." Other times the children would arm themselves with sticks, cardboard-tube telescopes, and masking-

tape "power stripes" to prepare for a long journey across the creek, through the brambles, and up the bank toward an unknown destination or challenge. The trek was usually filled with imagined dangers and enemies, such as wolves or robbers.

Children's inner voice—imagination—as well as their confidence and self-knowledge, is nurtured by their constructing and playing in wild places and secret spaces (Goodenough 2003). Children need to build places for play because the "imagination needs to feel protected as it expands within safe boundaries" (Goodenough 2003, 3). In my class, the boys who engaged in the long process of mixing paint to create camouflage masks and construction-paper weapons were creating their own world—an imaginary world in which they were hunters and heroes, in control of their environment.

Childhood and a sense of place: Making the space their own

Clearly, the children came to inhabit the forest—for them, the forest became part of school and part of their lives. Time to play in wild space is very important for children. It allows them to discover and test their own boundaries against a physical environment that can accept the changes children bring, while remaining essentially the same. The classroom can replicate some things in nature, but in the natural environment the learning seems so much more authentic. For instance, in a classroom, children may learn about wedges and levers in block play, but in the forest, children *use* such simple machines to build a shelter. Louv discusses how the tacit knowledge that grows from experiences in nature affects children's sense of self: "Natural play strengthens children's self-confidence and arouses their senses—their awareness of the world and all that moves in it, seen and unseen" (2008, 186). The young children at Sabot thoroughly explored the new space and made it their own. At the same time, the space is so big, and so many things are in it, that the children never exhausted their wonder of it.

In our school forest, where the creek bank is overgrown with tree roots and ivy, the children pulled themselves up to discover a little clearing in a dense thicket. After a few brambles were stomped down and some branches rearranged, this became the children's hideout. Building is a way for children to order and control their world, often in a cooperative way. In building forts and tree houses, digging holes and making dams in moving water, children deconstruct and reconstruct the landscape to suit their need for secret spaces, spaces they can define for themselves, away from adults (Moore 1986). Environments are often too controlled by adults to allow for children's spontaneous building. It is in the fringe, out-of-the-way places that children create their spaces—under tables and in closets, in alleys, fields, or vacant lots.

Childhood experiences and adult creativity

Do our childhood experiences with nature become a part of who we are as adults? Chawla (2002) reviewed autobiographies of prominent people to determine if early experiences with special places had any impact on adult creativity. She found that adults who were involved in creative fields described "magic or ecstatic" experiences with places in childhood they remembered (2002, 214). Bachelard also wrote about the link between secret spaces and artistic authenticity: "Inhabited space (the space where we think and daydream) transcends geometrical space (the actual physical place where we are)" ([1958] 1994, 47).

In undertaking the forest project at school, I realized that my artwork draws heavily on my memories of wild places. I have been making paintings of houses and imaginary landscapes for years. I never thought about what real places they represented, but they are strong, symbolic images that have a magical quality for me. Today, I wonder if my childhood explorations of parks, campgrounds, and waste places like vacant lots between houses and shopping centers may have been among my earliest aesthetic experiences and whether that is why they influence me now. Artists, like children, "enjoy harmonizing things in smaller, manageable worlds of their own" (Goodenough 2003, 9). Clearly, my own childhood experiences are embedded in my adult memory in a way that nurtures my creativity; but how important are these kinds of experiences to young children today?

Reflections and conclusions: Making connections

The most important questions I ask myself over and over again have to do with becoming a better teacher and a better artist. I want to know more about reflection and documentation. I want to read and understand the theories of important educational pioneers like Lev Vygotsky and Jerome Bruner. I wonder about the relationship between reading theory and putting it into practice in my classroom. I think about the connection between drawing and learning. As an artist, I feel that I can bring reflection and painting together in a mysterious way to create art that is very personal and that I don't know how to explain. But how does all of this thinking come together? I'm not sure I have found any answers, but somehow my work with my colleagues and the children in exploring the forest has brought my questions together in a new way.

Exploring the Sabot School forest with the children and documenting that experience, reading about children and nature, and working through my fathers' things became strongly connected in my mind. Never before had my artwork been so directly influenced by what was happening in my classroom, and never before had what happened in the classroom been so influenced by what I was reading and what was happening in my personal life. I began thinking about everything in a new way. More than any other time, my personal and work interests came together in the exploration of the forest, and I understood the idea of school as life.

Children need strong and satisfying connections to nature, but unfortunately, for too many, time spent outside and in wild places is a luxury rather than an everyday opportunity (Nabhan & Trimble 1994). Moore estimated in 1986 that "the current generation will spend 5/7 of their time in experientially deprived spaces" (p. 60). Experientially deprived spaces include the indoors, manicured suburban lawns, and school and park playgrounds that offer only very programmed and safe play. Moore advocates for changes in public policy that would make natural spaces more available to children. He believes that children must have access to wild places so they can learn about nature, face physical challenges, and learn how to be themselves. Children cannot learn the importance of adventure and exploration in natural spaces unless adults make that

possible, and sadly, many adults do not expose their children to nature play if they themselves have not experienced it in childhood.

Unfortunately, children are often taught that the natural world is perilous. In *Beyond Ecophobia*, Sobel (1996) laments that children hear about environmental disasters, like oil spills and loss of biodiversity and habitat, while they lack firsthand, authentic experiences with natural places. Indeed, some environmentalists worry that teaching children about distant environmental disasters can lead to apathy instead of activism (Nixon 1997).

Abstract discussions (e.g., about tropical deforestation) are completely different from allowing children to interact with nature in their own community.

The forest at Sabot School has become the piazza. It is a rich resource for teachers and families, as well as for children. I studied children's strategies to represent the forest and tried to find better ways to bring the outdoors into the classroom. Other teachers used the forest for an inquiry into light and dark, to study family involvement, and to see what would happen if a class spent the entire school year outdoors. The families of Sabot School have embraced this space, sharing the documentation, helping to maintain the land, and exploring the forest and creek with their children after school. For children, the forest is a place for exciting dramatic play, a place for discoveries, and a place to map through physical exploration. As the children grow up, I hope that they too will remember it as magical and inspiring.

In this experience, I began to better understand the way children learn and how they can thoroughly immerse themselves in a project. Exploring the forest coincided with an intensively reflective period in my life, as I experienced the loss of my father. The process of teacher research took on new meaning as I reflected not only on what was happening at school and the things I was reading, but also on my relationship with my dad and his love of nature and wilderness. I was learning as a teacher, as an artist, and as a person, just sorting things out in my mind, and this is the story of my learning.

Updated from *Voices of Practitioners: Teacher Research in Early Childhood Education* 5 (1). Copyright © 2010 NAEYC.

Photos courtesy of the author unless otherwise noted.

References

Bachelard, G. [1958] 1994. *The poetics of space: The classic look at how we experience intimate places.* Trans. © Orion Press 1964. Boston: Beacon Press.

Chawla, L. 2002. Spots of time: Manifold ways of being in nature in childhood. In *Children and nature: Psychological, sociocultural, and evolutionary investigations,* eds. P.H. Kahn & S.R. Kellert, 99–225. Cambridge, MA: MIT Press.

Goodenough, E.N., ed. 2003. *Secret spaces of childhood.* Ann Arbor, MI: University of Michigan Press.

Hart, R.A., J. Volkert & N. Walch. 1983. Rough housing. In *Home sweet home: American domestic vernacular architecture,* ed. C. Moore, 63–69. New York: Rizzoli.

Louv, R. 2008. *Last child in the woods.* Chapel Hill, NC: Algonquin Books.

Malaguzzi, L. 1993. History, ideas, and basic philosophy. In *The hundred languages of children: The Reggio Emilia approach to early childhood education,* eds. C. Edwards, L. Gandini & G. Foreman, 84. Norwood, NJ: Ablex.

Moore, R.C. 1986. *Childhood's domain: Play and place in child development.* London: Croom Helm.

Moore, R.C. 2003. Childhood's domain: Play and place in child development. In *Secret spaces of childhood,* ed. E.N. Goodenough, 57–61. Ann Arbor, MI: University of Michigan Press.

Nabhan, G.P., & S. Trimble. 1994. *The geography of childhood: Why children need wild spaces.* Boston: Beacon Press.

Nixon, W. 1997. Letting nature shape childhood. *Amicus Journal* 19 (3): 31–35.

Sobel, D. 1996. *Beyond ecophobia: Reclaiming the heart in nature education.* Nature Literacy series, vol. 1. Great Barrington, MA: The Orion Society.

If I were President I would tell the builders who build houses for rich people to build the homeless houses and I would give them food and a car.

Chapter

07

If I Were President:

Teaching Social Justice in the Primary Classroom

Elizabeth Goss

Liz Goss, a primary grade teacher in inner city Chicago, demonstrates how 6- and 7-year-olds can eagerly engage with difficult issues of social justice like slavery and collective action. In one set of lessons, she drew on popular culture by using the Disney movie *A Bug's Life* (1998) to help the children think about the oppression of one group by another.

Goss's teacher research illustrates an effective technique for analyzing a large body of data to represent children's thinking. Five emergent themes from the data were woven together to tell a story rich in examples of what really happens in urban primary grade classrooms. Little did this teacher know in January 2005, when she asked her African American students to think about what they would do if they were president, that four years later they would witness the inauguration of an African American as president of the United States.

Like President Obama, Goss's students reveal a deep level of hope and a desire for change. Goss offers insight into how to co-construct with students a curriculum that promotes social justice and yet is grounded in their everyday lives.

—Barbara Henderson

If I were President I would give poor people houses. If I were President I would tell the builders who build houses for rich people to build the homeless houses and I would give them food and a car.

If I were President I would stop wars from killing people and fighting and throwing bombs at people. They need to care for people. That's what I would do.

The 6- and 7-year-olds in my classroom created posters with drawings of themselves as president of the United States. Their statements completed the thought, "If I were President, I would . . ." I was teaching on Chicago's West Side in a small public school that stands in the shadows of one of the city's largest housing projects. My multiage first and second grade class was made up of 25 active, questioning, loved, curious, and sometimes worried and pained African American children.

The world of my first- and second-graders was a complicated one. They came to school rich in experiences of the world, garnered from both home and school. As young children, they still debated the existence of the tooth fairy but were painfully aware of the reality of gunfire in their neighborhood. I struggled to create with them a classroom full of wonder, love, joy, hope, and questions. I wanted my students to ask important questions, and I believed they were capable of finding answers and finding their way in the world. I envisioned a better world for them, one that is more just, more joyful, more inspiring. This was the setting for my action research project.

Undertaking action research

Looking for a new challenge after four years of teaching, I applied for and received a MetLife Fellowship at the Teachers Network Leadership Institute (TNLI) through the Chicago Foundation for Education. TNLI was a nonprofit educational organization established to improve student achievement by bringing teachers' expertise and experiences to education policy making. The institute awarded fellowships to full-time public school teachers to conduct action research in their classrooms and then connect their findings to local, state, and national policy discussions. MetLife Fellows met every three weeks to discuss their action research with each other under the aegis of a university mentor who provides technical assistance to the group. The fellows documented their work by writing papers and making presentations.

If I were President I would make things good. I would love the world and I would buy anthing for kids and I would help people get homes.

I had often asked myself, How do the students in my first- and second-grade classroom respond to ethical dilemmas? I wanted to give my students opportunities to explore large questions of justice. I wanted to set up learning experiences that pushed them to think critically about their world. I decided to see what would happen when I centered my teaching in the ethics of social justice. I also wanted to see whether my students could participate successfully in helping to determine the direction of the class curriculum. In essence, I wondered, What happens when teachers work collaboratively with children to investigate how to create a better world for all?

I believe in the power of education and critical thinking to transform the world. Therefore, there was no better place for me to situate this transformation than in my first- and second-grade classroom—a place affected by an overarching social system of inequality and injustice and yet also full of hope.

What is teaching for social justice?

At the turn of the 20th century, John Dewey captured the imaginations and hearts of many educators with his writings on the critical role that education plays in forming a democratic society. Dewey wrote in 1916:

> I appeal to teachers . . . to remember that they above all others are consecrated servants of the democratic ideas in which alone this country is truly a distinctive nation—ideas of friendly and helpful intercourse between all and the equipment of every individual to serve the community by his own best powers in his own best way. (Dewey 1976, 210)

If I were President I would make a park.

As the theories and practices of teaching evolved, the roles individual teachers and communities can play in the decisions regarding curriculum, methodology, and pedagogy have been limited (Edelsky 1999). Teachers have to contend with high-stakes tests that constrain curriculum. They find their hands tied in their own classrooms due to the district's, even the state's, adoption of the latest textbook or newest instructional system. Curriculum decisions are often made by bureaucrats far removed from classrooms, many with limited or no actual teaching experience. Despite this backdrop of increasing centralization of power, good teachers attempt to create curriculum and classrooms with democracy at their heart as a living, breathing, evolving metaphor (Bigelow 1997; Zinn 2002).

Teaching for social justice comes in many shapes and sizes. This research project is grounded in a framework developed by teachers committed to the idea that public education is central to the creation of a humane, multiracial democracy. The framework was presented in *Rethinking Our Classrooms: Teaching for Equity and Justice* in 1994 (Au et al. 2007) and adapted by a group of Chicago area educators, Teachers for Social Justice. It comprises eight principles, as follows.

A social justice curriculum and classroom practice should

- Be grounded in the lives of our students
- Equip students to pose critical questions about their world
- Be multicultural, anti-racist, pro-justice
- Be participatory, experiential
- Be hopeful, joyful, kind, visionary
- Encourage children to act on their ideas
- Be academically rigorous
- Be culturally and linguistically sensitive

(Au et al. 2007)

Research questions

My research questions were,

- How do first- and second-graders respond to questions of inequality?
- How do children's experiences outside of school influence their perspectives on social justice?

- How can the teacher integrate social justice into the design of the curriculum?
- What happens when teachers allow children to make some of the decisions about the direction of the curriculum?

Design of the study

During a five-month period, I initiated curriculum activities to solicit the children's views on and foster their understandings of social justice issues. The eight teaching principles mentioned earlier served as a framework for the curriculum planning and the activities. Most of the activities were planned for an eight-week unit on the Civil Rights Movement, which began with an introduction to slavery through the

movie *A Bug's Life*. I planned a brief discussion about slavery in the United States to provide the historical context for the Civil Rights Movement. Among the activities planned were listening to a guest speaker, Reverend Addie Wyatt (who had worked with Dr. Martin Luther King Jr.), and the development of an idea for our class's participation in the schoolwide assembly on Black history.

Another activity, If I Were President, followed the 2004 presidential elections and was related to current events rather than being part of the civil rights unit. This activity prompted responses from the children that reflected their thinking on social justice issues. I used the two activities, described below, in my study.

If I Were President

During the inauguration of President George W. Bush in January 2005, the class discussed the roles of the president. I then asked each child to create a page for a class book titled "If I Were President." Each page would begin with the phrase, "If I were President I would . . ." The pages included the children's illustrations of themselves as president of the United States and the completed phrase stating what they would do as president. I photocopied the pages to make the class book, and mounted the original pages on large sheets of construction paper, which I then laminated. I posted these posters in the classroom.

A Bug's Life

I introduced the topic of slavery by showing the children the animated movie *A Bug's Life*. The movie's premise is a Marxist take on the power struggles in the insect world. The main characters, the ants, are exploited by the grasshoppers, who rule by fear. The ants are forced to gather all the food for the grasshoppers. As the ants become aware of the unfairness of their lot, one ant stands up to the evil grasshopper leader. Ultimately, the ants realize that they outnumber the grasshoppers and simply have to work together to overthrow the grasshopper regime.

I explained to the class that we were going to watch an entertaining children's movie, but that I wanted them to think about its theme. I said that it reminded me of slavery. I led a brief discussion, eliciting their prior knowledge about slavery, and then we prepared to watch the movie. I explained that we would watch the first 20 minutes and then stop so that they could write about how the grasshoppers treated the ants and what they thought the ants should do.

I asked students to give their views by responding to three prompts:

I think the ants are treated _____ by the grasshoppers.

They have to _____ and _____.

I think _____.

Unit on the Civil Rights Movement Parents' Survey

Dear Parents:

Our class is just completing a unit on the Civil Rights Movement. Please take a moment to fill out this survey so I can evaluate the effectiveness of our studies. Circle yes or no in response to each question, and write additional comments you may have in the space under the question. I value your opinion and would very much like to hear from you.

1. My child talked with me about Reverend Wyatt's visit.	Yes / No
2. My child talked about the Underground Railroad and slavery.	Yes / No
3. My child talked about the Black History Assembly.	Yes / No
4. My child talked about the Civil Rights Movement (including Rosa Parks, Dr. King, Malcolm X, and boycotts).	Yes / No
5. I see my child applying lessons learned from the unit to her/his everyday life (issues of fairness, justice, race, etc.).	Yes / No

Do you have any comments about the unit on the Civil Rights Movement?

Do you think learning about African American history is important for the children?

Please return your response in your child's homework folder.

Thank you for your time.

—Ms. Goss

Data collection and analysis

Data collection

I collected data for my action research project from five sources over a period of five months:

Student work samples—written work from my students, including copies of their journal entries, writings from class projects, and written responses in classroom meetings.

Teacher journal—my observations of pertinent class lessons and discussions as well as reflections about the curriculum. I wrote in the journal at least twice a week, spending 15 minutes at lunch or at the end of the day recording my thoughts. After a few weeks, I realized I was questioning my own role as a teacher as much as recording the students' responses to activities.

Parent survey—parents' reports on the ideas the students were bringing home from their experiences at school (see the box "Unit on the Civil Rights Movement Parents' Survey").

Audiotapes—audio recordings of class meetings during social justice activities.

Informal conversations—my notes on conversations about social justice topics between students and teacher during the study.

If I were President I would say all the schools are to be great and no one can fight you and I would set every one free out of jail.

Analysis

At the end of five months, I read and analyzed the data. I looked for patterns in children's responses to questions of inequality and for evidence that students were using their experiences from outside of school to justify or explain their views on social justice. I also examined the data to determine what happened when the students participated in making decisions about the direction of the curriculum. I had collected a large amount of data but wasn't sure what it told me. However, on closer examination, as I read through the data, certain trends began to appear, which I explore below.

Findings

Students used main themes or categories when discussing issues of social justice

At the beginning of the research process, I was anxious about what I would find and how I was going to make sense of the children's thinking. What if I couldn't identify distinct threads of thought in the data? What if the students weren't interested in questions of justice? I was surprised, relieved, and intrigued by how clearly the categories of their thinking emerged. I found five recurring themes in their writing and conversations: empathy, identifying with the oppressed, collective action, standing up for oneself, and fairness.

Empathy. Students expressed empathy often. In the If I Were President activity, they showed empathy toward poor people ("I would give poor people houses. I would give them food and a car") and toward people involved in violent situations ("I would stop wars from killing people and fighting and throwing bombs").

Identifying with the oppressed. The children generally felt empathy for people who were hurt or sick or poor and for animals, but they had a more specific identification with people who were oppressed by others or whose freedom had been taken away. They used both fictional and real-life ideas when identifying with the oppressed. They saw the ants in *A Bug's Life* as oppressed because the grasshoppers made the ants do all the work, took away the ants' freedom, and did not treat the ants with respect ("I think the ants are treated desrespackful"). In the children's own experiences, people in jail are oppressed ("If I were President I would set every one free out of jail . . ."). Many of the children had had direct experiences with people whose freedom had been taken away. I believe this was part of their strong identification with the ants.

Collective action. The students referenced how the ants worked together to gain their freedom from the grasshoppers. They understood how people (or ants) work together to make a plan and carry it out. They wrote, "I would rather be an ant becuae we will work toghet and mak a plan to defet [defeat] the grasshopp" and "They have to try to escape and take all the food I think." They believed it was important to be brave and not just accept unfair treatment. When asked how the ants won, one student wrote, "The ants was braf enf to deft the grasshoppers togehr" [The ants was brave enough to defeat the grasshoppers together].

Standing up for oneself. Many of the students had been taught that they have to stand up for themselves and their family members. For example, if a younger brother is being bullied on the playground, the older sibling would be expected to stand up for him. In the *A Bug's Life* discussion I often heard, "I think they should fight back" and "I think they should stand up for ther self." When the children were asked if they would rather be an ant or a grasshopper, one responded: "I would rather be an ant because they is brave. They stand up for therself. Thay will scair the grasshopper. They is not scaide [scared] of the grasshopper no more."

Fairness. Primary-age children often say, "That's not fair." They can be very focused on equity and they look at equity in concrete terms. The children in my classroom judged the fairness of a situation by comparing themselves to their peers. For example, they would think, "If I have to do some work, then you should have to work also." If the cafeteria ran out of a favorite food, the children's response was not just "I can't have it," but "It is unfair because you got some and I didn't." The students expressed this view when discussing how to solve the problem between the grasshoppers and the ants: "I think the grasshoppers should give back their food." That is, the ants did all the work and the grasshoppers didn't work at all, and yet the grasshoppers got the food. Similarly, the children thought the homeless should have houses because rich people have houses: "If I were President I would tell the builders who build houses for rich people to build the homeless houses . . ."

Frequently, two or more themes are apparent in a single comment. For example, when the children identified with the oppressed, it was often because the oppressed subjects were treated unfairly and the children empathized regarding their situation ("If I were President I would help schools. I would let people out of jail, like my uncle" and "If I were President I would take care of the country and buy everybody games"). The responses told me a lot about the depth of their understanding of social justice issues. I learned more about teaching social justice to young children from my class's responses than from any textbook on teaching.

Findings linked to the main activities in the study

I began an analysis of the data by looking at students' work for the activity If I Were President and then at the activities connected to the movie *A Bug's Life*.

If I Were President class book and posters. I had asked the children what they would do if they were president of the United States. As is clear from the quotations at this chapter's opening, the children looked at their own communities' needs and decided how they could improve their world. The activity—to represent themselves as a Black president—was especially meaningful because the children placed themselves in the seat of power, visually and intellectually. It enabled them to visualize this within the context of a world that has a hard time imagining anyone who is not White, male, and wealthy running for president.

Nineteen of the 23 children wrote statements that showed their ideas about empathy, identifying with the oppressed, and fairness. Not all of the children responded by thinking of others. Of the remaining four, their plans for using presidential power

If I were President I would stop wars from killing people and fighting and throwing bombs at people. They need to care for people. That's what I would do.

represented the typical priorities of 6- and 7-year-olds, such as, "If I were President, I would ride a bike and roller-skate in the Oval Office" and "If I were President I would boss around my mom, dad, sister, and Ms. Goss."

A Bug's Life. In this movie the situation of the ants and the grasshoppers ignited the students' passion, and the children became deeply engaged in discussing and writing about its unfairness, how one ant stood up to a grasshopper, and how the ants as a group banded together to change their circumstances. Because of the children's strong interest and enthusiastic participation in the activities related to *A Bug's Life*, the movie became the cornerstone of our social justice curriculum.

In the activities that followed the children's viewing of *A Bug's Life*, it became clear that the children identified with the oppressed ants. When asked how the ants were treated by the grasshoppers and what the ants should do, in response to the prompts, "I think the ants are treated _____ by the grasshoppers" and "They have to _____ and _____," the children wrote,

I think the ants are treated badly.

I think the ants are treated desrespackful.

They have to give them all the food.

They have to think and then do it. I think they should excape.

They have to think of a plan.

In response to the prompt "I think _____," students wrote about collective action and standing up for oneself, and they expressed their empathy for the ants. One example of advocating collective action was Tameka's response: "They have to try to escape and take all the food I think." Two other children wrote about standing up for oneself:

I think they should fight back.

I think they should stand up for ther self.

Five children showed empathy toward the ants:

They wanted to be treated right and I think the grasshoppers is mean.

I think they [the grasshoppers] should give back there food.

They don't have to do wate thay don't wont to do.

I think the grassphoppers sould say sorry.

I think the grasshoppers have to do the work.

In the middle of viewing *A Bug's Life*, I stopped the movie and asked the students to write about whether they would like to be an ant or a grasshopper. (This pause is before the ants win the war.) Of the 16 responses, 15 students wanted to be ants and only one wanted to be a grasshopper. The lone grasshopper wannabe wrote, "I would rather be a grasshopper because I love bosting [bossing]. Bost [bossing] is fun."(It is interesting to note that this same child said if she were president, she would boss around her mom and her teacher.)

Of the 15 students who wanted to be ants, they again wrote about identifying with the oppressed, standing up for themselves, fairness, empathy, and collective action. Here are some representative responses:

> I would rather be an ant because they is brave. They stand up for therself. Thay will scair the grasshopper. They is not scaide of the grasshopper no more.

> I would rather be an ant becaue the ant make food. He stand up for all of them. The grasshopper did nothing.

> I would rather be an ant because when I grow up I wot to be goo giy [I want to be a good guy].

> I would rather be an ant because we will work toghet and mak a plan to defet the grasshopp.

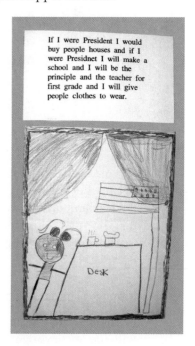

> If I were President I would buy people houses and if I were Presidnet I will make a school and I will be the principle and the teacher for first grade and I will give people clothes to wear.

> Desk

At the end of the movie, I asked the students to explain how the ants defeated the grasshoppers. The students wrote exclusively about collective action and standing up for oneself. Eight students used the concept of collective action to explain how the ants won:

> They stood up for each [other].

> Flick [an ant] stood up to the grasshopper and the ants took the grasshoppers down.

> The ants was braf enf to deft the grasshoppers togehr. [The ants was brave enough to defeat the grasshoppers together]

Children can take an active part in determining the curriculum

I thought a large part of my research project would focus on the Civil Rights Movement, and I had planned it accordingly. But the students really wanted to know more about slavery. So I thought I would split the class into two study groups, each working on its topic of choice, slavery or the Civil Rights Movement. We took a class vote, and slavery won by an overwhelming majority: 18 votes for studying slavery, 2 for going ahead with the civil rights unit.

If I were President I would give money to school and help all the people in the world improve their schools.

Although changing the curriculum plan required work on my part, I was pleased that the students wanted to learn more about slavery and that they were participating enthusiastically. I had taught a unit on the Underground Railroad a few years earlier, so I had some resources at hand. I kept the civil rights speaker I had invited, who brought to life the Civil Rights Movement, but we changed the plan for our contribution to the Black history assembly. We developed a performance about the Underground Railroad based on a hip-hop song, and the students choreographed a dance. They loved performing it during the school assembly. The children felt they owned their performance because they had chosen the topic and worked hard to create the performance piece. It is interesting to note that the assembly was the children's most popular topic of discussion at home, according to the parent survey.

While I had often thought about basing the curriculum on students' interests, I'd had a hard time imagining what that would look like in my classroom of first- and second-graders. They knew their learning was in their own hands, and they responded competently in helping make decisions about the curriculum. They were able to negotiate within boundaries that made sense for them as young students and within acceptable boundaries for me as a teacher. Following the interest of the children in planning the curriculum gave them an empowered voice in the classroom. I had always told the children it was their learning community, and now they were speaking out about what they wanted to learn. They were engaging in critical thinking and taking a stand about their own learning.

Families respond positively

I asked the children's families to respond to a parent survey, which I sent home with the homework in the children's book bags. I asked the parents five questions to gauge student interest in the Black history unit (see p. 82) At the time of the assembly, I had 20 students, and 14 of the students returned their parent surveys—a good rate of return (I typically receive homework from 10 or 12 students a week). I asked the parents to tell me if their child talked about the Black history curricular topics at home. The overwhelming response to each question was, "Yes, my child talked about this at home." On average 90 percent of the respondents marked yes for each question. Some responses were,

I thought the unit was very enlightening.

Please keep the unit going.

Jordan asked a lot of questions; some I can't answer, but I told him to put it on the library list.

Seven members from the children's families attended the Black history assembly, and two came to hear the talk by the civil rights activist.

Children can apply their classroom learning about social justice in everyday life

The following experience shows how opportunities to discuss social justice can arise spontaneously in the course of the day in ways we cannot always predict. On a typically cold January day, our school cafeteria decided to sell ice cream for the first time that year at lunch. Seven children had enough money to buy ice cream that day, and they did so, while the others did not. So there were seven children happily eating ice cream and 15 other upset children, some of whom were crying. I called a class meeting and asked the students what we should do in the future: should some students in the class continue to buy ice cream, even if everyone could not afford it? Or should no one buy ice cream? In the ensuing discussion, the students relied on the understandings of fairness they had developed in the classroom.

I asked the entire class how the children who had not bought ice cream felt, and if buying ice cream had caused any problems. The children debated for about 15 minutes. When children argued on the side of buying ice cream, they were often inclusive of others: "I can buy everyone ice cream," said Jacob, and "We should have ice cream because I like it. I would share," said Tameka. Most of the children were sensitive about others' feelings.

I asked them to write about what we should do. Seven children wrote, "Yes, we should buy ice cream," and 15 wrote, "No, we should not." There was a clear majority against buying ice cream, and as a class we decided that on the grounds of fairness, no one would buy ice cream. The children who said no showed empathy, and a sense of fairness. For instance, one child said "I think we should not buy ice cream at lunch because the kids dat buy ice cream daizt [doesn't] be nas [nice] to the ath [other] kids."

One student was even so moved by the lessons of the Montgomery bus boycott, which they had learned

If I were President I would take care of lots of people. People would have 3 day weekends. There would be no school for a week.

about, that she proposed planning collective action: "I think we should boycott them [the cafeteria] because it is not fair for other kids that don't have money. We should boycott tham for a year."

We knew that as a class we were looking for an answer that could balance individual wants with the collective good. This balance is often tenuous, as shown by the child who argued passionately for boycotting the cafeteria and then the next day sneaked out to eat ice cream. Deciding what is fair and equitable is a lifelong struggle, and it deserves a place in our curriculum and our classrooms. The children worked together to create a vision of a pro-justice and participatory classroom, and I gave them the tools and the space to work toward it for themselves.

Promoting social justice

I was considering my action research project somewhat when we began the discussion about ice cream, but much of this unplanned curriculum became the focal point for my research question about how children respond to issues of social justice. If curriculum is to be pro-justice and participatory, teachers must allow students to determine what justice looks like (and tastes like) to them. Students need real-world issues to wrangle with and to take stands on.

If I were President I would give poor people houses.

The If I Were President activity is an example of a critical curriculum that is grounded in the lives of the children. My class was able to talk back to the world. The children focused on better schools, less violence, and more freedom for everyone. They showed their feelings of empathy and sense of fairness when they imagined themselves with presidential power. Jordan stated, "I would tell the builders who build houses for rich people to build the homeless houses and I would give them food and a car." He took a critical dilemma—homelessness—and figured out a simple solution for giving everyone the basic necessities for living: shelter and food.

The children's writing about how the ants should solve their problems showed their vision of justice. I discovered how deeply primary-age students can feel about justice and fairness. However, I also believe our society works hard to discourage some of those feelings of empathy and fairness. To encourage social consciousness, I believe we must give students frequent opportunities within the curriculum to discuss and refine their ability to empathize and their thinking about fairness. These are some of the democratic ideas that Dewey challenged teachers to serve.

The value of teacher research

As I circled back to my original questions, I found that my thinking had shifted. I originally asked, Can first- and second-graders work with questions of inequality and change and examine social justice issues? What is the role of the teacher? How can teachers design the curriculum to support social justice? I found I had been most comfortable thinking about my role as a teacher and a social justice curriculum. However, I was surprised by the answer to my first question: Yes, first- and second-graders can work with questions of social justice. My class responded enthusiastically with their own categories of analysis.

I had never conducted action research in my classroom before. I enjoyed the space and support I received from the Teachers Network Leadership Institute for reflecting about my practice. During my four prior years of teaching, I had included many units around themes of social justice, but I had never had the tools or support to analyze my participation and the ways the children made sense of social justice. When I began the unit, I thought all of the children's social justice learning would come from the unit on the Civil Rights Movement. I learned that I had to shift my focus from a teacher-directed viewpoint to one that was about the children's responses to the curriculum. As it turned out, the children negotiated many concepts of social justice in their everyday lives. They had experienced homelessness, visited loved ones in prison, and witnessed violence on their block, and they used the hard lessons of life to promote justice and equity. I learned how they made sense of their world and which categories of social justice were meaningful to them.

Future changes to my social justice teaching

I learned that the most effective curriculum comes from the daily, lived experiences of the children. The curriculum that evolved during my action research project was not one that could have been planned by someone who had never met them. It did not fit neatly into a textbook. I did not plan to have a discussion about buying ice cream at 10:40 a.m. on January 22. It happened because it was important to my class at that moment. It was a curriculum focused on real, deep thinking. It met the standards for creating critical thinkers and creative problem solvers. It also met many of the state's language arts standards for articulating an opinion and speaking and writing on a topic, and the social studies standards for understanding the role individuals and groups play in history.

I learned to listen to the children. My class continually used five categories to make sense of social justice. No book told me to look for fairness, standing up for oneself, empathy, collective action, and identifying with the oppressed. They used these five concepts to figure out how to be a good president, whether they wanted to be an ant or a grasshopper, and whether it is acceptable for some of the class to buy something special that others cannot afford. These categories emerged from their thinking and were accessible to me only because I took the time, through my research, to discover how my students were learning. I also learned how to let the children negotiate the curriculum without allowing it to become overwhelming or too broad.

The project reinforced my belief that classroom community can be built around sharing, discussing, and working to resolve social justice issues. It showed what democracy in action looks like in my classroom. It reinforced my belief in using education to transform our ways of thinking and our ways of living in this complicated world.

Updated from *Voices of Practitioners: Teacher Research in Early Childhood Education* 4 (2). Copyright © 2009 NAEYC.

Photos courtesy of the author.

References

Au, W., B. Bigelow & S. Karp. 2007. *Rethinking our classrooms: Teaching for equity and justice*, vol. 1. Rev. ed. Milwaukee, WI: Rethinking Schools.

Bigelow, B. 1997. The human lives behind the labels. *Rethinking Schools* 1 (4): 1–16.

Dewey, J. 1976. *1916: Democracy and education*. Vol. 9 of *John Dewey: The middle works, 1899–1924*, ed. J.A. Boydston, 210. From the series *The collected works of John Dewey, 1882–1953*. Carbondale: Southern Illinois University Press.

Edelsky, C. 1999. Foreword in *Class actions: Teaching for social justice in the elementary and middle school*, ed. J. Allen, vii–xiii. New York: Teachers College Press.

Zinn, H. 2002. *You can't be neutral on a moving train: A personal history of our times*. Boston: Beacon Press.

© Ellen B. Senisi

Chapter

08

Getting Started
and Moving into
Teacher Research

Barbara Henderson and
Daniel R. Meier

Beginning a teacher research project and seeing yourself as a potential teacher researcher can be daunting. It is a process rarely taught in early childhood teacher education; nor is it emphasized in daily teaching responsibilities or in professional development. To succeed, you must pull together helpful resources and formulate a teacher research plan that starts with a focused question. With this framework, you can confidently embark on teacher research.

There are resources to help begin thinking about the focus for a teacher research project and to understand the processes of collecting data, analyzing the data, and sharing findings and ideas with colleagues and others. Print resources like this book are excellent for getting started. This book, *Our Inquiry, Our Practice: Undertaking, Supporting, and Learning from Early Childhood Teacher Research(ers)*, contains a range of relevant conceptual ideas and practical suggestions for thinking about what to research, how, and why. Online resources such as the journal *Voices of Practitioners* and other sources cited in this book can also provide examples of successful and effective teacher research projects, as well as demonstrate pitfalls to avoid as you conceptualize and begin your research.

Practical steps

High-quality teacher research is carried out in a conscious and systematic manner. Here is an outline of the steps within teacher research projects:

Curiosity: Wondering about an issue, challenge, new situation or special interest—this serves as a genuine prompt for inquiry that originates with the practitioner.

Feasibility: "Is the question I've asked researchable in a practical way? How can I set aside the time to observe, collect, and reflect on my data?"

Clarification: Using question frames to clarify the research. For example, "How can I improve my teaching with respect to . . . ?" or "What is happening when . . . and what accounts for this . . . ?"

Reviewing the literature: Reading to learn what others have found out about your topic and question.

Study design: Formulating how to address the research question through data collection and organization of the final research product.

Data collection: Determining what information to collect, when, and how.

Data analysis: Applying higher order, critical thinking to interpret data as evidence to support claims about what is truly going on. Data analysis in teacher research can use tools and techniques already formulated by other qualitative researchers, but most broadly, it is an approach where teacher researchers look at their data by questioning their assumptions, bringing their biases to light, and looking beyond the obvious.

Writing: Drawing together data collection, data analysis, and findings to reflect on the meaning and value of the data. Integrative and reflective writing should take place throughout the process of teacher research to permit self-dialogue around emerging findings and to invite feedback from others, which is particularly important since you are part of the setting you are researching.

Feedback: Critical information on in-progress findings and early drafts from colleagues and others.

Implications: Drawing connections and conclusions from your findings:

   a. Making links to relevant literature about your research focus and topic.

   b. Realizing the impact of findings for other teachers, as well as for families, educational leaders, and even policy makers, such that teacher research findings can impact the public decision making on educational reform.

Public presentation: Sharing research findings and products with relevant audiences.

Ask a genuine question, ask a researchable question

As an early childhood professional beginning teacher research, you should start with a real question, a problem, or puzzle about your work. It should be practical and based in research or teaching. Teacher researchers need a linguistic or visual way to break down and *narrow the teacher research focus*. One effective method is to think of a question or set of questions that encapsulate your research interests.

Examples of a single research question include:

- "Why don't the girls play with blocks even when I set up a girls-only block play time?"
- "What is the value of introducing more multicultural and multilingual songs and dances into my music and movement curriculum?"
- "What will happen if I implement a certain new curriculum designed to promote classroom community and help children make friends, and what accounts for those changes?"

Here is an example of a set of interrelated questions:

- "What are the views of teachers, children, and families regarding granting permission for children to do 'scribble scrabble' writing and drawing? To what extent do our cultural perspectives influence this process and these views? How can I integrate the frameworks of developmentally appropriate practice and culturally responsive teaching to understanding our views on scribble scrabble?"

Some teacher researchers look at a *persistent problem, issue,* or *puzzle* in their teaching—for example, the girls in our classroom never play with blocks, shy children have a hard time making friends, physically active children consistently get into trouble. Other teacher researchers look at *what is going well* in their teaching, in an effort to uncover why these aspects of their teaching are effective and successful—for example, music and movement activities allow boys and girls to play together well, a sand tray promotes the needed expression of difficult feelings in certain children, nursery rhymes are soothing to infants, use of a first language comforts and supports second language learners.

Here is an example of a problematic question one new teacher researcher started with: "Should war and weapon play ever be allowed in early childhood educational settings?" On the one hand this was a good starting question because it was an issue that she faced immediately in her work, and connected to a controversy about war play at her site. It is also a good question in that it is relevant to many others in early childhood education, as children typically play with themes of power and the dichotomy of good and evil. The problem was, however, that the question as she posed it was *not researchable*. It was, instead, a philosophical question. Here, then, are the ways she reformulated the question so that she could begin to research her interest. Her two researchable questions were:

1. *"What changes did I observe* in children's play when we shifted our policy so that certain kinds of war and weapon play were permitted?"

2. *"What effect did a change in policy have on my practice* as an educator, in particular how I viewed girls' and boys' play styles?"

Another way that many new teacher researchers find useful to frame a question is using an action research frame, beginning questions with "How can I . . . ?" Here are a few examples of successfully researched questions:
How can I improve . . .

- my teaching of emergent literacy with infants and toddlers?
- my practices for engaging children with clay?
- materials to develop children's concepts of number?
- children's observation of natural phenomenon in order to develop science concepts?
- my use of authentic experiences, such as field trips?

Another way to think of a good research question is to frame your query by thinking about daily events and routines in the classroom. These can serve as a strong and specific springboard for inquiry. Teacher researchers can also use the hypothetical frame, "What happens when . . . and what accounts for . . . ?" to look at classroom routines and events. Here are a few such examples from teacher researchers we have worked with who used this framework as their starting point:

1. What happens when *children are called to group meeting* and what accounts for *their behavior during this transition*?

2. What is happening when *children are in conflict,* and what accounts for *my reaction to step in and solve the situation*?

3. What is happening when *children engage together in "goofy" play,* and what accounts for *the energy this brings to their interactions*?

So far, we have focused on examples of questions that are purely linguistic. Some teacher researchers find it helpful to find an interesting focus both visually and also with text. This involves making a web or another kind of graphic showing how certain ideas, elements, and issues might be related to each other. For example, a teacher considering a project on how children learn about nature through outdoor exploration, might start with the word "nature" in the middle of a web diagram, and then brainstorm related associations and concepts, writing them down in web formation. In this kind of free-write, we can find related and connected ideas and suggest activities to explore further in the research process, like "hiding spaces," "toys," "time," "mud and water," "tools," "dirt," and perhaps also names of particular children who might exemplify interesting engagement with nature.

Thinking about the study design

Consulting the kinds of resources mentioned in this chapter and in this book as a whole will help you consider what you want to research and why, how to collect data, how to analyze data, and how to share and disseminate findings on what has been learned. But first, as we have been exploring, you must decide on a *relevant and meaningful research focus.* Questions will narrow as the teacher research project unfolds, but they may also shift. Both changes are positive. For example, what starts as a case study of a child may become a self-study of yourself as a teacher. So data collection and study design centers on the new focus.

Getting started with your research plan involves figuring out what to collect; how, when, and where to collect it; and how to analyze the data. It is also important to think about the logistics involved—

Do Teachers Have Time for Research?

—Gail Ritchie

As surprising as this may seem, teacher research may actually save teachers time in the long run. That's because the systematic collection (and subsequent analysis) of data by a teacher researcher is much more efficient and effective than a random, hit-or-miss, shot-in-the-dark approach to addressing classroom issues and concerns. Some school districts value collaborative teacher research to such an extent that they provide funding to pay for substitute teachers. This allows the teacher researcher groups to meet six times per year, during the school day, and support one another's inquiries.

Many new teacher researchers are amazed to discover that they were already engaged in actions similar to the teacher research process as a natural part of their classroom instruction/assessment cycle. Once they join a teacher research group, they become much more systematic and focused as they experience the energy derived from evidence-based inquiry and practice. They realize the interconnectedness between teaching and research, as their research informs their practice, and the realities of the classroom inform their understanding of educational theory. This promotes professionalism (in the form of reflective, inquiry-based practice and collaboration), and provides evidence (in the form of the data collected during the inquiries) to support innovative instructional practices.

Source: G. Ritchie, "Teacher research," *Teachers Count.org*. Available online at www.teachers count.org/topic/topic-ritchie.shtml. Accessed October 12, 2011. Used with permission of TeachersCount.org (www.teacherscount.org).

how to juggle teaching, observing, and collecting data at the same time; the best time to start your research; how long the project should run approximately; what data tools or strategies to employ; and what your system for collecting and organizing your data will be as the project begins and unfolds. Selected other chapters in this book discuss these factors in more depth, and provide real-life examples of successful teacher research.

In the end, you will want to organize your presentation as a coherent whole—that is, to tell a certain kind of story about your findings. Try to think early on about how the final product will be presented and the implications for the study design. Here are some examples of types of study design and paper organization:

Chronological: Document the changes that occur from the start to the end of a project.

Case study: Choose a child about whom you have a particular question and describe your teaching from the perspective of how it affects him or her. The use of case study in early childhood teacher research differs from a case study wherein the outside researcher uses a case study child to illustrate a certain process or mode of behavior. In early childhood teacher research, case study children are viewed as key actors and protagonists in the unfolding social and academic life of the classroom and the research journey. Therefore, the child's voice and intention is truthfully and vividly portrayed, and the child is seen through a lens of strength.

Comparative case study: Choose two children to illustrate how curriculum, materials, or the classroom environment are experienced differently by children and why.

Self-study: Conduct a case study of yourself as a teacher, looking at certain elements of your teaching philosophy, techniques, role, and image.

Thematic: Uncover a pattern of overarching themes that run through data, and then present excerpts of data to document these aspects of teaching, learning, and development. For example, in one project on conflict resolution in preschool children's play, the teacher researcher discovered a pattern in the conversational data of certain children who were able to vary their linguistic and nonlinguistic strategies to successfully engage and then re-engage peers when a conflict or misunderstanding arose.

Data collection & analysis

Teachers undertaking research should collect data from a variety of sources. Here is a list of some common resources to draw on:

1. Reflective teacher journals (These are personal documents that include reflection, critique, celebration, and feelings on teaching practices, reactions to instruction, students, administration, families, and the research process. Such notes can serve as data or may provide support and direction to the teacher researcher for data

collection in more public documents. These entries are dated and kept in chronological order so that the collection is systematic, and therefore serves as a trustworthy source of data.)

2. Observational field notes (This ethnographic term describes writing done in a classroom or community setting that captures details of research participants' words and actions.)

3. Children's work samples (for example, artwork, writing, constructions, child-photographed images)

4. Photographs of children, children's work, the setting, and materials

5. Audio recordings of class interactions, and selective transcriptions

6. Video recordings of class interactions, which can be selectively transcribed and that also serve as an excellent source for still photos, especially for photo series and for serendipitously captured moments within a stretch of video

7. Informal interviews with colleagues, families, or children

8. Questionnaires collected from parents, colleagues, or children

9. Chart paper and other documents used during lessons

10. School documents (for example, newsletters, faculty manuals)

11. Tallies of events or interactions (i.e., a data collection sheet)

Data analysis in teacher research also draws on many sources:

1. Discourse analysis of speech samples (where speech is transcribed as text, and taken apart to find patterns to better understand the complexities of conversations)

2. Analysis of photographs

3. Analysis of children's work

4. Quantitative summary and analysis of an event, response, words, time elapsed, or other occurrence

5. Analysis of interviews

6. Grounded theory or constant comparison analysis of field notes and teacher journals (developing an explanation to predict and account for recorded phenomena, then referring back to the original situation to verify it, modifying and fine-tuning the theory as events and analysis warrant)

7. Narrative inquiry, where narratives are used to present and interpret key data gems from data collection

8. Memoir, where personal and professional experiences are used to illuminate current teaching practices

Habits of writing

Writing is crucial to teacher research. It is a key part of data collection, integral to field notes, teacher journals, interviews, and more. Qualitative data analysis requires writing, as do data memos written to a collaborative group of teacher researchers to verify findings as research progresses. Sharing the results of teacher research is part of the cycle of inquiry, so teacher researchers must be prepared to write final products or share their findings orally with others. They also need to be supported in doing so. When teacher researchers' findings have implications for policy, documents should be distributed beyond the educational sphere (e.g., op-ed pieces, submissions to impact potential legislation).

For many teachers beginning teacher research, keeping a journal and conducting other forms of written records also means they must see themselves as writers. One major challenge for many early childhood teacher researchers will be the task of writing about their own practice and research. Writing within the inquiry cycle is seen by different audiences and serves different purposes. Good writing is well edited. All writing publicly presented will have gone through editing and revision. Teacher researchers learn more about the structure, content, and form of well-written research products when they are given opportunities to read and respond to the work of colleagues. Through this writing process, teachers may find their own voices, and see the impact they can make with the written word.

Giving and receiving feedback from critical colleagues

Collaboration with colleagues, especially team members in the same classroom, is an important part of successful teacher research. It is helpful to think of those you work and study with as *critical colleagues*—peers who participate in research to provide one another with feedback on the accuracy, trustworthiness, and depth of analysis, findings, and implications of an inquiry. Critical colleagues at your program can offer an important insider perspective. Critical colleagues from other sites provide distance that can strengthen the trustworthiness of an account. Data based on your own perceptions, practices, and judgments can be verified by external response. Teacher researchers see their own projects more clearly when they work with others, and collaboration provides emotional and practical support.

Collaborative teacher research projects are part and parcel of the overall communication and coteaching of the classroom. Sharing the work in a teacher research project often means that you can concentrate more fully and devote more time to an individual child or small group, or to a particular focus within the overall project focus chosen by a teaching team. It can also mean that colleagues can aid in data collection on your particular focus as you teach, offering a fresh pair of eyes and ears to observe and collect data.

It is also useful to enlist the help and guidance of mentors such as former or current early childhood education instructors. In addition, it is often critical to enlist the support of site administrators (especially if you are one of the first practitioners at your program to embark on teacher research). Since we want teacher research to grow and become a foundation of effective and high-quality early childhood teaching and professional development, we need administrators and directors to understand and promote teacher research on a long-term basis. For many of us, this might mean providing administrators and supervisors with background material and information on teacher research—what it is, how it works, its benefits, its potential drawbacks, and so on. Administrators can provide crucial support for our teacher research as both individual teachers and as colleagues and members of a teaching team; they can also communicate to families the value of teacher inquiry for the high-quality education of their children.

You also might decide that you'd like to embark on a teacher research project on your own. What are the advantages of going it alone, at least at the start of a teacher research project? For some early childhood teacher researchers, it's simply easier to think out thoughts on such a new and complicated process individually. You may need time and space to evaluate the process's initial ups and downs, and to revise and formulate changes in your research design and plan as issues arise.

The steps we've outlined here will go a long way in helping you take that initial step and move into teacher research. A successful beginning sets the tone for yourself ("Yes! I *do* know what I am doing!") and gives you the confidence and expertise needed to move forward with the inquiry process.

How Can Early Childhood Professionals Support Teacher Researchers?

Frances O'Connell Rust

A t the heart of all good teaching is a quest for knowledge—knowledge of whether, how, and what learners are learning. For teacher educators, this quest is both our own and our desired path for our students, who are tomorrow's teachers. In this section of *Our Inquiry, Our Practice: Undertaking, Supporting, and Learning from Early Childhood Teacher Research(ers)*, the reader will learn how teacher educators around the country are using teacher research with both preservice students and practicing teachers to develop what Cochran-Smith and Lytle (2009) describe as an *inquiry stance* toward their own teaching.

This second section of *Our Inquiry, Our Practice* focuses on teacher research in two ways: first, as an endeavor designed to support teacher research among preservice students; second, as an important form of teacher professional development for beginning and experienced teachers. The first three chapters of this section focus on critical issues faced by early childhood teacher educators who wish to make the inquiry stance of teacher research core to the preparation of new teachers. The fourth and fifth chapters describe ways in which teacher educators at both the undergraduate and graduate levels have successfully integrated teacher research into the programs. The final chapters provide wonderful examples of teacher research taking root in classrooms, centers, schools, and among inquiring professionals.

Andrew J. Stremmel leads off with "Reshaping the Landscape of Early Childhood Teaching Through Teacher Research." Here, Stremmel frames "research as something teachers do as part of their teaching" because, "in its truest sense teaching involves a dialectical relationship between critical theorizing and action." For teacher educators, Stremmel's chapter provides a powerful rationale for incorporating teacher research into the curriculum of teacher education. It positions both teacher educators and their students as professionals whose research, because it so intimately connects theory with practice, has "the potential to make a difference in the lives of those who confront real issues and problems in particular sites, at particular moments, and in the lives of particular individuals and groups" as well as in the larger sphere of local, state, and national policy.

The second chapter in this section is J. Amos Hatch's "Teacher Research: Questions for Teacher Educators" in which Hatch asks five critically important questions beginning with "What counts as teacher research?" What Hatch offers in answering this and other questions is a deep look at the critique leveled against teacher research and a powerful framework that is helpful not only for pushing back against the critique but also for demonstrating how this important form of inquiry can strengthen the early childhood field.

Lilian G. Katz takes up the discussion of teacher research in preservice education in her chapter "Developing Professional Insight." It is through the type of inquiry that is core to teacher research that teachers can do what Katz describes as "cultivating the life of the mind." "We" (teacher educators), she writes, "must tell students to see themselves as developing professionals; they must become students of their own teaching, and remain so throughout their careers." For teacher educators, this chapter, like the two before it, provides a helpful perspective about why the habits of reflection and inquiry that inform and guide teacher research are essential in the preparation of teachers.

The next two chapters focus on examples of ways in which teacher research has been incorporated into teacher education programs. Barbara Henderson's chapter "Teacher Research: Improving Practice and Amplifying Teacher Voice among Diverse Students in Early Childhood Education" not only provides the frame of an entire program and how it promotes inquiry among student teachers, but also provides a broad range of examples of student studies. Such student work suggests that developing an inquiry stance is not a matter of developing a course or two to give prospective teachers practice in shaping and pursuing questions. Rather, thoughtful inquiry that gives shape to one's practice comes through the careful calibration of experiences, reading, and conversation like that developed by Henderson and her colleagues at San Francisco State University.

In Shareen Abramson's "Co-Inquiry: Documentation, Communication, Action," co-inquiry (collaborative inquiry) meetings, as Abramson describes them, are designed "to produce new insights into how the teaching-learning relationship is realized in the everyday action of the classroom and to lead to improved teaching practices." Such meetings are a key component of Abramson's teacher education program at California State University. They represent a "collaborative process that involves joint action and interaction and is often used in human services settings to help effect change." It is because of their willingness to pursue inquiry together that Abramson and her colleagues have been able to develop this process, resulting in very deep knowledge of the children and families with whom they work. Their method, which is heavily influenced by the Reggio Emilia approach, is a powerful model of professional development.

"Zooms: Promoting Schoolwide Inquiry and Improving Practice," is an example of how teacher research can be carried out throughout an early education setting. Ben Mardell, Debbie LeeKeenan, Heidi Given, David Robinson, Becky Merino, and Yvonne Liu-Constant describe a remarkable inquiry community where the entire staff became teacher researchers who, through their collective inquiry, came to understand themselves as knowledge creators. The Zooms process builds collaboration in concrete and structured ways, a process through which the teachers provide both emotional and intellectual support for one another, the children, and their families.

The selections that follow take teacher research out of the college/university setting and into the practice of the everyday worlds that are early childhood settings. Two of the groups described here were initiated by teacher researchers, and though the reader will certainly see the background support of individual professors in several, these narratives demonstrate the transformative power of conversations about practice that emerge when teachers bring inquiry into their work.

In the short piece "Las Americas Early Education School Teacher Research Initiative in Collaboration with San Francisco State University," Isauro Michael Escamilla and his colleagues describe how reading Meier and Henderson's book *Learning from Young Children in the Classroom: The Art and Science of Teacher Research* (2007) instigated their inquiry and motivated them to meet with author Daniel Meier. As Escamilla relates,

> More than anything else, these meetings have given us the framework to acquire a common language. They offer the opportunity to learn or redefine the meaning of the following terms, to name a few: *observations, reflective practice, pedagogical reflections, teaching journal, documentation of children's learning experiences, classroom-based inquiry,* and *active listening*.

The perspective of these practitioners suggests most emphatically that teacher research encourages critical thinking along with self-reflection as common teaching practice. It can bring teacher educators and their students together as creators of general knowledge of teaching and children, and local knowledge of particular children and settings.

Two pieces by Mardell and colleagues demonstrate ways in which professional knowledge can grow across a school and into a community. "Making Learning Visible at the Lee Academy Pilot School" shows teachers presenting questions about practice and sharing related artifacts during inquiry sessions, gradually growing their collective inquiry by building on preceding sessions' conversations. Such conditions for growth happen in environments that are "safe"—where teachers can talk, share highs and lows, and inquire together.

"The Making Learning Visible/Ready to Learn Providence Peer Network" selection, which Mardell wrote with Bethany Carpenter, describes an exciting collaboration between Harvard's Project Zero and Ready to Learn Providence— "a community-based school readiness initiative." Mardell and Carpenter co-facilitated a teacher researcher peer network of 16 teachers who transformed their own teaching as they watched children take ownership of a project, a guidebook on the children's favorite places to play in Providence. This guidebook was designed for out of town visitors and reached the hands of the mayor, who used it to welcome NAEYC National Institute for Early Childhood Professional Development participants to Providence in the summer of 2011. Teachers shared their thinking and strategies with one another and enhanced their practice with children in their own schools through peer group meetings. They write, "Almost all the teachers increased their use of video documentation, both to examine their own practices and to share with children." For the teachers, the effort gave rise to the funding of a new teacher research group in Rhode Island.

Sometimes it is a teacher educator who is in various ways an outsider to the setting who helps to build a bridge between theory and practice. Such was the case as described in Carol Bersani's "Kent State University Child Development Center, Ongoing Teacher Research," where teachers, student teachers, and teacher educators came together in a beautiful natural setting

> to better understand the child's approach to natural outdoor spaces, to engage families in dialogue regarding the value of nature experiences, and to support preservice teachers' knowledge of the integrated learning opportunities when children explore natural spaces on campus, in the wetlands, on the school play-ground, and in their own neighborhoods.

They organized themselves into critical friends groups to support their inquiries and enable conversation between novice and experienced teachers to flower.

Deepening knowledge of young children and of early childhood practice in a collaborative environment is what makes "Reflective Early Childhood Educators' Social Seminar—RECESS" described by Jeff Daitsman, such a powerful example of a teacher research collaborative group. Daitsman's group of early childhood professionals in the Chicago area focused on improving the quality of education in their classrooms through visiting each other's sites and regular meetings.

Together, the articles here demonstrate what Marshall McLuhan ([1964] 1994) reminded us of so long ago: "The medium is the message." Teacher research can be a medium for collaborative learning, professional development, and keen understanding of teaching and learning. To engage in such inquiry is to enter into a space of deep thoughtfulness with the potential for powerful practice.

References

Cochran-Smith, M., & S.L. Lytle. 2009. *Inquiry as stance: Practitioner research for the next genera-tion*. New York: Teachers College Press.

McLuhan, M. [1964] 1994. *Understanding media: The extensions of man*. Cambridge, MA: MIT Press.

Meier, D., & B. Henderson. 2007. *Learning from young children in the classroom: The art and science of teacher research*. New York: Teachers College Press.

09

Reshaping the Landscape of Early Childhood Teaching through Teacher Research

Andrew J. Stremmel

A nyone who has ever been a teacher knows that teaching is a complex, challenging, and often uncertain process. There are no absolute answers for how best to teach young children. However, research has shown that students of teaching tend to believe there is some set of "right answers" to the problems of teaching, and they hold fast to the image of teachers as consumers and disseminators of information (e.g., Stremmel et al. 1995). If there is one thing confirmed by both the professional literature on teaching and the anecdotal experiences of many teacher educators, it is the assertion that teaching is more than technique (Ayers 1993; Cochran-Smith & Lytle 1999; Schön 1983). Teaching is a process involving continual inquiry and renewal, and a teacher, among other things, is first and foremost a questioner (Ayers 1993; Hansen 1997).

The conventional and restricted vision of the teacher as technician—consumer and dispenser of other people's knowledge—has been reinforced, however, by No Child Left Behind and its focus on high-stakes accountability and standards-based instruction (Liston et al. 2007). Nevertheless, Cochran-Smith and Lytle (2009) suggest that the narrow notion of teacher as technician has been a catalyst for the current teacher-as-researcher movement in the United States. This movement has helped re-unite two complementary and natural sides of teaching—reflection and action (thinking and doing). The teacher research movement also has helped teachers reclaim inquiry as a legitimate means of gaining knowledge and insights about teaching and learning.

In this chapter, I paint a more promising and encompassing view than that of the teacher as technician—one of teaching as an inquiry process, a view that sees teachers as researchers who take seriously the study of self with the aims of bringing about personal, social, and educational change (Dewey [1933] 1985; [1938] 1997; Meier & Henderson 2007).

Teacher research gives new meaning and value to the role of teachers and redefines the parameters of their work. Teacher research can effect positive changes in the quality of early childhood teaching, enhance the professional status of teachers, and acknowledge their important responsibility to both theory *and* practice.

Reframing the role of teacher through teacher research

The real value of engaging in teacher research at any level is that it may lead to rethinking and reconstructing what it means to be a teacher or teacher educator and, consequently, the way teachers relate to children and students. Teaching has typically been thought of as doing, acting, carrying out, and/or performing the work of teaching in the classroom. However, in its truest sense teaching involves a dialectical relationship between critical theorizing and action. Teachers do not act without thinking (theorizing), and when they think, they act. And because teachers are always observing, questioning, reflecting, interpreting, deciding, and acting, they are researching. The act of research must be redefined as something teachers do as part of their teaching. Teachers are "knowers" and agents in the classroom, not simply consumers of knowledge. As such, practitioner, theorist, and researcher are all inseparable and unifying elements of what it means to be a teacher.

When teachers reflect on and give voice to their questions and dilemmas, they demonstrate the notion that teaching is an inquiry process: learning to teach is inherently connected to learning to inquire (Borko et al. 2007). Cochran-Smith and Lytle (2009) have called this a stance or way of thinking and being in the classroom. Adopting an inquiry stance means learning to question or challenge what happens in the classroom. It also means helping children pursue their own questions and taking their inquiries seriously, as well as working with others to generate knowledge and understanding of what it means to teach and learn. As Vivian Paley (1997) states, once this mindset is achieved teachers may find their unique teaching and writing voices and make public the questions, discoveries, and continual rethinking, interpretations, and postulations they engage in each day.

But why should teachers, who are already overburdened with curriculum requirements, standards of learning, and the daily challenges of caring for young children, take on teacher research? Teachers need to know what is happening in their classrooms, and they want to know whether they are effective. Paley states (1997) that it is up to teachers themselves to wonder and write about something that no one else understands—their life in the classroom, their experiences with children, and those things that perplex and astonish them.

Making space for reflection, reading, writing, and inquiry, as well as providing the opportunity to discuss insights into often taken-for-granted aspects of their work, teachers learn to recognize and interpret key moments in the life of the classroom and focus on the meaningful issues of teaching and learning. Teacher research, then, has the potential to effect change both in terms of teacher professional development and the quality of teaching (Zeichner 1993).

When teachers engage in research on their practice, their immediate goal is to get better at what they do. Teachers who engage in research become learners in their own classrooms. They reflect on what they believe, the decisions they make, and reasons underlying what they do. Instead of implementing prescribed curriculum or following the methodologies of others, teachers become the source and creator of the theoretical basis of their own implementation techniques. In this way, teacher knowledge originates in a form of teaching that is grounded in research, a form of teaching that is much more than action, imparting information, or enhancing technical skills. By adopting a research stance, teachers become engaged in meaningful professional development and become more autonomous in judgments on their own practice.

When teachers embrace inquiry as a routine and expected function of their professional lives, they can see children and themselves in new and unexpected ways.

For example, consider a teacher who has been perplexed by her children's lack of motivation or sustained engagement with classroom activities. Through engaging in the process of disciplined inquiry, she might refocus her question to ask: "What motivates *me* as a teacher in the classroom?" "How does *my* motivation affect the children I work with?" In the messy, complex, and uncertain world of teaching, inquiry helps teachers be more responsive to children and the particular demands of their classroom contexts.

A generation ago, Frederick Erickson noted that if teaching is to come of age as a profession, then teachers will need to take seriously their roles as researchers who investigate their own practice systematically and critically, using methods appropriate to their practice (1986,157). Teachers are insiders who can see their work more fully than others might, and are motivated to observe and make sense of their work. Using methods consistent with everyday teaching (e.g., observation, document collection, journaling, discussions) teachers can generate data that cannot be captured by traditional methods of research. If done well, teacher research that is intentional, systematic, and relevant to problems of practice has the potential to change the kinds of questions we ask and the kinds of understandings that are produced.

The value of teacher research

Teacher research is largely about developing the professional dispositions of life-long learning, reflective and mindful teaching, and self-transformation (Mills 2000; Stringer 2007). The ultimate aim of teacher research is transformation, enabling teachers to develop a better understanding of themselves, their classrooms, and their practice through the act of reflective inquiry (Stremmel et al. 2002). Although its primary purpose is to help practitioners better understand teaching and learning and to improve practice in specific and concrete ways, teacher research can and often does lead to significant change—for example, in helping schools develop new curriculum methods or improving parent-teacher partnerships (see Fu et al. 2002).

Evidence suggests that teachers who have been involved in research may become more reflective, more critical and analytical in their teaching, and more open and committed to professional development (Henson 1996; Keyes 2000; Rust 2007). Participating in teacher research also helps teachers become more deliberate in their decision making and actions in the classroom. We live in an age of accountability, and more than ever teachers and schools are being held accountable for the policies, programs, and practices they implement. Teachers are called upon to make informed, data-driven decisions about what they do in the classroom; therefore, they need to be much more deliberate in documenting and evaluating their efforts. Teacher research is one means to that end.

Is teacher research real research?

While research by those outside the classroom is often criticized as focusing too narrowly on educational issues and problems in isolation from actual settings, teachers, and children (Zeni 2001), teacher research is often perceived as being a lesser form of scholarship, even though it may contribute to the knowledge base of teaching and learning. Attitudes about the rigor and status of practitioner research do still need to be addressed. In particular, there is the view held by academic scholars that teacher research as a form of local knowledge that leads to change within classrooms is acceptable, but that when it is presented as public knowledge with claims beyond the practice setting, validity may be questioned (Anderson & Herr 1999). While there may be disagreement over how to evaluate the quality of teacher research, there is agreement that standards for rigor must be maintained (Freeman et al. 2007; Zeichner & Noffke 2001).

Like any sound research, teacher research must be systematic and all procedures must be carefully documented. Second, multiple approaches to inquiry—multiple sources of data and multiple approaches to data analysis—are essential to the quality and authenticity of teacher research (Cochran-Smith & Donnell 2006). Third, teacher research must be relevant to problems of practice and provide legitimate bases for action. The findings and interpretations derived from the research must be trustworthy, addressing the question: "Can the findings be trusted enough to act upon them?" And they must be believable, or have verisimilitude, which addresses the question, "Do the findings appear to be true or real in the experience of teaching?"

Bell (1985) outlines four criteria that may be used to evaluate the quality or rigor of teacher research:

Credibility—Is the study believable to those who are competent to judge the subject of investigation?

Transferability—Does the study promote the exchange of experience from one practitioner to another?

Dependability—Does the study use reliable procedures and produce findings that are trustworthy?

Confirmability—Is the study capable of being scrutinized for absence of bias by making its evidence and methods of analysis available?

Teacher research that illuminates the complexity of teaching and relates it to learning is certainly likely to be viewed as credible. When it is well designed, teacher research has the potential to contribute substantially to the knowledge base of teaching and teacher education.

Primary among the factors creating renewed interest in teacher research was the growth in the appreciation and value of qualitative methods in educational research and the concurrent shift from thinking about teacher research as something done *to* teachers to something done *by* teachers (Lampert 2000; Zeichner 1999). Although debate continues about the value and limitations of quantitative versus qualitative inquiry in educational research (e.g., Davis 2007), there has been a shift from an exclusive reliance on quantitative methods to the use of a broader range of qualitative methodologies (e.g., ethnography, narrative inquiry, biography, and autobiography) in the study of teaching and teacher education (e.g., Borko et al. 2007; Hatch 2007). The growth in these qualitative methodologies occurred in response to questions regarding the relevance of quantitative inquiry in addressing the issues and concerns of teachers and to the changing perception of teachers as researchers, as opposed to passive consumers of research on teaching. Teachers have often felt that traditional educational research is not relevant to their needs or is written in a way that fails to help them understand their classroom situations. In short, traditional research on teaching often pursues the wrong questions and offers unusable answers. Furthermore, teachers have often felt left out of research activity. Missing, therefore, in the traditional educational research is the real-life context of the classroom and the voice of the teacher (Davis 2007; Lytle & Cochran-Smith 1990).

Whether it involves the daily observations of children and written reflections on what happens in the classroom, or the purposeful and solution-oriented investigation of particular classroom issues or problems, teacher research stems from questions and reflections on everyday practice and a desire to improve teaching and learning (Hansen 1997). Because teachers have established relationships with children, knowledge of their classroom culture, and insights into problems of daily practice, they have a distinct advantage over researchers based outside of the classroom in conducting ethnographic and interpretive research.

Making teacher research public

If teacher researchers are to make a large-scale impact, they need to have appropriate and accessible outlets for their discoveries. Over the last 10 years, there has been an increasing number of professional book publications devoted to teacher research (see, e.g., Castle 2011; Meier & Henderson 2007; Stringer 2007). Additionally, there are more published studies of teacher research appearing in both research- and practitioner-oriented journals. For example, NAEYC's early childhood teacher research journal, *Voices of Practitioners*, welcomes all forms of teacher research. The journals *Networks: An On-Line Journal for Teacher Research, Educational Action Research,* and *Studying Teacher Education: A Journal of Self-Study of Teacher Education Practices* are devoted entirely to teacher research. Several other journals, like *Harvard Educational Review, Teaching and Teacher Education,* and *Journal of Early Childhood Teacher Education* (a publication of the National Association of Early Childhood Teacher Educators), are very open to publishing the work of teachers, students, and teacher educators who engage in reflective inquiry. Increased interest in inquiry-based curriculum, Reggio

Emilia-inspired practices (e.g., pedagogical documentation and projects, or *progettazione*), and renewed interest in the philosophy of John Dewey may be associated with the growing amount of teacher research being published (Hill et al. 2005; Meier & Henderson 2007). Nevertheless, excepting in venues like *Voices of Practitioners*, comparatively little teacher research of any kind that is generated in local settings for local purposes gets published, though much of it is shared orally at regional and national teacher research or teacher education conferences such as the NAEYC's Annual Conference & Expo and National Institute for Early Childhood Professional Development and the American Educational Research Association's Annual Meeting (Zeichner & Noffke 2001).

It should be noted that although there is a tendency to think of the products of research as a presentation or publication directed to academic audiences, teacher research must be first and foremost accessible and relevant to those who conduct it and those in situations where it is immediately applicable. Teacher research must have the potential to make a difference in the lives of those who confront real issues and problems in particular sites, at particular moments, and in the lives of particular individuals and groups.

Partnerships in inquiry

As university-based researchers have become more interested in and involved with problems in teaching and schools, they have recognized teachers as knowledge generators, and there has been greater interest in seeing the development of a knowledge base for teaching practice as a shared responsibility (Bickel & Hattrup 1995; Lytle & Cochran-Smith 1990).

As documented in the other chapters in this section, increasingly, graduate and undergraduate programs in early childhood education are teaching students the skills and dispositions to be researchers in their classrooms and are offering courses that require them to conduct action research projects (see, e.g., Hatch et al. 2006; Henderson 2012; Hill et al. 2005; Moran 2007; Rust 2007). Many of these programs utilize university child development laboratories as the primary site for inquiry. As centers of critical and collaborative inquiry, lab schools offer opportunities for teachers to produce knowledge as they interact with children in complex and challenging teaching and learning situations (Zeichner 1999). These programs typically are philosophically grounded in social constructivist, reflective, inquiry-based, and Reggio Emilia-inspired approaches that have self-transformation and educational renewal as explicit goals. They help prospective teachers to think and act like researchers who rely on keen observation, reflection, and documentation to become better curriculum planners and to highlight or illuminate traces of experience from which learning can be inferred. Such programs are based on a belief in the value of integrating teaching and research and the notion of teaching and its study as legitimate scholarship.

This interest in shared responsibility has been evident not only in the growing emphasis on university-teacher collaborations but also in collaborations among teachers themselves, among teachers and school administrators, and among teachers and parents. Research that is conducted by teachers or among teachers in collaboration provides a unique look at the program from the differing perspectives of those who have special insights and knowledge of children, curriculum, and teaching and learning. When teachers form reciprocal and full partnerships with other teachers and university researchers, addressing shared concerns and questions, they increase the likelihood of developing richer understandings of their teaching, their students, and themselves. Furthermore, they can share in the professional responsibility of adding to the knowledge base on teaching and learning, and may potentially alter what we now consider to be the appropriate standards and practices in the dialogue of applied qualitative research (Freeman et al. 2007; Lampert 2000; Zeichner & Noffke 2001).

Whether in partnership with other teachers, teacher educators, or university researchers, teachers themselves must be viewed as knowledge generators and partnerships must allow for supportive and reciprocal relationships. To be maximally effective, all participants must be seen as equal and full partners in the research process (Bickel & Hattrup 1995).

In conclusion, teacher research is important because it repositions the meaning of teacher from one who simply performs or acts to someone who generates and contributes to the knowledge on which classroom practice is based and how decisions are made. Teacher research is liberating and empowering inquiry that allows teachers and teacher educators to take their lives as teachers seriously, to generate knowledge and understanding that can improve teaching and potentially create a more democratic and equitable learning community. Most important, teacher inquiry allows teachers to simultaneously study their teaching, their students, and themselves—the images they hold of children as learners and themselves as teachers—and as a result, it allows the possibility of transformation and renewal for both themselves and for the early childhood field as a whole.

Portions of this chapter were originally published as a Research in Review article in the September 2002 issue of Young Children *(57 [5]: 62–70).*

References

Anderson, G., & K. Herr. 1999. The new paradigm wars: Is there room for rigorous practitioner knowledge in schools and universities? *Educational Researcher* 28 (5): 12–21.

Ayers, W. 1993. *To teach: The journey of a teacher.* New York: Teachers College Press.

Bell, G.H. 1985. Can schools develop knowledge of their practice? *School Organization* 5 (2): 175–84.

Bickel, W.E., & R.A. Hattrup. 1995. Teachers and researchers in collaboration: Reflections on the process. *American Educational Research Journal* 32 (1): 35–62.

Borko, H., D. Liston & J. Whitcomb. 2007. Genres of empirical research in teacher education. *Journal of Teacher Education* 58 (1): 3–11.

Castle, K. 2012. *Early childhood teacher research: From questions to results.* New York: Routledge.

Cochran-Smith, M., & K. Donnell. 2006. Practitioner inquiry: Blurring the boundaries of research and practice. In *Handbook of complementary methods in education research,* eds. J. Green, G. Camilli & P.B. Elmore, 503–18. Mahwah, NJ: Lawrence Erlbaum.

Cochran-Smith, M., & S.L. Lytle. 1990. Teacher research and research on teaching: The issues that divide. *Educational Researcher* 19 (2): 2–11.

Cochran-Smith, M., & S. Lytle. 1993. *Inside/outside: Teacher research and knowledge.* New York: Teachers College Press.

Cochran-Smith, M., & S.L. Lytle. 1999. The teacher research movement: A decade later. *Educational Researcher* 28 (7): 15–25.

Cochran-Smith, M. & S.L. Lytle. 2009. *Inquiry as stance: Practitioner research for the next generation.* New York: Teachers College Press.

Davis, S. H. 2007. Bridging the gap between research and practice: What's good, what's bad, and how can one be sure? *Phi Delta Kappan* 88 (8): 568–78.

Dewey, J. [1933] 1985. *How we think, a restatement of the relation of reflective thinking to the educative process.* Boston: Heath.

Dewey, J. [1938] 1997. *Experience and education.* New York: Scribner.

Erickson, F. 1986. Qualitative methods in research on teaching. In *Handbook of research on teaching,* 3d ed., ed. M.C. Wittrock, 119–61. NY: Macmillan.

Freeman, M., K. deMarrais, J. Preissle, K. Roulston & E. St. Pierre. 2007. Standards of evidence in qualitative research: An incitement to discourse. *Educational Researcher* 36 (1): 25–32.

Fu, V.R., A.J. Stremmel & L.T. Hill. 2002. *Teaching and learning: Collaborative exploration of the Reggio Emilia approach.* Upper Saddle River, NJ: Merrill/Prentice Hall.

Hansen, J. 1997. Researchers in our classrooms: What propels teacher researchers? In *Literacies for the 21st century: Research and practice,* eds. D. Leu, C. Kinzer & K. Hinchman, 1–14. Chicago: National Reading Conference.

Hatch, J.A. 2007. *Early childhood qualitative research.* New York: Routledge.

Hatch, J.A., T. Greer, & K. Bailey. 2006. Student-produced action research in early childhood teacher education. *Journal of Early Childhood Teacher Education* 27 (2): 205–12.

Henderson B. 2012. Teacher research: Improving practice and amplifying teacher voice among diverse students in early childhood education. In *Our inquiry, our practice: Undertaking, supporting, and learning from early childhood teacher research(ers),* eds. G. Perry, D.R. Meier & B. Henderson, 133–46. Washington, DC: NAEYC.

Henson, K.T. 1996. Teachers as researchers. In *Handbook of research on teacher education,* 2d ed., eds. J. Sikula, T. Buttery & E. Guyton, 53–64. New York: Simon & Schuster.

Hill. L.T., A.J. Stremmel & V.R. Fu. 2005. *Teaching as inquiry: Rethinking curriculum in early childhood education.* New York: Pearson Education.

Keyes, C. 2000. The early childhood teacher's voice in the research community. *International Journal of Early Years Education* 8 (1): 3–13.

Lampert, M. 2000. Knowing teaching: The intersection of research on teaching and qualitative research. *Harvard Educational Review* 70 (1): 86–99.

Liston, D., J. Whitcomb & H. Borko. 2007. NCLB and scientifically-based research. *Journal of Teacher Education* 58 (2): 99–107.

Lytle, S.L., & M. Cochran-Smith. 1990. Learning from teacher research: A working typology. *Teachers College Record* 92 (1): 83–103.

Meier, D.R., & B. Henderson. 2007. *Learning from young children in the classroom: The art and science of teacher research.* New York: Teachers College Press.

Mills, G. 2000. *Action research: A guide for the teacher researcher.* Upper Saddle River, NJ: Merrill/Prentice-Hall.

Moran, M.J. 2007. Collaborative action research and project work: Promising practices for developing collaborative inquiry among early childhood preservice teachers. *Teaching and Teacher Education* 23: 418–31.

Oja, S.N., & G.J. Pine. 1989. Collaborative action research: Teachers' stages of development and school contexts. *Peabody Journal of Education* 64 (2): 96–115.

Paley, V.P. 1997. Foreword. In *Class acts: Teachers reflect on their own classroom practice*, Harvard Education Review Reprint Series, No. 29, eds. I. Hall, C.H. Campbell & E.J. Miech, vii–ix. Cambridge, MA: Harvard Educational Review.

Rust, F.O. 2007. Action research in early childhood contexts. In *Early childhood qualitative research,* ed. J.A. Hatch, 95–108. New York: Routledge.

Schön, D. 1983. *The reflective practitioner.* New York: Basic Books.

Stremmel, A.J, V.R. Fu & L.T. Hill. 2002. The transformation of self in early childhood teacher education: Connections to the Reggio Emilia approach. In *Teaching and learning: Collaborative exploration of the Reggio Emilia approach,* eds. V.R. Fu, A.J. Stremmel & L.T. Hill, 135–45. Upper Saddle River, NJ: Merrill/Prentice Hall.

Stremmel, A.J, V.R. Fu, P. Patet & H. Shah. 1995. Images of teaching: Prospective early childhood teachers' constructions of the teaching-learning process of young children. In *Advances in early education and day care: Vol. 7. Social contexts of early development and education,* series ed. S. Reifel, 253–70. Greenwich, CT: JAI.

Stringer, E.T. 2007. *Action research.* 3d ed. Thousand Oaks, CA: Sage.

Zeichner, K. 1993. Action research: Personal renewal and social reconstruction. *Educational Action Research* 1: 199–219.

Zeichner, K. 1999. The new scholarship in teacher education. *Educational Researcher* 28 (9): 4–15.

Zeichner, K.M., & S.E. Noffke. 2001. Practitioner research. In *Handbook of research on teaching,* 4th ed., ed. V. Richardson, 298–330. Washington, DC: American Educational Research Association.

Zeni, J., ed. 2001. *Ethical issues in practitioner research.* New York: Teachers College Press.

© iStockphoto

Chapter

10

Teacher Research:

Questions for
Teacher Educators

J. Amos Hatch

P rofessors have great jobs. Even low-status, overworked, and underloved early childhood education professors have it pretty good. I count myself lucky because a big part of my work is getting other early childhood professionals (at all levels) to think in different ways about what they do and what it means for the children they teach.

I remember a "Peanuts" comic strip from years ago in which Sally says to Marcie as they chat in school, "I have it all figured out. The way I see it, there seem to be more questions than there are answers." Marcie says, "So?" and Sally replies, "So try to be the one who asks the questions!"

In this chapter, I take the role of the one who asks the questions. While I offer some possible answers, my intent is to get the questions on the table for discussion. If the questions stimulate teacher educators responsible for guiding the teacher research of their students to think in new ways, then I will have accomplished my goal.

What counts as teacher research?

Is teacher research equivalent to action research? Is Reggio-style documentation synonymous with teacher research? Are qualitative data collection and interpretive analysis essential to teacher research? The issues embedded in these questions are more than semantic. Being clearer about what we actually mean by teacher research is important if we want it to be taken seriously.

I offer the following as a working definition: Teacher research is systematic, data-based inquiry that teachers use to improve their professional practice. At their best, teacher researchers tell stories of how they deal with real problems in real classrooms. Their stories bring to life the complexities of working in those real-world settings. However if it is really research, then it must be done systematically—as opposed to randomly or haphazardly. It is not just a random set of stories—the teacher researcher has carefully planned ways to address a classroom issue, and he or she has carefully documented exactly what happened during the "action" and "research" parts of the study. The teacher researcher's narratives of practice are stories that include evidence supporting the conclusions of the inquiry.

Teacher research is still research. For me, that means that it does not ignore the "paradigmatic" dimensions of systematic inquiry. It must be data-based (empirical)—as opposed to experiential or impressionistic. This means that an organized plan for executing the inquiry must be laid out before the project is begun—as opposed to trying to figure out what happened after the fact. It means that a design for carefully collecting and analyzing data must be in place at the outset of the inquiry—as opposed to making judgments about the outcomes of their efforts based only on impressions or feelings. It means that teacher researchers must collect evidence that accurately represents what is going on in the settings they are studying. It means that data collection options (qualitative and/or quantitative) must be applied based on the best fit for the issues at hand—as opposed to a dogmatic insistence on one kind of data collection over another.

If it is *teacher* research, then it must be done by teachers in a self-conscious effort to make improvements in their work—as opposed to studying educational phenomena for pedantic or purely scholarly reasons. That means that teacher researchers must be reflective about their professional practices to the point where they can see issues that they need to address in order to improve—as opposed to seeing only forces outside their control. It means that teacher researchers see their inquiries as opportunities to get better at doing what they do in the settings where they do it—as opposed to doing traditional research that is disconnected from the contexts in which they work.

By starting with a definition like the one I have suggested, we can get closer to figuring out what counts as teacher research. Action research models that have been applied to education and many other disciplines fit within the discussion above, as does documentation as it is usually described in relation to the Reggio Emilia philosophy. That means that the preservice and in-service teachers we are working with can do action research or Reggio-style documentation as teacher research, but that other kinds of inquiry are legitimate teacher research as well. Since data collection and analysis strategies are appropriate insofar as they give teacher researchers evidence on which to assess what's going on in their work settings, limiting choices to either qualitative or quantitative seems wrongheaded.

Can teacher research add to the knowledge base in early childhood education?

Who is the audience for teacher research findings? Who owns teacher research data? I count these as genuine questions to which a number of answers are possible.

In the current climate of No Child Left Behind and official proclamations that stipulate a narrow set of criteria for studies to be considered scientifically based, teacher research does not meet the standard. Even without the heavy-handed imposition of one view of science on the educational research community, it's not self-evident that teacher research has something important to add to the early education knowledge base. If teacher research is, by definition, focused on the immediate contexts of one teacher's professional practice, then it is fair to ask what it has to do with the practices of others.

However, I believe that teacher research can make a unique contribution to the understanding of teaching and learning in early childhood settings. Teacher research provides credibility and on-the-ground information that improves the likelihood that early childhood practitioners' voices will be heard and respected. A look at the recent history of initiatives to build new foundations for teaching excellence (e.g., Howes & Pianta 2011) reveals that far too little teacher input has been solicited and even less has been taken seriously as policy decisions have been made and implemented. Except in isolated, local cases, the overall trend is for decisions to be made in rooms and corridors far removed from settings where teaching and learning actually happen.

I, for one, believe that teacher research that is well done and well described has plenty to contribute to the knowledge base in early childhood education. By *well done*, I mean that it meets the definition offered earlier—it's systematic, data-based, and focused on professional practice. By *well described*, I mean that it is communicated with enough detail and clarity to reveal what happened in the study so that other professionals can make up their own minds about the meaningfulness of the findings to their own work settings.

This gets a little tricky for me because I insist that the primary audience for any teacher research project be the teacher her- or himself. The whole point of teacher research is to improve professional practice through systematic, planned inquiry. If the intent from the beginning is for the research to generate publishable findings, that's fine; but is it still teacher research? I can see that it's possible to have it both ways, but I worry that the essence of teacher research may be compromised if publishing and presenting become the primary aim.

This also points to tricky territory for those of us who support teachers and teachers-to-be who are designing and doing teacher research projects. As university-based scholars, it's part of our job to generate knowledge. Those of us who guide the implementation of teacher research projects have an important place in the process, and we have experience and expertise that can help well-done teacher research become well-described teacher research. But the limits of our place need to be carefully drawn so that teachers own their own research and we are not appropriating the work of our colleagues. I tell the teacher researchers with whom I work that they own the data. I sometimes work with students to help them present their projects at professional conferences and publish descriptions of their research, but they report their studies under their own names.

There is another strong argument for the idea that teacher research like the kind reported in this collection has an important place in the literature and practice of our profession. That is the premise that narrative knowledge is essential in professional practice in any field. Bruner (1986) makes a powerful distinction between what he calls paradigmatic and narrative ways of knowing. The production of paradigmatic knowledge is based on the "rational" methods of the Western scientific tradition: advancing hypotheses, reporting evidence, and inferring conclusions. "True" knowledge is held to be the exclusive province of this logical and verifiable discourse. In contrast, Bruner argues that narrative ways of knowing produce storied understandings that cannot be captured via paradigmatic thought. Even though it has been treated as inferior in the Western world, narrative knowledge in the form of stories is specifically suited to making sense of human action. In Polkinghorne's words,

> While paradigmatic knowledge is maintained in individual words that name a
> concept, narrative knowledge is maintained in emplotted stories. Narrative cogni-

tion gives us explanatory knowledge of why a person acted as he or she did; it makes another's action, as well as our own, understandable. (1995, 11)

Bruner reminds us that stories of experience represent valid and important sources of knowledge. I argue that stories of early childhood teacher research are valid and important ways to generate and share knowledge of professional practice.

Although the stories that teacher researchers produce are treated as inferior knowledge forms in traditional Western thought and teacher research is treated as an inferior form of research by those currently in a position to decide what constitutes knowledge in the field of education, narrative knowledge has a vital place in all human endeavors, including professional practices in all arenas. Individuals who are trained to be physicians, engineers, and even scientists learn what constitutes professional practices in their fields from stories. Physicians, engineers, and scientists, like teachers, continue to develop professional expertise over the course of their careers because they accumulate storied knowledge of their own practices and the practices of others. Like teachers, they process paradigmatic information generated from within and without their professions. However, they can only make sense of paradigmatic knowledge in terms of individual applications in complex, real-life settings (i.e., through storied understandings).

So, narrative ways of knowing are important in all human activity, even in professions that are held up as "scientifically-based." Scientifically-based practices are based on knowledge generated using traditional, quantitative research designs like those used in medicine (large numbers, control groups, and double-blind experimental procedures). Just because a piece of research passes the scientifically-based litmus test does not mean that it provides inherently useful knowledge. If fact, the "rigor" required may so restrict the human dimensions of the study, that findings never fit an actual classroom setting. Scientifically-based knowledge ought to be available for teachers to use as they see fit. This works within the teacher research model because teachers are trying to improve their practice through their action research efforts— they should tap into all the knowledge available as they examine their own practices and seek to make improvements.

Action research provides a vehicle for generating narrative understanding that has a legitimate place in the knowledge base of any profession, and early childhood teacher research is a powerful tool for producing storied knowledge that informs early education practice and policy.

How are participants in teacher research projects protected?

Are parents, teachers, and especially children put at risk by the dissemination of teacher research? Should human subjects reviews and informed-consent protocols be required for teacher research projects?

Universities are careful about safeguarding the rights of individuals who volunteer to participate in the research efforts of faculty and students. Institutional review boards (IRBs) screen research protocols, adding a layer of bureaucracy to university-based research projects. At my university, every teacher licensure candidate completes a teacher research project (using an action research model) during her or his full-year internship. We have a blanket IRB approval that covers all of the teacher research being done as part of the teacher education programs, except when findings from the studies are to be made public beyond program requirements.

The logic of the blanket approval is that our interns are doing only what good teachers ought to be doing, so they don't need informed consent from parents or assent from children. It follows that if the interns intend to go beyond the classroom and course requirements (that is, to present and publish), then they need an IRB approval that includes appropriate consents.

Even though it is cumbersome and sometimes limits the pool of participants, I generally agree with the policy that when students or teachers plan to disseminate their findings, children, parents, and other adults who are human subjects in those teacher research projects should be informed regarding the extent of their participation in the study, what is intended for the results of the study, and to what degree their identities will be kept confidential. And they must be given the option of refusing participation without penalty.

It's hard to imagine any kind of treatment that would put participants at physical or psychological risk in an early childhood teacher research project. As a teacher educator, I guide my interns' project development at every step of the process, so I would know if a design included anything that might be perceived as involving a risk. But if findings are to be shared in public settings, there is some risk (depending on the data and how they are displayed in the final report) that participants could be identified.

So when students or teachers do teacher research that they have no intention of disseminating to a wider audience, I don't think it's necessary to get IRB approval and participant consent. But if they want to publish or present their work, the same criteria that fit other university-based research should be applied.

Is it ethical to do transformative teacher research in settings in which we are guests?

Is it right to encourage transformative teacher research when our students working with children in grades K–3 will likely be employed in school settings dominated by conservative forces? By *transformative*, I mean designed to challenge the racial, cultural, and socioeconomic inequalities that are imbedded in education settings.

A major thread in the action research tradition is the application of critical/feminist perspectives to transform social contexts characterized by the unequal treatment of historically marginalized groups. Those of us who teach, guide, and support teacher research need to examine what we believe, say, and do as we work with practitioners who bring a critical/feminist edge to their teacher research projects.

This is a tough issue for me. I work in a program designed to prepare teachers for work in urban-multicultural settings. Students have to apply to be in the program, and we select only those who are open to working in diverse settings. Critical pedagogy and critical literacy are key elements of our teacher preparation curriculum. We want the teachers we prepare for multicultural environments to be aware of and equipped to resist the historical and structural inequalities that characterize society. We want them to be critical in their thinking and transformative in their teaching. When it's time for them to design and implement their teacher research projects, we want our students to apply their critical thinking and generate transformative teaching.

It turns out that most do not—and I don't blame them. After all, they are guests in the schools in which they do their internships and implement their teacher research projects. It seems just plain rude to ask teachers, principals, and parents to let students learn how to teach in urban settings and then have them develop plans to systematically expose racism, ethnocentrism, or other prejudicial treatment in or around the school.

However, many of the interns with whom I work do find ways to generate transformative action plans as part of their teacher research projects. They use culturally relevant pedagogical approaches, but almost always in the context of improving academic achievement. That way, they are being true to their own convictions while helping the schools move toward their primary objective of educating children and getting off or staying off the No Child Left Behind lists.

Yes, teacher research can be transformative. Nothing in the definition of teacher research limits teacher inquiries to certain political perspectives. But university educators responsible for guiding teacher research should help students balance their political beliefs with the realities of contemporary school settings.

I am a firm believer that institutional change has to come from within. We have to support our future teachers' efforts to first get inside systems, where they can then make changes in ways that do not threaten their careers. My students have taught me that teacher research is one avenue to change that can be shaped so that transformation can happen.

Can teacher research be its own reward?

Part of my job as a teacher education professor is to guide preservice teachers through the processes of designing, implementing, and writing up an action research project. They do this project as part of a full-year's internship that takes place at the master's level, after the completion of a bachelor's degree in an arts and sciences major. Because my students do action research while they are learning everything else associated with being a first-year teacher, it is an intense, time-consuming process. So while they are engaged in their inquiry projects, few students would claim that teacher research is its own reward. However, when they finish their projects, write their conclusions and implications, and present their work to peers, professors, and professionals at an annual intern conference their views change—most recognize the significant role that the action research process plays in their development as reflective, thoughtful, problem-solvers in the classroom.

Regardless of the outcomes of the inquiry or the writing expertise of the author, the credibility of teacher research as a distinct form of inquiry is based on the assumption that it improves professional practice. I've seen action research projects that generate exciting and positive outcomes, and some are close to doctoral dissertations in quality. I've also seen final reports that are not well written, even after three or four edits. What I hope my students come to understand is that teacher research is a tool for improving professional practice, that learning the processes of systematically addressing classroom issues is the goal, and that writing it up is a way to help internalize the processes and share insights with others.

All new teachers benefit from connecting to support groups in their early childhood practice communities so that the teacher research skills and dispositions developed in teacher education programs like mine can be nurtured and validated. Practicing teachers who have conducted teacher research as part of their classroom practice believe that engagement in action research positively impacts their teaching. They describe themselves as "becoming more reflective, more critical and more aware, regardless of how many years they have been teaching" (Rust & Meyers 2006, 81). They claim that research helped them become stronger teachers and enabled them to assume a voice in policy making in their schools, communities, and beyond (Rust 2007). If early childhood teacher research is not its own reward, it comes close because of the benefits it provides to those who undertake it.

In conclusion

To return to where I began, it's the questions that matter. As early childhood education professionals responsible for directing the teacher research of our students, we need to spend some time reflecting on our own thinking about the issues raised in the questions that organized this essay. My answers are not *the* answers; others have to figure out what their own answers are, given who and where they are.

Teacher research provides many opportunities for encouraging the development of thoughtful, action-oriented teachers who are willing to take responsibility for the improvement of their own practices. It also generates meaningful ways to bring the authentic voices of frontline educators to the professional discourses of our field. Smart, dedicated, well-prepared teachers who systematically study their own practice provide a powerful model for improving the quality of early childhood practice in general. When teachers collaborate and discuss their work in peer networks, demonstrate they can effect genuine change in classrooms, and lay claim to professional expertise and commitment, their chances of being heard are greatly enhanced.

Early childhood teacher researchers are in a position to show policy makers and others what is possible when teachers are supported in the exercise of their professionalism. Teacher research projects take readers inside real classrooms and tell real stories of teaching and learning. They demonstrate the power of narrative ways of knowing to illuminate the complexities of contemporary early childhood teaching. They make plain the limitations of overly relying on so-called "scientifically-based" knowledge to address the many issues that face teachers and students. They make the case that teacher research provides opportunities for renewing a sense of professional efficacy that is sometimes hard to find in the socio-political climate we currently face. And, high-quality teacher research projects further the notion that increasing teacher autonomy is an essential component of moving the early childhood field forward.

I hope the questions, possible answers, and discussions I have shared will help other teacher educators take better advantage of opportunities and create sensible responses to the challenges associated with teacher research in early childhood settings.

This chapter is based in part on the introduction "Teacher Research, Narrative Knowing, Classroom Practice, and Education Policy," by J. Amos Hatch, previously published in The Missing Link: Connecting Teacher Research, Practice & Policy to Improve Student Learning, *by E. Meyers & F. Rust, eds.*

References

Bruner, J. 1986. *Actual minds, possible worlds.* Cambridge, MA: Harvard University Press.

Howes, C., & R.C. Pianta. 2011. *Foundations for teaching excellence: Connecting early childhood quality rating, professional development, and competency systems in states.* Baltimore, MD: Brookes.

Polkinghorne, D.E. 1995. Narrative configuration in qualitative analysis. In *Life history and narrative,* eds. J.A. Hatch & R. Wisniewski, 113–35. London: Falmer Press.

Rust, F.O. 2007. Action research in early childhood contexts. In *Early childhood qualitative research,* ed. J.A. Hatch, 95–108. New York: Routledge/Taylor & Francis.

Rust, F.O., & E. Meyers. 2006. The bright side: Teacher research in the context of educational reform and policy-making. *Teachers and Teaching: Theory and Practice* 12: 69–86.

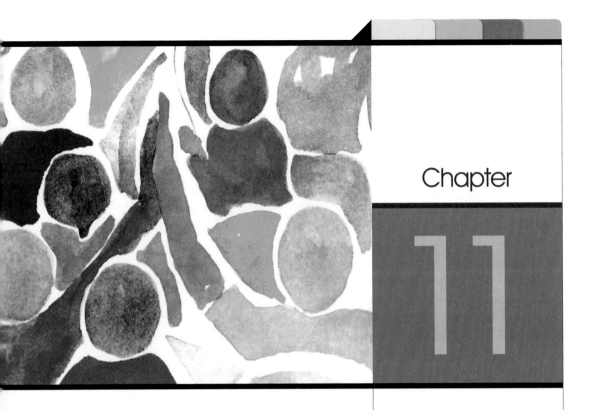

Developing
Professional Insight

Lilian G. Katz

S ome time ago, as often happens during stormy weather, I spent a very long time in one of our big airports waiting to be re-booked because I had missed a connecting flight. After a while, to relieve the tedium, I turned to the man standing next to me in the long line and asked him where he was trying to go and why. He told me his destination and then talked about his work in a large food production company. "Sounds interesting," I said. "Must be lots to think about in that kind of work," I added, and he modestly agreed. He then asked me where I was going and why. I explained that I was on my way to a conference of preschool teachers. "Oh, well," he said, "that kind of work sounds easy enough; anybody can do that!"

As we know, however, teaching young children is not easy. I offered him the following principle—*only from a distance does someone else's job look easy.*

The deeper and closer we get to the classroom and the teaching-learning process, the better able we are to appreciate its complexities. This is especially true for pre-service teachers—an early childhood education student armed with a set of creative activities is eager to jump right in and try them out, but cannot yet understand all of the responsibilities entailed in managing a classroom. It seems easy until you are actually responsible for it.

In the classroom, teachers are faced with a wide range of contextual, situational, and ethical constraints, the pros and cons of various practices, and other professional complexities. As teachers become more experienced and more knowledgeable about the nature of teaching, they become more aware of the complexities of being competent teachers. They develop new criteria for what it means to be a good teacher; their thinking is deeper and more detailed. The teacher research studies in this book help us appreciate the many complexities of the lively environments in the classrooms of young children and the challenges encountered by their teachers, just about daily.

What does it mean to be an early childhood professional? A professional is able to exercise judgment based on specialized knowledge, principles, and techniques. An early childhood professional

- is committed to serving the needs of children, parents, and society
- responds to children with reasoned judgment, in thoughtful and informative ways, and with warmth
- acts on the basis of principles that are taken into account in the formulation of professional judgment
- is thoughtful and responsive
- is self-respecting

The goal of education is to engage the minds of learners so that their understanding of significant phenomena and events becomes deeper and clearer. We want to impart intellectual content of lasting import, instilling a strong intellectual ethos in the process. Our message to teachers needs to be: Cultivate your own intellect and nourish the life of your own mind. For teachers, this intellectual cultivation is as important as growing our capacities for compassion and caring—not less, not more, but equally important. In other words, we must tell students to see themselves as developing professionals; they must become students of their own teaching, and remain so throughout their careers.

What can be learned in advance about actual practice? Becoming an early childhood professional

Much of what needs to be learned about how to teach young children cannot be mastered beforehand in professional preparation outside of a classroom setting where a teacher is responsible for the decision making. A great deal of education consists of providing learners with information and knowledge they do not yet want, or experiences they cannot imagine ever drawing from. This predicament in preservice teacher education is caused by the fact that it very largely consists of providing undergraduate students with answers to questions they have not yet asked, and strategies and solutions for problems not yet encountered—of preparing them for eventualities rather than actualities. Some matters learned during teacher education seem useful, practical, and helpful, but in retrospect later during actual practice seem irrelevant to the current issues the teacher faces. And vice versa—much that is taught may seem irrelevant while actually being studied and learned, but will become relevant and even useful later on in unanticipated ways. Because our graduates are likely to be employed in settings in which the diversity of children and communities may be very wide, it is difficult to predict what knowledge and which skills will be essential and which are merely traditional or simply desirable.

All teachers at every level of education face conflicting pressures concerning the extent to which they should emphasize *coverage* versus *mastery* of the content and skills to be learned. In our field, students are expected to become generalists in possession of a wide range of knowledge, understanding, and skills needed to teach the whole early childhood curriculum. We are under constant pressure to expand the teacher education curriculum to cover more content and skills. No one ever offers to drop a program component! So—there's a lot to cover! However, if we try to address too much, it can result in superficial, shallow learning on the part of students. Some of the pressure to expand content and skills coverage comes from teacher educators themselves, who urge expansion to include such important aspects of teaching as sensitizing students to minority cultures, gender stereotyping, mainstreaming, parent-school relations, computer literacy, and so on and so forth. Expansion of knowledge applies also to what I call "supply disciplines," such as child development, psychology of learning, methods of teaching phonics, language development, math and science, and special education. While the underlying intention to cover as much as possible is admirable, overall this approach is detrimental to student preparation. Certainly the disposition to be reflective is unlikely to thrive when the teacher education program opts for coverage versus mastery.

The main problem in opting for coverage is that the teacher education program may easily become a "smattering" approach to education. A bit of this and a bit of that, but little real depth and mastery. What is covered in the program may indeed be learned by students, but is unlikely to be sufficiently grasped to permit retrieval and application when the candidate is subsequently under fire in the trenches. A smattering of many subjects and teaching methods courses is likely to have a weak impact on our college students' ultimate professional competence in the workplace.

The greater the coverage, the more likely students will feel under pressure to "cram" the course content just to cope with the assignments, examinations, and to just get through. Their main concerns will be stuffing their heads with collections of vaguely related facts and satisfying performance criteria on a laundry list of techniques and competencies. But being good at being a student is not necessarily equal to being good at teaching. The knowledge covered is likely to be inert rather than applicable. Mastery of topics needs to be deep enough to withstand the pressure of later "real world" demands. The advantage of reducing the breadth of content and skills covered is that it could allow the faculty to focus on strengthening dispositions relevant to students' professional development in the long term (Katz & Raths 1985).

How does teacher research help address the breadth and depth issue?

The collection of studies in Part I of this book in which teachers of young children share their experiences conducting research on their own teaching is very welcome. The studies offer a sense of what is possible when teachers conduct research on their own work, often in association with other contributing and supportive specialists, as well as families and even the children themselves. We can easily see that teachers are in a good position to gain new knowledge about the intricacies of the particular situations in which they are working. In addition, they offer us deeper understandings of the complex environments involved in the education and care of young children—often contexts characterized by a wide range of physical, social, and financial constraints and pressures.

Competent teachers are those who are open to fresh ideas and take responsibility for their own continuous learning seriously. They need to know how to look up topics of interest and tap into the existing knowledge bases of the field. Hatch provides a rich discussion of basic aspects of the teacher research process and the ways it can support the teacher's own professional development. In the teacher research process, early childhood teachers engage in serious in-depth studies of their most pressing and relevant issues and concerns about their practice. The process engages teachers in looking at current professional literature and examining prior knowledge in light of new understandings, assessing their own values and beliefs and measuring how well they are or are not addressing the challenges of their practice. We can help by encouraging initiative and independent study in our students. As Henderson, Meier, Perry, and Stremmel state earlier in this volume, teacher research studies can "help teachers gain new ways of seeing children, develop deeper understandings of children's feelings and growth, and help teachers become more responsive to children" (see p. 5).

As Stremmel points out so convincingly in his chapter on "Reshaping the Landscape of Early Childhood Teaching through Teacher Research," teaching is an "inquiry process." The inquiry stance (Cochran-Smith & Lytle 2009) on teaching fostered via teacher research increases depth of learning and mastery as teachers study and understand an important issue or interest at a deeper level (Cochran-Smith & Lytle 2009).

Developing professional insight

Much of the literature for teachers, especially as learned during preliminary and formal training, addresses what is often referred to as "professional knowledge." This would include a full grasp of what is known about the norms of development and the typical ages and stages during which a range of abilities are normally acquired. In addition, professional knowledge includes familiarity and understanding of the typical schedule of activities appropriate to given age groups, standard environmental arrangements, equipment, play materials, teaching strategies, and so forth—part of a list much too long to include here. A teacher's knowledge would also most likely include familiarity with the many curriculum models that are constantly referred to in contentious discussions within the early childhood profession (e.g., House 2011; Zigler et al. 2011).

Teaching young children involves constant decision making. Some decisions are simple—almost automatic. Many are related to daily routines without which the teacher could risk suffering from "analysis paralysis." But many decisions are complex and have a range of implications for the individual child as well as for the whole group. Such cases may benefit from some reflection, deeper analysis, and the teachers' *insights*.

The term *insight* is very difficult to define. As I have discussed it with very many colleagues, we seem to agree that it refers to putting together in a less-than-conscious way all we know that could possibly be relevant to a given situation and/or person. I think of insight as the act of compiling—on a deep level—knowledge, facts, and hunches about many aspects of a predicament. A teacher reflecting on what is happening in the classroom might consider such factors as knowledge about children in general (i.e., norms and stages), what is known about individual children, and what the teacher knows based on personal relationships with children. Together these sources of information serve as a basis of insight—a deep intuitive understanding of all the children for whom the teacher is responsible.

Somehow, by putting together all we know, what we understand, and our best guesses, we develop a deep understanding that can serve as a basis for decision making and action. This volume offers ample examples of how such insights can be developed and strengthened by teachers conducting and learning from their own research. Such study not only benefits the children they teach, but adds to the sense of satisfaction gained from working with children at such an important time in their lives.

I continue to believe that it is useful to think of teachers, as indeed all other professionals, as moving through stages of development—beginning with a "survival" stage and with enough experience, support, and encouragement ultimately reaching a stage of "maturity." The reports included in this volume suggest that when teachers conduct their own research on their own teaching their path to maturity can be strengthened, fostering continuous professional growth throughout their careers.

References

Cochran-Smith, M., & S.L. Lytle. 2009. *Inquiry as stance: Practitioner research for the next generation.* New York: Teachers College Press.

House, R., ed. 2011. *Too much, too soon? Early learning and the erosion of childhood.* Gloucestershire, UK: Hawthorne Press.

Katz, L.G., & J.D. Raths. 1985. Dispositions as goals for teacher education. *Teaching and Teacher Education* 1 (4): 301–07.

Zigler, E., W.S. Gilliam & W.S. Barnett, eds. 2011. *The pre-k debates: Current controversies and issues.* Baltimore, MD: Brookes.

© Mac H. Brown

Teacher Research:

Improving Practice and Amplifying Teacher Voice among Diverse Students in Early Childhood Education

Barbara Henderson

Thischapter offers a comprehensive description of the teacher research program at San Francisco State University and shows how the concepts and skills of teacher research and values of the faculty are introduced to graduate students and upper level undergraduates. I focus specifically on materials describing teacher research and how professors Daniel Meier, Mina Kim, and I use it as the organizing framework for the graduate program in Early Childhood Education at San Francisco State University.

Teacher research education—the graduate program at San Francisco State University

Teacher research is the centerpiece of graduate work in early childhood education at San Francisco State University. San Francisco State is one of the California State Universities; we are primarily an undergraduate and master's level institution, although we also have a few small doctoral programs. We have a population of approximately 30,000 students, with 25,000 undergraduates and 5,000 at graduate-level. Our program serves 75–90 active students, graduating an average of 25 students each year. The program consists of 33 units, which a majority of students take part-time over 2–3 years.

The graduate program in Early Childhood Education features a diverse student body—our students are predominantly of color, and nearly half of them speak English as a second or additional language (including international students, adult immigrants to the United States, those who immigrated as children, and those who grew up in homes where the family spoke languages other than English).

Our students are also diverse professionally. The largest portion of our students consists of practicing teachers, at approximately 60 percent. Teachers include preschool teachers, infant-toddler caregivers, and a few elementary teachers working in the primary grades. The second largest group includes about 20 percent of our students who are volunteering or substituting in centers, or working in private settings as nannies. About 15 percent of our students are school leaders who administer early childhood and after-school programs. Our early childhood education teachers and administrators work at a range of sites, including university child care, district-run sites, private non- and for-profits, corporate child care, state-sponsored preschools, home-based programs, and Head Start centers. About 5 percent of students are in allied fields, including early childhood education evaluators, teacher trainers, and social service professionals.

Courses focus on teaching teacher research skills along with course content. Four foundational courses are:

1. Cognitive Development in Early Childhood Education

2. Social, Emotional, and Physical Development in Early Childhood Education

3. First and Second Language Development in Early Childhood Education

4. Narrative Inquiry and Memoir in Early Childhood Education

Students integrate teacher research skills through a fifth course:

5. Practitioner Research in Early Childhood Education

All of our courses have a sociocultural perspective and value students' and children's home language and culture. We work to build skills and knowledge of teacher research throughout our courses, which culminate in a field study—the term we use for the master's thesis—and most of these projects are examples of teacher research. Courses and the major papers for each course are laid out in the following figure. In this flowchart, four of the major courses are shown across the top of the figure as sails, with each of the final course projects shown as attached tags. The practitioner research course, shown as a flattened diamond, has arrows feeding into it to indicate how the other required classes contribute to students' skills prior to this class. The flowchart shows how courses lead to the culminating field study or master's thesis, which is depicted as a flattened oval at the bottom.

The flowchart shows how elements of teacher research are taught in five of our required courses and lead to the culminating field study.

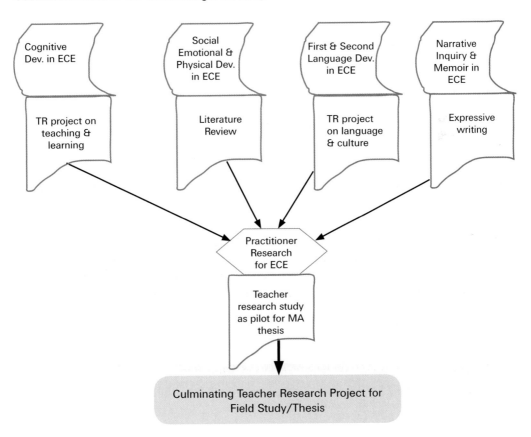

Teacher research skills taught in the course on cognitive development

The major assignment for this course is a teacher research study focused on one's own teaching and the learning and development of a focal child or group of children. A specific study design is required for the project; that is, students use a traditional pre-test to post-test continuum, and seek to identify the outcomes of the teaching-learning exchanges. Papers are written chronologically to describe the course of the children's learning and to trace how the teacher-planned environments, materials, and interactions build upon the children's interests and partial understandings.

For data analysis, we focus on teaching students how to use photo analysis, analysis of children's work samples, and conversational analysis. Students need the most direct instruction on conversational analysis; that is, learning how to draw deeper meaning from children's transcribed speech. Perhaps because speech is so integrated into human understanding, it is hard at first for students to think beyond the surface content of an exchange. Conversational analysis, which relates to discourse analysis and a range of other sociolinguistic research tools, is an approach to interpreting oral discourse where transcribed speech is treated as text and taken apart to find patterns. We focus on a range of elements, for example:

1. Turn-taking
2. Initiation and uptake of content that creates episodes within an exchange
3. Variation in linguistic style or language
4. Uses of non-linguistic communication, including silence, tone, gesture, verbal interjections, babbling, and laughter
5. Identifying where and how power relations arise

For example, here is a selection from a video transcript of an interaction between an older infant, Lizzie, and her preschool-aged brother, Aaron. They interact with their caregiver, Elaine, at a park with a small merry-go-round. Both children are on the equipment at the start of this excerpt. They have played here together before.

Aaron: Go round and round!

(Uses left leg to move the merry-go-round and other leg to swing around a bar to hang on. Looks at Lizzie as he is spinning the merry-go-round. Lizzie grins, standing and holding on to the bar. Then she starts stomping both feet, gripping harder on the bars.)

Lizzie: Ehhh ehhh! Ehhhh ehhhh! Ehhhhhhhhh.

Elaine: Lizzie, are you asking to slow down?
(Aaron puts his leg out and lowers his foot to the ground.)

Elaine: Thank you, Aaron.
(Lizzie starts swinging on the bars with both hands as the merry-go-round slows down. Aaron watches her, then starts spinning the merry-go-round faster.)

Lizzie (stomping with both feet): Eh eh ehhhh!

Elaine: Aaron, I think that when she makes that sound, she is asking you to slow down.

Lizzie: Ah ahhh. (stomp stomp)

Elaine: When she is stomp-stomping her feet, slow down, hon.
(Aaron slows the merry-go-round.)

Elaine: Thank you.

This was at the start of their play, and shows an equal flow of turn-taking among the three participants. Aaron speeds up the spinning ride, and Lizzie requests that it be slowed down—requests that are facilitated by Elaine. At the start of the interaction, Lizzie first communicates her pleasure at the spinning with a smile, and then her increasing concern with gripped hands, stomps, and cries of "Ehh, ehhh!" Elaine tries an indirect scaffold first, restating what she sees Lizzie requesting, to which Aaron responds. A new sub-episode starts as the merry-go-round slows and Lizzie initiates a new action, swinging, to which Aaron responds by increasing the speed again. Lizzie then repeats her insistence that they slow down, which Elaine and then Lizzie both reinforce several times until Aaron complies.

Overall, this example shows how even preverbal children can communicate as conversational partners to engage in play that would be well beyond their capacities without social scaffolds, and to show how such scaffolds allow them to participate in turn-taking and decision making. In this case Lizzie was interested in challenging her motor planning skills; she found her older brother an exciting model, but also responded to internal limits about what felt manageable.

The focus of students' analysis in the cognitive development class is children's skill and conceptual development. I encourage students to select a topic related to science, math, logic, moral development, music, or visual arts. For infants and young toddlers I suggest they focus on sand or water play, motor planning, children's understanding of routines, self-regulation in social situations, or turn-taking. One of my goals is for students to choose a topic differentiated from their learning in our courses on children's language and literacy development. The other challenge for topic selection is choosing a narrow enough focus such that projects present clear outcome measures within the few months of research time allotted by the semester. Finally, students need to understand how to construct and facilitate projects built on children's prior knowledge and interests that can extend over several weeks or even several months and show a wealth of involvement and opportunities for children's insight. Project topics have included toddlers learning through expressive drawing, 3-year-olds' understanding of hide-and-seek, and preschoolers' development of the deep concepts of fairness and reciprocity.

Most students take this course early in the program, and the assignments build through use of data memos (described below) and drafts. The projects on children's cognition provide students with a well-guided yet rigorous introduction to teacher research.

Teacher research skills taught in the course on social, emotional, and physical development

In this course, students undertake a literature review while integrating their own observations of children on social, emotional, and physical topics. The goal of this project is to help teacher researchers understand how to gather and critically interpret literature from the field. As early childhood education draws from a range of related fields, this study also facilitates comparison of literature from journals in curriculum and instruction, child development, brain-based studies, occupational therapy, and physical and social development. The course instructs students on how to integrate literature into their written arguments; it also aids students in integrating ideas from the literature with their experiences and data drawn from their close observation of children. Ultimately, the goal is for students to improve the clarity of their academic writing and to learn how to enter into dialogue with the relevant literature from our field.

Many students begin discussing the literature as though writing a series of book reports. However, the academic writing we wish to engender involves students seeing themselves as knowledge brokers among different disciplines that all talk about children, but do not talk much to each other. At the same time, we want students to see themselves as knowledge creators—their own careful observations of children in early childhood settings can add to our understanding of how children behave and what children know from a very early age. In their writing, students eventually gain the ability to synthesize literature about children's social, emotional, and physical development into a kind of conversation among the authors. As authors themselves, students become the facilitative and evaluative voice that helps the reader understand, apply, and appreciate the significance of the material.

Teacher research skills taught in the course on first and second language development

This course takes a strongly cultural emphasis on language acquisition, beginning with the assumption that many children grow up as speakers of multiple languages or dialects and that essentially all of the preservice early childhood professionals in our program will be working in multilingual early childhood settings. Topics include early language acquisition, storytelling, power and equity issues regarding language in multilingual societies, critical literacy, and children's early literacy experiences. The major course project is an empirical study of children's language acquisition; this also helps teacher researchers understand how to take and analyze language samples from children in natural settings. Students are expected to conduct a study that spans at least five observational settings and develops over 3–4 weeks. A two-and-half-month time frame is suggested for data collection, early drafting, and final write-up of the paper.

To prepare for the final research project, an early course assignment requires students to create a relevant data collection sheet to efficiently capture and record children's behavior, gestures, verbal language, non-verbal language, artwork, and writing as they unfold in natural settings. Students are encouraged to ensure they have sufficient and sufficiently interesting data to write a strong paper. Papers also need to integrate relevant literature, which can easily stretch beyond course readings. In fact, using course readings as references in the paper is wholly optional; we emphasize instead that the materials be relevant to the paper topic, and that students come to know the research literature most closely tied to their growing areas of expertise. Some recent examples of projects titles include "Bilingual Families and Autistic Children," "Code-Switching and African American Children in Preschool," "How Mothers Use 'Motherese' with Infants," and "The Language of Friendship, a Study of Two Toddlers."

Teacher research skills taught in the course on narrative inquiry and memoir in early childhood education

This course emphasizes arts-based inquiry, specifically focusing on forms of narrative inquiry and memoir as alternative tools for enacting teacher research. The course helps students explore their personal, professional, and cultural memories to better understand the social, educational, and cultural forces that shape teaching and learning. Course readings include memoirs of teachers and others, as well as narrative accounts of teaching, learning, and language in and out of educational settings.

The writing that students do in this course is, then, quite different from traditional academic writing; the final course project consists of a collection of personal narratives, professional narratives, and other expressive writing around a theme. Meier has developed the course over the past 10 years, modifying the final project over time from what was at first an amalgam of stories and memoirs to collections that now often include a wide range of media, such as paintings, sketches, photographic portraiture and landscapes, video collage, poetry, short story, and myth. General elements of the collection include vignettes that capture moments of life, narratives about children people have worked with, themselves as children, or their own children, and poetry and visual arts that express life experience about teaching and identity.

The students do three separate assignments to prepare for the photographic, narrative, and poetry-based elements of the final collection. Two photographic assignments are a study of a child and of murals in San Francisco's Mission District. The murals study connects with an important cultural aspect of our city, and requires students to evaluate how murals use narrative elements such as plot, character, tone, voice, and setting. The write-ups for these two photographic assignments are brief, but require students to explicitly connect what they have learned to their work in early childhood education.

For the story and poetry collections, the goal is creativity and personally grounded meaning, without governance from heavy-handed guidelines. Students sometimes struggle to understand what is expected from them here, especially since this particular class is required and not everyone feels comfortable as an author of personally revealing material. To help students, Meier provides them with evaluative questions to guide their efforts, such as:

- Is your story something others will want to hear about because you have a strong desire to tell it?
- Do you make the apparently insignificant significant?
- Do you show rather than tell what is going on?
- Does the story rely on our senses?
- Does your beginning draw the reader in, and make them want to find out what will happen?
- Can anything be cut or changed to make it better?
- Have you as the author avoided cliché?
- Which images drive the story and stay with us as readers after the reading of the story is over?
- Is there a twist or a surprise or a new feeling or thought that we take away as readers by the end of the story?

Similarly for the poetry collection, Meier asks these key questions:

- Is the language original? Do you avoid cliché?
- Does your poem have a depth of feeling, ideas, and experience?
- Does it have music and rhythm? Is there a distinct tone?
- Does the punctuation enhance the reading, and does it provide cues to the reader?
- Are there strong images that stay with us?
- If you are writing from personal memory and experience, do you tell us just enough "truth" so that it's believable?

Students choose such topics as small moments of children learning and growing in preschool, personal memories of childhood, and reflection on their own children's experiences.

Our narrative inquiry and memoir class changes the nature and feel of the overall program, and echoes of it can be felt in the written style, structure, and data representation of nearly all of the culminating research projects. This kind of arts-based inquiry and focus on expressive writing has helped our students become more willing to take risks and reveal themselves in their teacher research projects. One student described this course as a lifeline, and wondered if she would have persisted in the program without it. Indeed, for many of our students this class gives them the permission and the skills to bring their whole selves to their writing and their academic studies. Whether or not they maintain a narrative focus in their later work, the experience impacts their writing skills for the better.

The teacher research course

This course is intended as the penultimate class, taken just prior to the master's thesis or culminating field study. Students take the full semester to research and write a teacher research paper on a topic of their choice. Given the timing of the class, this project serves as a pilot for many students' culminating field studies.

A key skill developed during this project is identifying a question that holds one's passionate interest; this must also be a question about one's own practice in a venue with easy and regular access to data throughout the semester, and in a setting one can potentially impact. Students learn to shape inquiry to make their question researchable through objective means. They then collect relevant data, organize and analyze that data, and collaborate with and critique other teacher researchers in class using "data memos," which are brief papers that present a bit of raw data and some tentative analysis for others in each student's research group to comment on. Data memos include the following elements:

1. The context of the selected data (who, when, where, what, how)

2. Analysis of the selected data, which may be shown as a list of points

3. Interpretation of the data with respect to course literature (or to fiction, poetry, memoir, visual arts, film, cultural, or political events)

4. The data to be discussed (e.g., transcript, copies of student work, or photos—this is attached to the 1–2 page write-up)

Another major assignment that helps students prepare for the final paper is our "Starting Point Speech" assignment—a write-up and oral presentation five weeks into the term where students describe to a small group what they plan to study and why it matters (see box). Although students are encouraged to explore topics and collect preliminary data from the start of the semester, this presentation, developed by our colleague Allan Feldman, marks the formal start of the students' commitment to follow through on a topic of inquiry for the semester. The assignment mixes narrative with more standard academic research elements.

Students develop further data analysis skills through an indexing assignment that guides them to find emerging themes in their data (see the box "Indexing Assignment"). In particular, students are expected to draw upon observational field notes and material from reflective journals.

Starting Point Speech

1. Key Anecdote

Write a vignette that captures the heart of your project. It should be short, and present some kind of problem or paradox. You may draw the story directly from your work in schools or you may use a bit of memoir. Your goal is to envision a vignette that could begin your final paper, although you may come up with a better one later in the semester.

2. Research Protocol

a. State your research question(s) and sub-questions (if any). Teacher research is primarily qualitative research, so your question will likely be more about opening up your understanding of the process than measuring discrete outcomes. However, you are using a mixed methods design (integrating both qualitative and quantitative data); you might measure some outcomes, but the qualitative data will need to open up these findings. Cycles of teacher action research look at evolving reform, which is a type of outcome, although the focus is still on the processes of that change.

b. Provide a brief overview of your planned research.

1. Explain what kind of teacher research design you have chosen (e.g., qualitative or mixed methods teacher research, teacher action research, self-study, narrative inquiry).

2. Give a brief description of your participants and setting.

3. Describe data sources and plans for data collection (use at least three different sources of data, such as: observational field notes, collections of children's work products, interviews, reflective journaling, photography, video, audio, and collection of school documents).

c. How do these data sources and collections address your research question?

d. Why does this study matter? That is, how can what you are looking at in your local setting inform others in the field of early childhood education, and how might recommendations arising from your findings relate to current policy (e.g., preparation of early childhood teachers, quality initiatives, curriculum adoption, funding, professional development, or other political issues affecting families and children in society)?

3. Ethics and Values Statement

a. How have you ensured your research is ethical in terms of informing and getting consent from your participants?

b. How have you made sure your research question(s), methods of data collection, and data analysis are in tune with your values? Is the action you are taking through this project addressing an existing situation that counters your values?

Throughout the semester, students develop skills in study design, data collection and analysis, and professional writing habits. Overall, students gain confidence as teacher researchers and become aware of how their findings might have a broader impact, influencing other teachers and potentially educational policy makers. The end-of-semester project guides students in integrating their data memos, Starting

Indexing Assignment

1. Data Index

Create a thematic summary, from which you will index your research notebook(s) and other data. The index should catalogue your field notes, reflective writing, and all the other data in your data archive box. This indexing exercise requires you to use a grounded theory approach to analyze your full data collection to date, and will contribute heavily to your final project. Turn in a photocopy of the index you have handwritten in your teacher research journal.

2. Defining and Illustrating Themes

Define each of the themes you've captured in your index. If you have more than 15 themes, find ways to collapse them, or omit those tangential to your research question. Then, draw examples from your data to illustrate four themes you expect to be most central to your final paper. As you discuss these key themes, make relevant connections to course readings. This section should appear as a list of terms or phrases, each defined. Then pull out the top four and provide extended definitions, one illustrative data excerpt, and interpretations that link these to the course readings.

3. Evaluating Project Scope

Evaluate the state of your research project, again making relevant connections to course readings throughout this section. Include the following four subsections. Each of the points below can be sufficiently addressed by a paragraph of text.

   a. Describe the impact of having made this index and pruned to four key concepts;

   b. Evaluate the scope and quality of your data, and effectiveness of your analysis;

   c. Highlight what is working well in your data collection and analysis and what you need to change;

   d. Given the pattern that emerged from your indexing, describe what data you need to collect next to confirm or disprove your emerging theory.

Point Speech, index of emerging themes, and course readings with other data in order to write up their full studies. We use *Voices of Practitioners* articles as models, and the journal's manuscript guidelines help students write papers that truly communicate with fellow practitioners and policy makers.

Part of the cycle of research is presenting one's findings, and so to close this circle, we make the students' research locally available and public by immediately self-publishing a teacher research journal that includes all of the students' papers. This journal is distributed to students on the final day of class. Some examples of recent teacher research papers written for this class include "Conducting Science Inquiry in a Preschool Classroom: An Adventure in Discovery for Students and Teachers," "Bridging Home and School Connections through Language: My Role in Supporting Spanish Speaking Toddlers' Cultural Identities," and "Dancing Together, Growing Together: One Teacher's Exploration into How Dance Class Supports Social-Emotional Development."

Evaluating the teacher research field study or thesis

Teacher research field studies and theses are assessed for quality via a set of criteria. Briefly, the elements considered include the following:

1. Is the question posed researchable?

2. Is the question significant within the field of early childhood education (i.e., current and relevant, original, of the right scope)?

3. Has the author made links to the relevant literature?

4. Was the study designed to effectively address the research question?

5. Does the paper use an effective writing style?

6. Do the findings use a range of qualitative and/or narrative inquiry methodologies to present evidence for claims?

7. Are there implications from the findings for others outside of the teacher him- or herself?

Reflective thinking

Reflective thinking is a critical part of our program at San Francisco State University. Teacher research is at its heart inquiry-based. It is work that practitioners undertake freely, based on their own curiosity—this then sparks reflective thinking. Reflective thinking is a term that appears frequently in the work of John Dewey, and is a phrase common throughout much of the professional development and teacher preparation literature. It is particularly appropriate in this context, as a full definition of reflective thought demands the same kind of disciplined, critical, evidence-based, and collaborative process as teacher research. Indeed, Dewey's work stands as a primary reference source for teacher research—beginning as early as 1899 his work called for a science of pedagogy in universities where practicing teachers would be the experts (Tanner 1997).

As Zeichner and Liston (1996) and Rodgers (2002) highlight, reflective thinking also requires a certain set of attitudes that include wholeheartedness, open-mindedness, directness, and responsibility. Wholeheartedness suggests enthusiasm, vigor, and a way of working that seeks engagement and willingly risks occasional failure in the attempt to improve. Open-mindedness is the ability to hear others' opinions and be open to contrasting perspectives, even when they challenge long-held beliefs; it is the willingness to negotiate perspectives with others and leave with opinions broadened and strengthened by those exchanges. Directness is an attitude of confident knowing, as Rodgers emphasizes from Dewey's classic edition of *How We Think* (1910). She explains that an experienced teacher who has had educative experiences (i.e., positive and allowing one to leverage greater control) will be more likely to embody directness than the novice. For example, the veteran teacher knows the content well enough to teach it from any angle, in a manner that is most responsive to the students at hand. Finally, reflective thinking encompasses a sense of responsibility that emphasizes the morally grounded aspects of one's work. That is, reflective thinking is done in the service of bettering the society and contributing to a just and equitable system. Teacher research seeks to improve our teaching and administrative practice to bring to light bias, inequities, or limited access to quality teaching-learning environments that some children and families may receive in educational settings.

Implications

The aim of research by teachers and others who work directly with children and families is first and foremost to improve the quality of teaching and learning, as well as the depth of thinking by children and early childhood professionals within their sites. A strong education—which incorporates inquiry, curiosity, a willingness to be critical, and self-motivated discovery—is a key foundational component of a democratic society. Teacher research can improve conditions at school sites for children, families, and teaching staff, and classroom-based, insider, qualitative inquiry like teacher research also has implications that stretch beyond a classroom's walls. Teacher research requires a systematic approach and a clear grounding in the justness of what we seek to do as we reform our teaching lives. As McDermott and Raley (2007) state in their article on the application of Dewey's ideas to educational reform:

> Systematic inquiry into how people nurture conditions for telling the truth requires both the flexibility to see the world from multiple angles, from inside the nuanced work people do with each other, and a fierce, but not too constraining, commitment to doing it carefully, to getting it at least workably right. (1822)

Teacher educators are in a position to broaden the professional role of the early childhood practitioner by making teacher research a central element in their university programs. In addition to focusing on the implementation of best practices, early childhood professionals can be educated as critical thinkers and knowledge creators based on their original research on teaching and learning in early education settings. Teacher education practices emphasizing the equal importance of quality pedagogical practices along with knowledge creation can transform the early childhood profession and contribute to a radical shift in the nature and scope of education research.

References

Dewey, J. 1910. *How we think*. New York: DC Heath and Co.

Rodgers, C. 2002. Defining reflection: Another look at John Dewey and reflective thinking. *Teachers College Record* 104 (4): 842–66.

McDermott, R., & J.D. Raley. 2007. From John Dewey to an anthropology of education. *Teachers College Record* 109 (7): 1820–35.

Tanner, L. 1997. *Dewey's laboratory school: Lessons for today*. New York: Teachers College Press.

Zeichner, K.M., & D.P. Liston. 1996. *Reflective teaching: An introduction*. Mahwah, NJ: Lawrence Erlbaum.

Co-Inquiry:

Documentation, Communication, Action

Shareen Abramson

One afternoon while the preschoolers nap under the supervision of her coteacher, Monica heads for the staff meeting room at the Huggins Early Education Center. It is time for the center's weekly collaborative inquiry, or *co-inquiry*, meeting—a structured, professional dialogue on classroom projects. Monica is making today's staff presentation on her class's investigation of road construction.

The teachers take their seats in a circle, facing one another. One is ready to videotape the presentation so that it can be reviewed later. The center director is serving as facilitator for the meeting. Monica is well prepared with documentation of the children's activities and learning as they investigate road building. Her project notebook is organized in chronological order, with written notes and observations, including the children's comments during construction activities and group discussions and a number of photographs showing specific interactions and examples of block constructions. A bigger folder holds a collection of the children's drawings of roads, which include their captions and descriptions. She has even prepared a two-minute video clip of the children working with large blocks on the playground.

Some of the participants did not attend the previous co-inquiry meeting on Monica's project, so she begins with some background information. She tells how the project emerged from preschoolers' interest in making roads for their cars, and summarizes the work. The 3- and 4-year-olds have pondered, "What is a road?" From her notebook, Monica reads aloud some of her observations and some of the children's initial comments:

Kayla: "It is a street that cars drive on."

Jacob: "It has signs with it and dots with it."

Hailey: "Where the bikes go."

Braelen: "It's where you race on and where you drive on. The pipes are under the road."

Colten: "A motorcycle. It's a road, motorcycle drive, go beep beep. My mommy go to work and my daddy go to work."

Joey: "Street is like metal stuff, glass. Trucks drive on it."

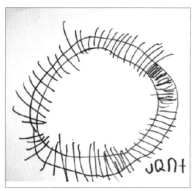

Monica next moves to the main focus of her presentation. She explains that whenever a specific problem or question comes up in her classroom, the teachers try to extend the children's thinking. In this case, when the children wondered how roads were constructed and what they were used for, the teachers initially asked the children if they'd like to draw some of the roads they envisioned. Monica displays several of the drawings and reads the children's descriptions, revealing their different conceptions of roads.

She tells how the teachers then invited the children to use their drawings as a blueprint to build a road. Five children volunteered to re-create their road drawings using the large outdoor blocks. The children decided to work together on the constructions, one drawing at a time. They succeeded in making a rectangular road from Kayla's drawing, but they encountered problems in making a round road from another child's drawing. Finally, Monica shows the video clip of the children working on the project. After the presentation, the co-inquiry group begins its dialogue, starting with comments and questions then offering ideas to further expand the road investigation the following week.

This exchange among teachers is an example of a co-inquiry meeting, which is a key component of the teacher education program at California State University where I teach. These meetings provide regular opportunities for teachers to engage in a dialogue about their own questions on teaching and learning. Documentation of a classroom event like the one described by Monica serves as a "memory" of experience. As the roads project unfolds, the co-inquiry group engages in animated discussion, examining the words and actions of the children and teachers. Co-inquiry meetings are designed to produce new insights into how the teaching-learning relationship is realized in the everyday action of the classroom and to lead to improved teaching practices.

What is co-inquiry?

The co-inquiry process was originally introduced by John Dewey. Dewey (1933; 1938) believed that teachers construct knowledge through inquiry with the assistance of colleagues and faculty, who help them refine and clarify their ideas about their learning and

teaching experiences in the classroom. Teachers see classroom problems or questions as possibilities for learning and growth rather than as stressful and inhibiting. To address an issue, it may be necessary to seek out information and other resources, consult with others, and acquire new skills. Over time, a problem can lead to new experiences, deeper understanding, and positive changes. The inquiry proceeds through a series of steps based on the scientific method (Dewey 1938). (See "Co-Inquiry and the Scientific Method.")

Co-inquiry is very similar to standard inquiry in teacher research, except it is carried out by a group rather than an individual. It is a collaborative process that involves joint action and interaction and is often used in human services settings to help effect change (Bray et al. 2000; Wells 1999). A group of people agrees to study a problem over a period of time by conducting research and holding meetings to examine findings and arrive at solutions. The group establishes a common purpose, research orientation, and commitment to action. Such projects sustain the group's interest, questions, and search for solutions. When undertaken by a small group of learners, co-inquiry stimulates different ideas and perspectives. As a result, participants acquire knowledge, skills, dispositions, and values.

Communication processes play a central role in the co-inquiry process. Co-inquiry relies on the sharing of ideas and understandings in both capturing and conveying the children's experience through documentation and through the exchange of ideas in the meeting discussions. Wells (1999) proposed the term *communicative literacy* to describe the ability to express meaning using the standard symbols of the culture—such as language, music, visual arts, and drama. Different ways to communicate ideas expand understanding and multiply the possibilities for meaningful, high-level exchanges of ideas.

Co-inquiry can enhance adult learning and professional development in a variety of settings (Bray et al. 2000). Studies in early childhood settings show a positive correlation between professional development experiences, teacher collaboration, and program quality/child outcomes (EdSource 2005; Honig & Hirallal 1998). Co-inquiry also leads to better understanding of children's learning styles, abilities, and interests, as well as new ideas for improving teaching (Hatch et al. 2005; Himley & Carini 2000; Kasl & Yorks 2002; King 2002; Langer et al. 2003).

The co-inquiry process at the Huggins Center

The Joyce M. Huggins Early Education Center (Huggins Center) is a demonstration training and research center serving families with children from 3 months to 10 years old. Huggins is also a student teaching site for early childhood majors at California State University.

Since the center opened in 1994, we have evolved our own particular way of doing co-inquiry. Our process represents a synthesis of ideas from the last 13 years of our professional development experiences, which have included workshops and sessions on the Reggio Emilia approach at NAEYC conferences, programs hosted by Reggio-inspired schools, and the traveling exhibit of children's work from Reggio schools in Italy.

The co-inquiry meeting has been used successfully by teachers in the center, student teachers, and student groups, and by teachers with parents and with children in the classroom. These meetings help create a culture of dynamic, professional interchange with the goal of improving teaching and learning. We have found that it is a practical way for a group to collaborate and learn from one another. For participants, co-inquiry heightens the focus on the meaning of development and learning and promotes study and research.

In our co-inquiry process, participants progress through three stages: **documentation**, **communication**, and **action**. As the opening vignette illustrates, professional learning experiences focus on a question, issue, or interest rather than on a topic or curriculum area. Teachers assume the role of researchers through inquiry and co-inquiry (Hill et al. 2005). As their "evidence," they use documentation—a multisymbolic tool for recording and representing children's learning experiences (Edwards et al.1998; Rinaldi 1998). Documentation of children's learning is essential to our inquiry process. It provides a common reference point for teachers in talking about children's learning experiences and the challenges of teaching (Abramson & Atwal 2003; Cadwell 2003; Carter 2002; Project Zero 2003). It also serves a dual purpose by providing specific observations and examples of children's early learning for meeting standards or other performance-based assessments (Edwards 2006).

Documentation facilitates interchange among children, families, teachers, and the larger community by improving communication and understanding of the importance of early education. Through this documentation process, educators can explore questions, examine children's thinking, and plan and respond to new problems, situations, and ideas (Gandini & Goldhaber 2001).

In presenting documentation and engaging in dialogue, Huggins teachers learn from each other's responses and questions, gain new perspectives, and gather ideas for future classroom experiences. In this supportive atmosphere, newer staff and less experienced teachers learn about the school philosophy, get to know the program and the teachers in other classrooms, and appreciate the value of meeting together to examine documentation. The meetings foster mentoring relationships, teacher confidence, and renewed classroom enthusiasm.

Three-stage structure

A key feature of the Huggins co-inquiry process is the explicit structure used for the co-inquiry meeting. This three-stage structure—documentation, communication, and action—helps the group move toward tentative hypotheses and planning. A protocol or structured format fosters the teacher's skill in reflecting on children's work and analyzing it in greater detail, resulting in improved student performances. (A good method is described in the website Looking at Student Work—www.lasw.org/primer.html.) This protocol ensures that everyone has an equal chance to speak, and it leads to thoughtful listening because participants are clear on their roles and when to offer their comments. Below is an outline of the protocol we use at Huggins. Each of the six steps is illustrated by an example from a co-inquiry investigation into a peer-relations problem experienced in one classroom. Together, the steps show how to conduct a co-inquiry meeting.

Documentation

1. A teacher begins by presenting documentation of a classroom experience to the group. The presentation should consider a problem, an observation of a situation of interest, or an area of confusion.

> *Example*: A Huggins preschool teacher who changed classrooms midyear is the presenter. She shares her observation notes on an issue concerning peer relationships. The children seem to be having difficulties in waiting their turn, sharing materials, and limiting their disagreements and conflicts during play.

Communication

2. Each participant takes a turn responding to the issue, describing an interesting, important, or provocative aspect of the experience.

> *Example*: The other teachers comment on aspects they see as important. One teacher points out that the midyear arrival of the teacher may have caused stress for the children. Another teacher observes that the issue seems to involve taking turns rather than personal animosities or differences. The group discusses why children who have been together for some time might be having these difficulties.

3. In turn, each participant asks a meaningful question concerning the implications for teaching or learning. (Questions are not necessarily answered at this time; they may require additional reading or classroom research.)

> *Example*: Teachers ask: "Are the same children involved in most of the conflicts?" "How are activities organized?" "Are there possible parental influences?" One teacher wonders, "How do children acquire skills in taking turns, anyhow?" The director describes an article on peer conflicts (Katz 1984) that she thinks may be useful and offers to make copies for the group.

Action

4. Participants continue to talk, and they brainstorm about how the classroom experiences could continue to develop.

> *Example*: The presenting teacher's colleagues suggest possible actions to take, such as talking with the children about problems; reading the documentation of conflicts to the children; and offering learning experiences that require turn-taking and cooperation, like a science experiment or cooking project.

5. Based on the comments, questions, and ideas from the co-inquiry, the presenter creates a "plan of possibility" to explore with the children in the coming week.

> *Example*: Returning to the classroom, the presenter shares her meeting notes with others on the teaching team. They have a class discussion with the children and suggest doing a group project. The children talk about what it means to take turns, and they share activities they like to do with others at school and at home.

The classroom teachers plan and carry out several activities, and cooking emerges as a favorite of the children. The teachers know that cooking is both educationally complex and socially challenging. It requires children to do many things cooperatively (such as reading recipes; using ingredients and utensils; following directions; measuring, pouring, and stirring; and watching the time), and the teachers can document each step. Cooking also invites family participation, because parents can send in recipes and ingredients or visit the classroom to make favorite recipes with a small group. In cooking together, the children not only practice taking turns and cooperating, but also discover the importance of individual and group efforts. The teachers learn new strategies for developing positive peer relations and parent participation. The classroom becomes a more communicative, collaborative, and caring community.

> **To read the Co-Inquiry Journal:** Interchange in Education, view multimedia documentation, and join the discussion,
>
> go to the co-inquiry website and blog: www.coinquiry.org

6. Documentation of the new classroom experiences is discussed in future inquiry meetings, continuing the co-inquiry process.

This protocol provides structure but allows flexibility. At times, some questions or comments may lead participants away from the topic, but they still should be addressed. After such discussions the facilitator suggests a return to the protocol.

The role of the meeting facilitator

As coach, model, and catalyst, the facilitator's role is to be a bridge: helping connect and build ideas, expanding on key points, providing history and other contextual information, giving examples and definitions from relevant research, and recommending further reading (Kennedy 2004). The facilitator helps the group accomplish its goals in the time allotted for the meeting and in a fair and respectful manner.

Typically, the facilitator is someone with experience in and knowledge of early education—for example, an experienced teacher or a director who is good at abstract thinking but who also can enter the day-to-day world of the teachers. Often the program administrator has the background to offer expertise on teaching and learning and identify resources for taking next steps. Serving as meeting facilitator helps this individual grow along with the teachers, because co-inquiry helps her or him become more aware of program and staff assets.

The facilitator encourages active, open, and sensitive listening (Rinaldi 2002) and assists the group in doing action research with documentation. He or she helps the group work through their differences and observes group dynamics. Facilitators demonstrate an attitude of acceptance for divergent interpretations, raise new questions, and suggest alternative viewpoints regarding a child or situation. It is important for them to acknowledge and recognize everyone's efforts. For example, here is what the facilitator said at the end of the meeting described in the vignette:

> The more we experience this co-inquiry process of sharing, the more I can see how it affects the work you are doing as teachers. Our reflection causes all of us to think more about our work and its importance and value in children's lives. It's a privilege and an honor to work with you and see the great work you are doing . . . an unfolding journey for all of us, speaking of roads. Many times I think back over our meetings and about what happened, and I wonder what the next part of this co-inquiry is going to reveal.

Co-inquiry's benefits to teachers

Co-inquiry is a low-cost, practical strategy that offers enormous benefits. At Huggins, we continue to experiment with the process and extend its use to various situations, such as college courses, meetings of student teachers, and discussion groups for workshops and conferences. (See "Holding a Co-Inquiry Meeting".) It helps teachers see the significance of their work, gain fresh insights, improve their documentation skills, and acquire communicative literacy. Teachers also learn to better understand and assess children's abilities so they can address learning standards (Langer et

Holding a Co-Inquiry Meeting

Reserve a quiet, pleasant room with comfortable seating to promote an atmosphere of congeniality and trust.

Provide a computer workstation as well as a TV and VCR/DVD player if needed. Participants will be able to view audiovisual documentation and access the internet to find additional resources.

Stock a nearby shelf with professional books, articles, and other materials to stimulate ongoing learning and professional dialogue.

Consider weekly meetings lasting one to two hours. To allow sufficient time for dialogue (10–30 minutes per presentation), schedule no more than two presentations (10–20 minutes each) per meeting.

Prepare an agenda with the names of presenters and their projects, and distribute it prior to the meeting.

Give all staff, whether teacher or assistant, novice or veteran, a chance to take part. Teachers can rotate their attendance so classroom activities can go on without requiring additional help. In early education programs, afternoon naptime is ideal. In schools serving older students, co-inquiry can be part of the weekly staff meeting.

Ask teachers to take notes in a designated meeting notebook to maintain continuity. One notebook per classroom works well. The teacher who attends the meeting adds to the notebook and then uses it to update classroom co-teachers.

Require staff to get written parental permission for documenting children and to explain to families how the documentation will be collected, used, shared, and displayed.

Use an educational video, professional article, or notes from a tour of another school to spark discussion if the whole group is new to documentation. The teachers can brainstorm and plan how to create their own documentation for a later meeting.

Ask the director to support documentation by supplying each classroom with a digital camera (or several classrooms could share a video camera). A teacher familiar with photography can demonstrate some camera techniques, especially how to take close-up shots to show what children are doing.

Encourage teachers to work in pairs or with volunteers to take notes, photos, or videos for documentation.

Open co-inquiry meetings to others gradually. As teachers become more comfortable with the process, they can invite parents or teachers from other programs to attend the meeting and participate, a few at a time.

Encourage interested staff from the same or different programs to organize their own group if co-inquiry is not possible during school hours. Such a group is often referred to as a learning circle or teacher study group. The participants may meet on a regular basis (perhaps once a month) before or after work, or on the weekend.

Consider electronic co-inquiry via email or listservs designed for networking and collaboration, such as Projects-L and Reggio-L. The Co-Inquiry Journal and its blog (www.coinquiry.org) are new tools to facilitate virtual interchange among educators (Abramson et al. 2005).

al. 2003). They become more passionate about their work and their school and feel revitalized in working with children and families (Abramson & Atwal 2003; Tegano 2002).

As part of a co-inquiry group, teachers develop a sense of belonging and closeness with other teachers. The process helps create a culture of professional development in which teachers learn to accept differences of opinion, articulate their thoughts, and project and plan constructive action to improve teaching and learning. As Rinaldi observes,

> Knowing how to work in a group—appreciating its inherent qualities and value, and understanding the dynamics, the complexity, and benefits involved—constitutes a level of awareness that is indispensable for those who want to participate, at both the personal and professional levels, in effecting change and building the future (2001, 29).

Updated from *Voices of Practitioners: Teacher Research in Early Childhood Education* 3 (2). Copyright © 2008 NAEYC. Photos courtesy of the author.

References

Abramson, S., & K. Atwal. 2003. Teachers as co-inquirers. In *Next steps in teaching the Reggio way*, ed. J. Hendrick, 86–95. Englewood Cliffs, NJ: Merrill.

Abramson, S., O. Benavides, G. Rogers & C. Ratzlaff. 2005. *Co-inquiry blogs: A semiotic tool for teaching and learning.* Paper presented at the NAEYC Annual Conference, Washington, DC, December 7–10.

Bray, J.N., J. Lee, L.L. Smith & L. Yorks. 2000. *Collaborative inquiry in practice: Action, reflection and making meaning.* Thousand Oaks, CA: Sage.

Cadwell, L.B. 2003. *Bringing learning to life.* New York: Teachers College Press.

Carter, M. 2002. Mobilizing new leadership. *Child Care Information Exchange* 148 (November/December): 75–78.

Dewey, J. 1933. *How we think.* Rev. ed. Boston: Heath.

Dewey, J. 1938. *Logic: The theory of inquiry.* New York: Holt.

EdSource. 2005. *Similar students, different results: Why do some schools do better?* Online: www.edsource.org/pub_abs_simstu05.cfm.

Edwards, C. 2006. *Digital documental: Identifying the competence of children without testing.* Preconference presentation, Annual Conference of the Midwest AEYC, Omaha, Nebraska, April.

Edwards, C., L. Gandini & G. Forman. 1998. *The hundred languages of children: The Reggio Emilia approach—Advanced reflections.* 2d ed. Norwood, NJ: Ablex.

Gandini, L., & J. Goldhaber. 2001. Two Reflections about Documentation. In *Bambini: The Italian approach to infant/toddler care*, eds. L. Gandini & C. Edwards, 124–45. New York: Teachers College Press.

Hatch, T., D. Ahmed, A. Leiberman, D. Faigenbaum, M.E. White & D.H. Pointer Mace, eds. 2005. *Going public with our teaching: An anthology of practice.* New York: Teachers College Press.

Hill, L.T., A. Stremmel & V. Fu. 2005. *Teaching as inquiry: Rethinking curriculum in early childhood education.* New York: Pearson Education.

Himley, M., with P.F. Carini. 2000. *Another angle: Children's strengths and school standards.* New York: Teachers College Press.

Honig, A.S., & A. Hirallel. 1998. Which counts more for excellence in childcare staff: Years in service, education level, or ECE coursework? *Early Child Development and Care* 45 (June): 31–46.

Kasl, E., & L. Yorks. 2002. Learning from the inquiries: Lessons for using collaborative inquiry as an adult learning strategy. *New Directions for Adult and Continuing Education* 94 (Summer): 93–104.

Katz, L.G. 1984. The professional early childhood teacher. *Young Children* 39 (5): 3–10.

Katz, L.G., & S. Chard. 2000. *Engaging children's minds*. 2d ed. Norwood, NJ: Ablex.

Kennedy, D. 2004. The role of the facilitator in a community of philosophical inquiry. *Metaphilosophy* 35 (5): 744–65.

King, M.B. 2002. Professional development to promote schoolwide inquiry. *Teacher and Teaching Education* 18: 243–57.

Krechevsky, M., & B. Mardell. 2001. Form, function, and understanding in learning groups: Propositions from Reggio classrooms. In *Making learning visible: Children as individual and group learners*, ed. Project Zero/Reggio Children, 284–95. Reggio Emilia, Italy: Reggio Children.

Langer, G.M., A.B. Colton & L.S. Goff. 2003. *Collaborative analysis of student work*. Alexandria, VA: Association for Supervision and Curriculum Development.

Looking at Student Work [website]. n.d. Primer for Looking at Student Work. Online: www.lasw.org/primer.html.

Project Zero. 2003. *Making teaching visible: Documenting individual and group learning as professional development*. Cambridge, MA: Project Zero.

Rinaldi, C. 1998. Projected curriculum constructed through documentation—Progettazione. In *The hundred languages of children: The Reggio Emilia approach—Advanced reflections*, 2d ed., eds. C. Edwards, L. Gandini & G. Forman, 113–25. Norwood, NJ: Ablex.

Rinaldi, C. 2001. Introductions. In *Making learning visible: Children as individual and group learners*, ed. Project Zero/Reggio Children, 28–31. Reggio Emilia, Italy: Reggio Children.

Rinaldi, C. 2002. The pedagogy of listening: The listening perspective from Reggio Emilia. *Innovations in Early Education: The International Reggio Exchange* 8 (4): 1–4.

Tegano, D. 2002. Passion and the art of teaching. In *Teaching and learning: Collaborative exploration of the Reggio Emilia approach*, eds. V.R. Fu, A.J. Stremmel & L.T. Hill, 161–77. Upper Saddle River, NJ: Merrill Prentice Hall.

Yorks, L. 2005. Adult learning and the generation of new knowledge and meaning: Creating liberating spaces for fostering adult learning through practitioner-based collaborative action inquiry. *Teachers College Record* 107 (6): 1217–44.

Wells, G. 1999. *Dialogic inquiry*. New York: Cambridge University Press.

Zooms:

Promoting Schoolwide Inquiry and Improving Practice

Ben Mardell, Debbie Lee-Keenan, Heidi Given, David Robinson, Becky Merino, and Yvonne Liu-Constant

A group of teachers and the program director describe a powerful collaborative and interactive teacher research process they developed at their school. The process engages teachers in generating new insights about teaching and learning. This chapter provides a road map for creating Zooms—documentation panels that are snapshots of classroom life—as unique, concrete models of teacher research. The authors illustrate how constructing Zooms helps teachers focus on children's learning when so much is going on in a lively classroom.

Ben Mardell and colleagues show how they created a professional learning community—a culture of inquiry—in their early childhood school that also enhanced staff collegiality. The teachers evolved from individual, reflective practitioners to collaborative, schoolwide teacher researchers. A real strength of the project is its emphasis on the teachers as knowledge creators. The Zooms process builds collaboration in concrete and structured ways and makes schoolwide inquiry key in teachers' professional development.

—Barbara Henderson

The teachers and administrators at the Eliot-Pearson Children's School in Medford, Massachusetts, have worked over a period of years to create a culture of research and reflection by conducting schoolwide inquiries into teaching and learning. Near the end of the 2005–06 school year, the staff developed a documentation technique called *Zooms* to improve teachers' abilities to respond to children in new ways and help children listen and learn from each other. Each teaching team created a Zoom panel that focused on a "moment" from their classroom.

The main purpose of this chapter is to describe a collaborative teacher research project examining how the Zooms contribute to the way we foster children's learning. The study begins by describing the evolution of the schoolwide inquiry from which the Zooms emerged. At the end of the chapter, we reflect on whether the Zooms helped promote a culture of inquiry among the educators at the Children's School, and we discuss the way Zooms influenced the quality of our staff meetings.

The evolution of a schoolwide culture of inquiry and the Zooms

The Eliot-Pearson Children's School is a laboratory school at Tufts University. The school's five classes serve 78 children, 3 to 8 years old: a first/second grade class, a kindergarten class, a mixed-age (3- and 4-year-olds) class, a two-day-a-week preschool (3-year-olds) class, and a three-day-a-week preschool class. Each class has a head teacher and a graduate teaching assistant who work as a team. The school serves families from a variety of cultural, racial, and linguistic backgrounds and family structures. As an inclusion model school, we work closely with several school districts to serve many students with special needs—or special rights, as we prefer to say.

Part of the school's mission is to generate new knowledge about teaching and learning. Staff undertake this task individually, in teaching teams, and for the past several years, through collaborative schoolwide teacher inquiry. As a community, we value the spirit of collegiality among the teachers, and in the past we established this spirit by sharing common curricular topics, such as the civil rights movement or families. Our evolution from individual reflective practitioners to collaborative teacher researchers built on this collegiality. In the schoolwide inquiry, the entire staff of the Children's School explores a common interest related to teaching and learning. The goal of the investigations is to develop shared understandings about our teaching practices. In this way, the inquiry is a central feature of the staff's professional development. It is, in the words of Reggio Emilia educator Carlina Rinaldi, "how we learn to teach" (Project Zero 2002, 13).

In 2004 a part-time research coordinator position was created to guide the schoolwide inquiry. It was filled by the kindergarten teacher, who served as both teacher and research coordinator. The research coordinator works in partnership with the director through weekly meetings, consults with each teaching team about its inquiry project, and facilitates staff meetings. Listening to recordings of staff meeting conversations helps the research coordinator plan the direction of the inquiry. The research coordinator helps each teaching team frame more focused questions that are relevant to the learning and interactions in their classrooms but within the broad inquiry topic.

Over the years we learned a great deal from the initial inquiries. In 2003–04, the first year of this approach, we selected a piece of equipment—the overhead projector—as the inquiry's focus. Each teaching team documented and interpreted children's investigations with the overhead projector as the children explored light, shadow, transparency, and color. At the end of the school year, we agreed that having a common topic supported our learning, but we felt the topic should have a broader impact on teaching and learning. The second

Chronology of Events Leading to Zooms

2003 Faculty shifts from collaborative curriculum to schoolwide inquiry with a common inquiry focus

2003–04 First schoolwide teacher inquiry documents children's exploration of the overhead projector

Spring 2004 Faculty wants to form a more intellectual learning group among the adults at the school

2004 Appointment of a part-time research coordinator

2004–05 Second year of schoolwide inquiry focuses on children's use of clay

2005–06 Third year of schoolwide inquiry focuses on children's power and engagement in the classroom

Spring 2006 Staff become interested in Rinaldi's pedagogy of listening; faculty creates the Zooms

2006–07 Fourth year of schoolwide teacher inquiry focuses on listening and learning

Spring 2007 Staff identify five domains central to creating spaces for listening—setting, activities, values/beliefs, social overlay, and cognitive factors—and each teaching team is assigned one of the five domains to investigate

2007–Present Ongoing teacher inquiry

year, the inquiry focused on children's use of clay. Again, the shared topic was important, yet we found the materials theme limiting.

During the third year, in 2005–06, we decided to focus on a more abstract concept in our schoolwide inquiry: power and engagement in small groups. We chose to view our practice through the two lenses of power and engagement because both are central themes played out in the lives of children in early childhood classrooms. By *power*, we mean the dynamics between children and adults and among children regarding the control of any interaction's agenda (e.g., play, conversation). *Engagement* is a choice all learners make about learning activities: how much, if at all, to attend, participate, and care. We felt that studying power and engagement would have great educational value for us as staff.

Development of the Zooms

It was also during this third year of implementing schoolwide inquiry that we initiated the use of Zooms. Rinaldi's idea of a *pedagogy of listening* (Rinaldi 2006) provides an expanded understanding of listening that helped us think about our schoolwide inquiry. For Rinaldi, listening involves, but is far more than, paying attention. It should also not be confounded with obedience (e.g., as used in the common adult statement, "You're not listening," when a child does not comply with directions). *Listening* is an active verb, involving interpretation. It requires a welcoming attitude— an openness and sensitivity to emotions and ideas. Listening formulates questions. It is essential for learning relationships. Listening helps connect people and ideas.

Such listening is not easy, but it is a skill and a disposition that people can develop. Rinaldi talks about *capacity for listening*. This capacity involves individuals but can also be applied to groups—we posited that **the staff of the Children's School collectively could become better able to listen and learn together**. Like other learning, our capacity to listen could be deepened by supportive colleagues and teaching tools. Regarding the latter, Rinaldi describes documentation as *visible listening*. She argues that one of the main purposes of documentation is to facilitate listening, a critical component of a learning community. The sense that documentation could be a tool to develop the capacity for listening gave rise to staff's creation of the Zooms.

What is a Zoom?

A Zoom is a three- by four-foot documentation panel that offers a close look, as with a zoom lens, at the children's and teachers' responses and understandings of their classroom's research question. *Zoom* is both a verb and a noun. The dual usage encompasses a way of zooming in (verb) and creating a snapshot of particular moments of classroom life, and it refers to a specific type of documentation—a Zoom panel (noun). The goal of the Zooms is to capture key aspects of the larger picture of unfolding relationships and understandings between children and between the teacher and the children as they consider an inquiry question in small groups. Zooms include images and words: photographs, quotes from children's discussions with each other and with teachers, and children's artwork representing their ideas. The teaching team incorporates their analysis of what the small group sessions say about the teacher inquiry question. Zoom panels are the culmination of the yearlong process of schoolwide teacher inquiry wherein the teachers document the teaching and learning relationships as they take place in everyday classroom interactions. Reading about the topic and having discussions focused on the classroom inquiry questions—at staff meetings and informally between teachers—enhance teachers' learning. Toward the end of the year, each teaching team selects a classroom episode to delve into that accurately represents what the teachers have learned about the classroom inquiry question.

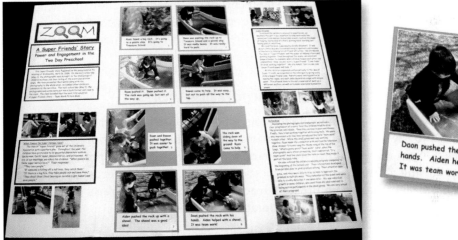

Daon pushed the rock with his hands. Aiden helped with a shovel. It was team work!

8

Here is how a Zoom develops, starting with conceiving the year's inquiry topic:

From concept to display

The notion of focusing on listening emerged when the research coordinator was looking over a set of documentation panels—Zooms—from the previous year's inquiry. He noticed that *listening* as an idea came to the forefront in all the classrooms. For example, as the teachers of 3-year-olds wrote about a small group working together, "Each child is careful to capture the attention of the other group members before fully sharing her/his idea. Each child listens fully before responding."

At the first staff meeting about the schoolwide inquiry, we decided that listening would be the focus that year. We spent the fall discussing what we meant by listening and honing in on more specific questions. We analyzed Rinaldi's article (2006) and watched videotapes of the students to identify where listening was taking place. And we hypothesized about which features of the context promoted listening. Based on these conversations, the research coordinator put together a draft analysis of listening and the conditions that promote it. We put our thinking up on a board in order to revisit and revise our theories further.

In the winter, teaching teams began bringing to staff meetings stories about their students' learning that were relevant to the issue of promoting listening. The stories were often supported by photographs, videotapes, or transcripts of conversations with children. In the end, we identified five domains that we felt were central to creating spaces for listening: setting, activities, values/beliefs, social overlay, and cognitive factors. Each teaching team investigated one of the five domains and selected a classroom episode that captured their thinking about how children learn to listen to each other and connect their ideas to the ideas of others. The teaching teams created their Zoom panels to document these moments of classroom life, showing the interplay between listening and one of the five domains. The Zooms included an analysis written by the teachers, describing the children's and their own interactions promoting listening.

Zooms sparks a teacher research question

Six members of our staff wanted to find out whether constructing Zooms was helpful in generating new understandings about the children and about our practice. So we six—the authors of this chapter—embarked on the teacher research project described in the following pages. Our research question was this: **How can focusing on a particular moment of classroom life help teachers understand children's capabilities and concerns and support their collaborations with peers?**

Data collection and analysis

Zooms were first used in the 2005–06 school year. That year, the schoolwide teacher inquiry focus was children's engagement and power. We gathered the following data for our teacher research:

- Transcripts collected in the classrooms during the preparation of the Zooms
- The audio and video transcripts of the presentations of and discussions about the Zoom panels during staff meetings
- Informal conversations within classroom teaching teams and between teachers in different classrooms while creating the Zooms
- Feedback from families and others attending the end-of-year exhibit as they viewed the Zooms panels

The final Zooms are analyzed individually by teachers, between teaching teams, at informal gatherings of faculty, and during whole-group staff meetings. They are read by families, colleagues from outside the school, and by new staff in the following school year. Teachers look for patterns of children's and teachers' responses to the schoolwide inquiry questions of the teaching teams and for teacher-child interactions that offer new insights about children's capabilities and concerns and about peer collaboration.

Findings—learning about children's capabilities and concerns and ways to support their collaboration

The process of zooming in on and carefully considering a particular classroom episode is a powerful learning experience for staff. Capturing these moments in documentation panels allows staff to collectively revisit and reflect on their questions and theories about teaching and learning. The full impact of Zooms on the school was not apparent immediately; however, it has become clearer over time.

So much goes on in a classroom that it can be difficult for teachers to focus. By allowing us to look closely at the students' learning, Zooms help us better understand the children's capabilities and emotional concerns and suggest ways to support their collaboration. This section provides excerpts from Zooms—class questions (in boxes), classroom moments, and teacher discussion—illustrating these findings.

Children's capabilities

While the faculty of the Eliot-Pearson Children's School embrace an image of children as competent, our young charges' specific capabilities are something we are constantly learning about. This Zoom, created by the first/second grade teaching team, enlarges our understandings of children's capabilities.

First/second grade Zoom—"Connections." In this Zoom, the children's drawings from their study of Boston are paired with work from their Boston curriculum (a map of the city, sketches of the state house, and a model of Paul Revere's house). The Zoom begins:

> Group work is challenging! It is a challenge for students as they work through the many issues that arise both in building and in sharing their ideas and opinions. It is a challenge for teachers to provide the right amount of scaffolding to help the group achieve its goals while still allowing the children to work through problems on their own. We often met as a class to discuss the challenges and successes each small group experienced. In one discussion, children shared comments about everyone in a group not doing the same amount of work:
>
> Becky [the teacher]: What if someone in your group isn't helping? What should you do?
>
> Amelia: You can tell them, "You have to work with us."
>
> Becky: Why do you think a person might not be helping as much?
>
> Jackie: Maybe they missed something or they don't have an idea.

Sophie: You could remind them of the directions and tell them you want them to be a part of the group.

Olivia: Maybe they're not helping as much and they're tired.

Becky: And they need to wake up a bit? Definitely! And sometimes people just need to step back and look at the work and see the whole project. Do any of you ever need to do that?

Group: Yes!

We have found that young children are capable of providing thoughtful feedback to one another. Indeed, the following year David (the preschool teacher) began facilitating such conversations in September rather than waiting until May. Asking children to comment on each other's work has become standard practice across the school. The first/second-graders' conversation underscores children's abilities to reflect on issues of engagement and power in group settings. Again, teachers across the school now invite children's input on learning about how groups work and solicit suggestions about how they might work better.

Supporting children's collaboration

Just as we embrace adult collaboration, we support children learning from and with each other (Project Zero & Reggio Children 2001). Insights on how to support children's collaborations, when adults are present and intentionally absent, emerge from the Zooms.

Three-day preschool classroom question
What does it mean to be a powerful participant in a classroom community?

© Heidi Givens

Three-day preschool classroom's Zoom—"The Searcher and the Merry-Go-Round: Moments of Insight into the Power of Sharing and Communication." The three-day preschool class has constructed a train from recycled materials for their Zoom. Accompanying it is a Zoom titled, "The Searcher and the Merry-Go-Round: Moments of Insight into the Power of Sharing and Communication." The Zoom explains that the train was constructed by pairs of children, each planning and building one car. It describes Phaidra, Eduardo, and their teacher Eva's effort to create a train car in which babies could play:

> Phaidra states, "This [tall foam triangle] could be a searching one, so if they lose something, they search with that. 'Cause it's kind of spinny." But Eduardo has a different idea: "No, no, no . . . this is for the kids to jump in here."
>
> In order to support the sharing of ideas and dialogue between the children, Eva adds, "Eduardo, share your idea with Phaidra. Tell her what you were thinking about this piece. Phaidra, Eduardo had an idea about what this piece of the train was for." Phaidra looks toward the train. Eduardo looks to Phaidra, establishing eye contact before he begins. Then he demonstrates his idea for how the kids will jump from piece to piece—his finger becomes a tiny baby excitedly jumping from one piece to the next. Phaidra is convinced by Eduardo's demonstration. She points to a tall pole at the front of the car and adds, "Oh, yeah! So maybe . . . so, the idea is that this piece could be the searcher, 'cause I put it in."
>
> Both children's ideas have been seen and heard by all three members of the group, and both ideas have become a part of the train car. . . . Each child is careful to capture the attention of the other group members before fully sharing her/his idea. Each child listens fully before responding. In the moments in which an idea is shared directly with the adult member, Eva is sure to engage the other child by directing the children to one another, encouraging them to speak with and listen to each other. Agreement is reached, as a space is created in which the children are able to articulate their motivations and be understood.

Kindergarten class question

What do power and engagement look like in study groups? How can kindergartners engage themselves and their peers in small group learning? How can teachers facilitate their students' abilities to engage in these activities? Having a specific purpose and teachers providing structure for the session contributes to these 5- and 6-year-olds' ability to collaborate without direct adult supervision.

Kindergarten class's Zoom—"Making a Plan: The Construction Area Design Group." This Zoom accompanies the children's guidebook for their redesigned classroom. The Zoom analyzes a session in which three children, Eamonn, Henry, and Luis, without direct adult supervision, make a plan for their redesigned classroom's new construction area. Bringing together three perspectives about the construction area is not an easy task. The Zoom relates the small group's conversation outlining the work of the design group:

> Henry worried, "What if we can't agree about what to do?" The teachers' response was to note that throughout the year, the kindergartners had learned about making small groups fun, fair, and good places to learn, and the teachers expressed confidence in the children's abilities to work together.

Eamonn, Henry, and Luis then began to work, taking turns making proposals by describing their ideas and moving sticky notes around a floor plan. Their conversation was filled with the language of collaboration:

© Ben Mardell

Luis: How about putting the risers here.

Henry: Yeah, yeah, yeah!

Eamonn: I was thinking the risers could be here and the blocks here.

Henry: How about the blocks on the risers?

Eamonn: No, not there.

Luis: What about next to them, here?

Eamonn: That's what I was thinking!

Henry: What do you think if we put the Legos here?

Eamonn: Good idea!

The Zoom goes on to describe the next 50 minutes of the boys' work, concluding with the teachers' analysis:

> We find it striking how easily the boys accepted each other's critiques. While at times there were disagreements, conflict was nearly absent. Each boy had a say in the negotiations. Fairness seemed to be a guiding principle as Eamonn, Henry, and Luis worked to craft a collective plan. After our yearlong effort to build a democratic learning community, the boys' efforts during this session are gratifying.

After further reflection, we would add that having a specific purpose and teachers providing structure for the session (e.g., using sticky notes) also contributes to these 5- and 6-year-olds' ability to collaborate without direct adult supervision. For Phaidra and Eduardo in the three-day classroom, the teacher's gentle social cues create a common focus for the children without curtailing their initiative.

Reflections: Learning about creating a culture of inquiry in an entire school

Prior to the development of the Zooms, staff meetings were largely devoted to teachers bringing artifacts (videotapes, children's work, transcripts) that shed light on their classrooms' schoolwide inquiry questions. We used a protocol to structure our staff discussions. The goal was to create a learning community among the staff by sharing perspectives and expertise that would in turn generate insights about our practice. Our faith in group learning was strengthened by examples of powerful collaborations from across the disciplines and professions (John-Steiner 2000). We were influenced by the *Making Learning Visible* project (Project Zero & Reggio Children 2001) as well as by other thinkers who emphasize the value of collaboration in creating innovations. There was a vision of a school where adults provide not only emotional support but also intellectual support for each other.

The tricky part, of course, is putting this theory of group learning into practice. Formal discussions of the schoolwide inquiry topic are confined to monthly, hour-and-a-half staff meetings. An analysis of audiotapes of these meetings confirms that staff felt frustrated by the lack of time to listen to each other during the meetings. Ninety minutes is an inadequate amount of time for 15 people to voice their opinions. Quality of time is also an issue. Hearing about teaching and learning issues just once a month makes it challenging to focus on the concerns of colleagues from different classrooms. Overall, conversations were rushed. They did not achieve the depth possible for this group of educators.

So have schoolwide inquiry and Zooms, the data-driven reflections on teaching and learning, contributed to making our school a good place for teachers to get some serious thinking done about early childhood education? We are convinced that the Zooms contribute to staff efforts to create a community of inquiry for the adults at the Children's School. The public nature of Zooms allows for the sharing of and reflections on children and teaching practices. The Zooms make it possible to discuss and modify ideas, which leads to collective understandings about teaching and learning.

Specifically, Zooms increase the amount of time adults can communicate with one another outside the monthly 90-minute staff meetings. From reading and rereading the panels, teachers note patterns and connections among the five classrooms. Zooms also change the quality of our listening at staff meetings. They remind us of our questions and interests. Staff are now more familiar with one another's theories. We don't start our conversations from zero, and we can listen to each other with greater sensitivity. Zooms are particularly helpful to new staff members, introducing them to the school's culture of inquiry.

This is true not only for the faculty, but for families as well. After visiting the exhibition, parents commented on learning about educational practices at the school through the Zooms. One parent explained, "I didn't realize how everything [my child] was doing at school worked together until I read the Zoom." Other families expressed their appreciation for learning about the approaches taken in all the classrooms.

While the process—conversations that stretch over the year—is critical to our learning, having a product to strive for—Zooms—is also important. This assignment turns each teaching team's efforts into a project. Rather than just reporting on problems (e.g., Rich and Martha are having trouble getting along), creating a Zoom points us in the direction of what each team considers an ongoing, epistemological question (How can we help Rich and Martha learn together?).

Listening is an essential element in all the interactions described in the Zooms, including the two-day preschool class's work moving a rock up a slide, Eduardo and

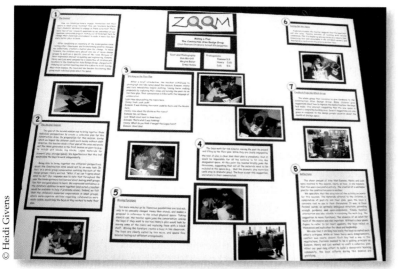

Phaidra's discussion about their train car, and Emily and Joe's dialogue about what they learned from their conversation. Listening is also an essential element in considering our staff meetings. This reinforces Rinaldi's idea of listening having importance for both adults' and children's learning.

Finally, Zooms influence the entire staff's identities as educators. Here, we teachers put forward our own thoughts and interpretations about teaching and learning. Rather than just being consumers of education theory, teachers become creators of knowledge about the field. The Zooms validate one of the rationales for undertaking teacher research: to give teachers a voice in the conversation about teaching and learning.

Conclusion: The relationship between adults' and children's learning

One of the guiding principles our director, Debbie LeeKeenan, uses in her leadership is that there is a strong relationship between what happens in the staff room and the classroom. How teachers are treated influences how they treat children. How teachers learn influences how they teach.

Megina Baker's experience as a new graduate teaching assistant at the school speaks to this relationship. Megina found she gained a better understanding of the inquiry-based instruction in the kindergarten room, where she teaches, after engaging in the schoolwide inquiry method and discussion of it at staff meetings. The Zooms are an integral part of this inquiry process, highlighting how documentation can support learning. Similarly, for many at the school, the honesty, directness, and caring seen in Emily and Joe's conversation is inspirational to staff communication. If 4-year-olds can give each other useful feedback, then certainly adults can as well.

Thus the reciprocal relationship between the children's and teachers' approaches to learning is highlighted in this teacher research project. As we promote the culture of inquiry, we learn about teaching young children; and as we learn about supporting children's capabilities, we strengthen our adult culture of inquiry.

The practice of collective inquiry is evolving at the Eliot-Pearson Children's School. It has become one of the cornerstones of our professional development as we educators continue to work together to increase our understanding of teaching and learning. Although the Zooms continue to capture exemplary moments from our classrooms, the structure of how we use this tool has evolved. We have developed a unifying aesthetic for the panels that considers layout, ratio of pictures to text, graphics (such as the use of mounting and font style and size), text structure and flow, and balance of child and adult voices. All of these elements contribute to better communication of a Zoom's message.

We have also begun to think about each Zoom as an integral piece of a whole—unique in its classroom story, yet part of the answer to our common questions. An examination of classroom moments in a later inquiry—a look at Rinaldi's pedagogy of listening within the school context—revealed common trends and insights into classroom practice. Over several months, we have refined our understanding into five interrelated yet distinct aspects of practice: consideration of activities, setting, values and beliefs, social overlay, and cognitive factors. Once defined, each of the final Zooms not only tells the story of an insightful classroom moment, but also reflects one of these five valued aspects of our teaching and learning. Collectively, these Zooms tell a more complete story of the process of our schoolwide inquiry and growth as a community of learners.

Going public in multiple arenas has served to both deepen and muddy our work. In our attempts to invite multiple stakeholders into the dialogue, we have made an already challenging process even more complex. Yet, it is this very complexity that pushes us to more clearly define and articulate our own thinking and values—in fact, to tell our own story. As our collaborative questions continue to emerge and grow, so too does the evolution of the Zooms; and with the evolution of the Zooms comes the wisdom and identity of our community.

References

John-Steiner, V. 2000. *Creative collaboration*. Oxford, UK: Oxford University Press.
Project Zero & Reggio Children. 2001. *Making learning visible: Children as individual and group learners*. Reggio Emilia, Italy: Reggio Children.
Project Zero, Cambridgeport School, Cambridgeport Children's Center, Ezra H. Baker School & John Simpkins School. 2002. *Making teaching visible: Documenting individual and group learning as professional development*. Cambridge, MA: Project Zero.
Rinaldi, C. 2006. *In dialogue with Reggio Emilia: Listening, researching and learning*. London: Routledge.

Supporting Teacher Research in Communities of Practice

Teacher research is increasingly recognized nationally and internationally as a critical part of early childhood professional development, and noted for its role in advancing knowledge about teaching and learning. The following chapters highlight the wide range of early childhood teacher research initiatives and inquiry communities through summaries of their work. They include contact information for educators interested in learning more about specific project goals and methods.

Las Americas Early Education School Teacher Research Initiative in Collabration with San Francisco State University

San Francisco, California

Isauro Michael Escamilla

L|ocated in the heart of the Mission District of San Francisco, California, Las Americas Early Education School is part of the San Francisco Unified School District Child Development Program. Our school provides a nurturing educational program inspired by the project approach, an academic philosophy that embraces children's interests as the starting point for in-depth study of specific topics through multiple media: reading, writing, drawing, field trips, and creative arts such as painting, collage-making, music, and movement.

Reflecting the ethnic, economic, cultural, and linguistic tapestry of our city, our school includes a multiage preschool program for children ages 3 to 5, a mainstreamed special education preK program, and an educational after-school and summer program for children in kindergarten through fifth grade. We aim to provide an environment-based curriculum using our school garden to connect nature, outdoor learning, and academic success. In our classrooms we offer children a rich variety of materials to explore and represent their ideas and emergent understanding on a variety of topics; in the process they create their own knowledge, with teachers offering support as needed at specific points of the learning experience.

Our staff has a commitment to support children's interests and curiosity by listening, observing, and documenting. We document their theories, ideas, and feelings through stories, photographs, dictations, audiotaped conversations, and drawings. We believe that when children work and play in small groups they are better able to explore and understand concepts of literacy, numeracy, nature, and the creative arts. Besides ensuring the safety of the children and their social-emotional well-being, we believe that one of the most important and challenging roles as teachers is to present children with thought-provoking questions or situations that encourage them to expand their emergent analytical thinking.

Preschool head teachers Isauro Michael Escamilla and Mary Lin graduated from the master's program in education with a concentration in early childhood from San Francisco State University, and consider teacher research an art as much as a science. Both are experienced teachers with a personal interest in pursuing the underpinnings of teacher research as a pedagogical tool to guide their own professional growth. Some of their work with children has been published in *Learning from Young Children: The Art and Science of Teacher Research* (Meier & Henderson 2007), *Young Children* (Escamilla 2004), and more recently in *Teaching Young Children* (NAEYC 2010).

The other teachers in our program have different levels of expertise and knowledge about the inquiry process and systematic documentation of children's learning experiences. Our inquiry group, described below, has provided the right context to share experiences, find answers to common questions, and more importantly develop the habit of collaborative reflection as a strategy to gain a better understanding of our role as educators of young children.

Our teacher research inquiry group

Our monthly teacher research team meetings help us further our understanding of the research process as it relates to documentation of children's learning experiences based on classroom projects. These meetings, supported by professor Daniel Meier, provide the pedagogical framework needed to reflect on practical day-to-day decisions about children's interests, and possibilities for inquiry based on those interests and activities. We hope to provide an on-site pedagogical forum to further our understanding of our role as educators and to improve our skills as critical thinkers and teacher researchers.

Our inquiry group is composed of two head teachers, two associate teachers, and two assistant teachers. All teachers are bilingual and speak Spanish, Cantonese, or Mandarin. We have different levels of expertise in the field, with a range of four to almost 15 years in the classroom.

We consistently meet approximately once a month for an hour and a half to discuss the progress of our class projects and the content of assigned readings. In order to create a common experience we decided to read the book *Learning from Young Children in the Classroom: The Art and Science of Teacher Research* (Meier & Henderson 2007) as a way to reflect on our job as educators, develop a common professional language, learn specific data collection strategies, and further our understanding of classroom-based research. From the outset, each teacher received a copy of the book; a teaching journal to keep up with the development of class projects, observations, and pedagogical reflections; a notebook for note taking during meetings; a calendar and folders; and one digital camera per room in addition to a tape recorder and a computer.

An important aspect of our inquiry group is the relaxed atmosphere and flexible formality of our meetings, with teacher researcher Isauro Michael Escamilla serving as group coordinator. Our meetings are not mandatory for the staff, but have become a forum where we can present to colleagues our ongoing projects, samples of children's work, emerging documentation panels, and the challenges we face to move projects forward. During these meetings we get constructive feedback, ideas, or strategies and we set new goals for the next meeting. More than anything else, these sessions have provided a framework to acquire a common language and the opportunity to learn or redefine the meaning of terms such as *observations*, *reflective practice*, *pedagogical reflections*, *teaching journal*, *documentation of children's learning experiences*, *classroom-based inquiry*, and *active listening*, to name a few.

Research examples

Our inquiry group explores a wide variety of topics. For example, in a recent meeting teacher Mary Lin focused her attention on an emergent interest in writing from a small group of kindergarten-bound children, and the strategies that teachers could use to help these children become proficient in holding different writing tools.

Throughout this richly documented project—which included photographs, teacher reflections, children's dictations, and writing samples dating back several months—Mary Lin discovered and confirmed that strategies are subject to differences in cultural beliefs, the involved adults' personal upbringing, and each child's skills, age, and dispositions to learning. She shared specific activities that helped children gain a more meaningful understanding of the writing process. Some of these activities were sensory, such as when she gently traced letters and other shapes with her fingers on the children's backs while they simultaneously wrote down the same letters or shapes they were feeling (and reading) with their bodies.

Other examples included writing in the air and manipulating playdough or sticky foam to engage the children in creative writing. She discovered that "playdough and sticky foam lead children to the sensory exploration of the abstract concept of letters, as the children represented the letters in a more concrete manner by manipulating, bending, and twisting the sticky foam to form random and letter-like symbols that had meaning for the children." She explains the influence of teacher research on her teaching:

> My participation in the teacher research meetings has encouraged me to question the status quo and to challenge my own assumptions and beliefs. The group has opened my mind to new possibilities in the way I teach children and collaborate with colleagues. Most importantly, it has made me be fully aware of how much I actually learn from coteachers and children.

The parents and guardians of the children who participated in this particular writing project shared that they observed great improvement in how their children held their pencils, crayons, or markers. Lin's coteachers Edwin Serrano and Sahara Gonzalez also noticed an increase in children's motivation to write, either with a marker on paper, a stick in the sand, or with plain water and a paintbrush on the walls in the school yard. Suddenly, writing became an enjoyable, stress-free activity for both children and teachers. The inquisitive nature of project-based learning and teacher research opened multiple perspectives on how to best support our young learners to develop a disposition to engage in real or imaginary writing. In this context, Lin and her coteachers promoted an optimal environment for creativity, laying a solid foundation for learning to take place.

Some of the projects we are currently working on and that are still in different stages of development are:

- Celebration of Chinese New Year, initiated by associate teacher Joanne Yu
- The Importance of Sand Play in the Classroom, documented by assistant teacher Sahara Gonzalez
- The Children's Creative Process in Collage-Making Using Recycled Materials, by head teacher Isauro Michael Escamilla

• Supporting Children's Literacy Development by Role-Playing Stories Read in Class, documented by assistant teacher Edwin Serrano and head teacher Mary Lin

Reflecting on our teacher research

In our first 18 months, our teacher research inquiry group has accomplished several objectives in accordance with our original goals. Some further questions we would like to reflect on, regardless of our topic of investigation, are:

• How do we find a balance between children leading the projects and teachers' guidance?

• How can we teach and at the same time collect data from multiple children?

• How can we deepen our reflective practice skills to find the pedagogical meaning behind the activities?

• How can we facilitate school-home connections when working on long-term projects?

Although most of the staff have embraced the principles of teacher research and the role of the teacher as observer, recorder, and interpreter of children's learning experiences, the premise of teacher research still remains thought-provoking. Perhaps this is because it contradicts the common perception that teachers are not deep thinkers and theory-makers. In many ways, teacher research breaks the stereotype of teachers as holders of knowledge and children as recipients of information; it encourages critical thinking along with self-reflection as common teaching practice. In any case, one of the themes that has emerged from our discussions is how to listen to the children and to ourselves, which has led us to the exploration of a *pedagogy of listening* within the teacher research context. The more we explore this topic, the more we discover that the traditional roles of teacher and learner as opposites tend to blend; the inquiry process helps us understand that these roles can and should be interchangeable.

Being a part of this group makes us feel a responsibility not only towards the children, but also towards each one of our members—when we commit to carry out a specific task, most of us tend to follow through and come fully prepared to the next meeting. Moreover, these gatherings may also count as professional growth hours to fulfill SF CARES requirements in order to obtain an annual monetary stipend. Professor Meier is also investigating how staff might be able to gain a college credit for professional development through local colleges and universities.

The success of our teacher research group at Las Americas Early Education School is in great measure the result of a staff-driven idea, as opposed to a top-down mandate. In a way, just like children, we are creators of our own knowledge. However, these opportunities for professional growth would have been more challenging without both the administration's support and funding from the Preschool For All

(PFA) program, which is part of the First 5 San Francisco initiative. Our current site manager, David Hollands, has expressed that our group provides a unique scholarly forum for teacher-initiated inquiry, in-depth observations, and interpretations and discourse, which only improve the teaching/learning experience of both teachers and students. Funding for substitutes has been possible through PFA and the First 5 San Francisco initiative, allowing our group to meet for more time.

In a recent staff meeting, Hollands outlined the expectation that our expanded support will provide more opportunities for enhanced class project developments, field research, innovative data collecting strategies, and field trips to exemplary schools in our area. He added: "The teacher research group . . . has been central to our faculty's team building and core competence. The individual and collective professional development of this diverse group of educators has been impressive and will continue to evolve."

Teaching can become quite an isolating profession; our teacher research group has made it possible to create a community of educators brought together by the need to make visible their voices, ideas, and learning journeys, with the ultimate goal of offering young children meaningful educational experiences.

References

Escamilla, I.M. 2004. A dialogue with the shadows. *Young Children* 59 (2): 96–100.
Meier, D.R., & B. Henderson. 2007. *Learning from young children in the classroom: The art and science of teacher research*. New York: Teacher College Press.
NAEYC. 2010. Collage. What do I do? I teach! Isauro Michael Escamilla. *Teaching Young Children* 3 (3): 4–5.

© Shari Schmidt

Making Learning Visible at the Lee Academy Pilot School

Boston, Massachusetts

Ben Mardell

For several years, the Lee Academy Pilot School, a preK through grade 5 Boston public school, has partnered with the staff of the Making Learning Visible Project—a research project of Project Zero at the Harvard Graduate School of Education—to promote learning communities among children and adults. During the 2009–2010 academic year, instructional coach Marina Boni of the Early Childhood Division of Boston Public Schools joined our effort. We are focusing on how to best support conversations and storytelling among the 3- to 5-year-old children in the school's early academy.

Our guiding inquiry questions are,

- How can teachers best support the oral language development of a diverse group of young children at an urban public school?
- How can a school faculty come together to build knowledge and improve their instructional practices?

Every other week, Marina or Ben Mardell and Mara Krechevsky, staff of the Making Learning Visible Project, facilitate a discussion among the six preschool teachers and two kindergarten teachers during their common planning time, a 45-minute period during the school day. Teachers take turns bringing a question about their practice and a related artifact to these meetings. For example, a teacher who wondered what questions to ask to extend his students' conversations brought a transcript of a conversation from his class. A teacher wanting to refine her prompts to promote storytelling brought a videotape of her eliciting a story from a child.

The protocol guiding our conversations includes the following steps:

- The presenting teacher describes her question and provides a brief context for the artifact shared.
- Teachers carefully review the artifact, make observations, and discuss the material the presenting teacher shared.
- The teachers discuss the presenting teacher's questions.
- During a few minutes of silent, individual reflection time, the teachers consider the feedback provided during the session and think about how it might influence their teaching practice. The facilitators encourage the teachers to share their reflections.

Each session builds on the preceding session's conversation. Teachers report on strategies related to the previous meeting's topic that they have tried, and discuss new questions that have emerged.

Kindergarten teacher Erin Daly feels that the time to reflect at the end of the conversation, even if only a few minutes, is very valuable, giving her a chance to plan how she can move her practice forward. Preschool teacher David Ramsey appreciates the chance to talk to colleagues about teaching and learning.

Building knowledge and influencing practice through collaborative teacher research requires a culture in which teachers are accountable to themselves and each other. The facilitators, Marina, Ben, and Mara, support this culture in several ways. As noted above, we bring teachers' ideas and practice to the forefront by beginning each session with teachers' descriptions of how they have tried to support conversations and storytelling in their classrooms since the last meeting. We reproduce the teachers' insights in several documents (e.g., a list of prompts for supporting storytelling) and bring these documents back to the group for feedback. We check in with the teachers—individually and as a group—to see if there are ways our work can better support their teaching.

Given the multiple demands teachers face, helping them focus on one topic is a challenge. However, real learning comes when teachers have opportunities to carefully track, collect evidence, and reflect on one aspect of children's learning over time. It is a process for which teacher research is well suited.

For more information, visit Making Learning Visible: Understanding, Documenting, and Supporting Individual and Group Learning at www.pz.harvard.edu/mlv. See also Project Zero and Reggio Children's *Making Learning Visible: Children as Individual and Group Learners* (Cambridge, MA: Project Zero, 2001).

Information about the Lee Academy can be found at: www.bostonpublicschools.org/school/lee-academy-pilot-school

---

Updated from "Teacher research initiatives: Inquiry work by early childhood teachers" in *Voices of Practitioners: Teacher Research in Early Childhood Education*, 5–6. Copyright © 2011 NAEYC.

Places to Play

In Providence

A guide to the city by our youngest citizens

"Waterplace Park is across the street from the Mall near the Statehouse and train station. The sun shines through the whole city."

Christian, Age 4

The Making Learning Visible/ Ready to Learn Providence Peer Network

Cambridge, Massachusetts
& Providence, Rhode Island

Ben Mardell and
Bethany Carpenter

I n April 2011, a teacher researcher peer network consisting of 16 early childhood educators in the Providence, Rhode Island area (center-based teachers and family childcare providers) began to collaborate to improve their teaching. The peer network was co-facilitated by Making Learning Visible (MLV), a research group based at Project Zero at the Harvard Graduate School of Education and Ready to Learn Providence (R2LP), a community-based school readiness initiative with a vision that all young children will be healthy and ready to learn. The network was supported by a grant from the Rhode Island Association for the Education of Young Children (RIAEYC) and Bright Stars (Rhode Island's Quality Rating and Improvement System). The teacher research network held six whole group sessions, the facilitators visited the centers twice, and the teachers visited each other's schools.

Places to Play in Providence: A Guide to the City by Our Youngest Citizens

At the network's initial session, the facilitators proposed that teachers work with children to make a guidebook to welcome the participants of the June 2011 NAEYC National Institute for Early Childhood Professional Development to Providence. To help in this process, the group decided to implement several strategies when working with the children:

1. encourage children to give each other feedback supporting multiple drafts of drawings and text

2. use documentation (especially video) to help teachers and children better understand learning processes

3. craft curriculum emphasizing children's contributions to their community

The notion of welcoming 2,000 early childhood educators to their city was engaging to the teachers and children. Throughout May, the teachers supported children in drawing and describing favorite places to play. There were successes and challenges in these efforts. When network participants came together for a second time they shared documentation from their settings, and discussed questions. These included:

• How can we best support children who are resistant to receiving feedback?

• How can we ensure that children's initiative and creativity are not curtailed by feedback?

Through conversations about their documentation teachers generated a method for introducing the concept of feedback to children via modeling. They also adopted developmentally appropriate language for describing helpful feedback, comments that are "kind, specific, and can be taken or left."

By the end of May, over a hundred pages with colorful drawings and thoughtful comments had been created. Some examples of the children's contributions were

- Alfie recommended the Providence Performing Arts Center because, "You can hear the Lion King. . . . Kids can sleep there because it's a long show."
- Pascal recommended Water Place Park because you can dream that the steps "Climb up to the sky."
- Paola recommended Lippitt Park because, "You could bring chalk and play with it. You could bring toys from home and play with them. You could make new friends."

The guide was presented to Institute participants by Mayor Angel Taveras at a Sunday evening session. The next day, in response to children's desires to meet "the 2,000 teachers coming to Providence" several centers brought their children to the Institute. At a Making Learning Visible workshop, they were greeted by a hundred appreciative early childhood educators.

Places to Play in Providence has attracted the attention of educators from as close to home as Somerville, Massachusetts and as far as Tokyo, Japan. It has been viewed over 2,400 times online. To read the book, see http://issuu.com/r2lp/docs/places_to_play_in_pvd.

Continuing conversation

The network met four times after the presentation of the book, and teachers continued to bring documentation from their classrooms to ground their discussions. To focus the conversations on teaching and learning, the facilitators introduced a protocol developed at Project Zero that separated noticing from interpretation and suggestions; hearing different perspectives on the documentation providing a stronger basis from which to offer feedback. The protocol suggested that the presenting teacher act as a listener for the majority of the conversation in order to maximize the opportunity for feedback from the group (see "Network Protocol" box).

Initially, the teachers' questions grew out of issues that had emerged during the creation of the book. Having witnessed children's ability to give each other feedback, teachers pondered how to facilitate and promote the process of children learning from and with one another. Impressed with the depth of engagement engendered by the draft making process, teachers discussed how to slow down curriculum in other areas in order to create deeper learning.

As the months went by, the topics considered broadened. One teaching team focused on promoting oral language through music and visuals so that children who needed this support could eventually give each other feedback. Another teacher evaluated changes to whole group meetings times. In an effort to increase engagement, she experimented with making attendance optional and started inserting meeting-type activities (e.g., group games) at choice times, often drawing large groups of children. Almost all the teachers increased their use of video documentation, both to examine their own practices and to share with children.

A new network is formed

The success of the MLV/R2LP peer network led to the funding of a new teacher research group in Rhode Island. In September, 22 community-based and Head Start teachers and family child care providers began meeting to examine their teaching practices.

As with the initial network, a common experience was provided: engaging children in creating how-to books. Again, questions about teaching and learning emerged. For example, the teachers found that while 4-year-old children could give directions of how to do something, 3-year-olds found the task much more challenging. Teachers developed a procedure of photographing children demonstrating steps of a process. Children were then given the chance to explain the photos—something they were able to do.

Children are now creating books about how to tie your shoes, draw the face of a T. rex, pretend to fly like Superman, be a big brother, and more. These books will be displayed at the Providence Children's Museum and the Providence Public Library.

The power of the group

At the sixth and final MLV/R2LP peer network session in December, teachers shared what they had learned, provided feedback about the process, and voiced new and continuing questions. Several themes emerged.

Teachers frequently drew parallels between their own learning and the children's. In May, the notion of children giving and receiving feedback was a new and emotionally fraught practice. Getting feedback about their own teaching at network meetings, in ways similar to what the children were doing, helped teachers understand the process better.

In the teachers' minds, feedback was closely related to the idea of "making learning visible." As participant Joe Mirsky explained, "I love this term. It's a great way to foster teachers' and children's learning." Specifically, teachers talked of using documentation (video, photography, and children's work) to ground conversations. At the meeting, Joe demonstrated the value of making learning visible by sharing a nine-minute video about a literacy curriculum where 2-, 3- and 4-year-olds learned from and with one another and he learned about his teaching. The video can be viewed at www.facebook.com/RIHomeSchoolConnection.

The intellectual and emotional support the network provided was also highly important, as many of our participants shared. Becky Dirrane noted "the importance of teachers learning together." Ted Weber explained his conviction that it "takes a community of educators to support learning." Andree Howard noted how the support of her colleagues in the network provided her with "the courage to try new practices." The most frequent question raised by the teachers was how to maintain these "engaging, professional conversations." All left the meeting committed to continuing this work individually and collectively.

Kent State University Child Development Center

Ongoing Teacher Research

Kent, Ohio

Carol Bersani

The teachers at the Kent State University Child Development Center, a laboratory school for children 18 months through kindergarten, are engaged in teacher research with children and families about the nature of relationships formed in the outdoors. The context for this research is a campus full of hills, trees, gardens, and an adjacent wetland area with a variety of plant and animal life, creeks, ponds, and woods.

The goals of our project are to better understand the child's approach to natural outdoor spaces, to engage families in dialogue regarding the value of nature experiences, and to support preservice teachers' knowledge of the integrated learning opportunities possible when children explore natural spaces on campus, in the wetlands, on the school playground, and in their own neighborhoods.

The following are some of our findings:

- As small groups of children and teachers explore natural places, they can listen to each other on a level not always possible indoors. This ability to listen closely to others supports group decisionmaking, negotiation, and problem-solving experiences that occur naturally in the outdoors.

- As the children establish their own landmarks in the outdoors, they begin to form an identity with these outdoor places (e.g., a drainpipe covered by a grill becomes "a bear cage"; a group of trees becomes the "whispering woods"). In these places, the children engage in rich, imaginative storytelling that blends science and fantasy. They also desire to bring the outdoors back to their classroom through dramatic play and the creation of maps of the wetland with the landmarks as points of reference.

- Children engage in more positive risk-taking in the outdoors. They test their physical capabilities and share their thinking and stories. We've observed that children who engage in less verbal communication indoors often become eager to talk when outdoors. Individual learning styles often become more visible in the outdoors.

- Children are able to slow down, observe carefully, explore intentionally, and make many discoveries that are later shared with other children and adults. Gardening on the playground becomes an opportunity for children to study the life cycle of plants.

- Children become caretakers of their outdoor environments. They develop habits related to honoring and protecting the natural environment. In a book written by a group of preschoolers, they stated their rights and responsibilities in the outdoors (e.g., "We never pick anything that is living").

As the children document their encounters in the outdoors and represent their findings through drawing, painting, and other forms of expression, they begin to understand the connectedness of all living things.

On Our Rights and Responsibilities in the Meadow

All children have the right to run down the hill.

All children have the right to play in the meadow.

All children have to keep themselves safe.

All children have the right to hold hands.

All children have the right to check on each other.

All children have the right to sing.

> We love each other!

> We love each other!

> We love each other!

When we go to the meadow, we stay together. We hold hands until we are past the parking lot.

We take care of each other.

We never pick anything that is living, but we can pick up leaves or plants that have fallen.

We don't kill anything in the meadow. We always pick up trash.

We go to the places we love and play there.

We always draw in our sketchbooks to remember.

These teacher-and-child research projects depend on a support system for conducting teacher research with children. Teachers have studied teacher research methodology, including framing the question, observing and documenting, interpreting, and communicating findings. They have organized themselves into critical friends groups, small groups of teachers exploring a particular aspect of the school-wide nature studies—for example, two teachers are studying the ways toddlers and preschoolers communicate their findings to each other about the birds that feed just outside their windows. Other aspects of the support system include resource people to support the process of teacher research and time for study together.

One of our research projects was published in the July 2009 issue of *Young Children* ("We Need a Way to Get to the Other Side: Exploring the Possibilities for Learning in Natural Spaces," by Galizio, Stoll, and Hutchins). We also share research projects with families and visitors by displaying collaborative hallway panels that communicate the importance of outdoor explorations for young children's learning.

Updated from "Teacher research initiatives: Inquiry work by early childhood teachers" in *Voices of Practitioners: Teacher Research in Early Childhood Education*, 7–8. Copyright © 2011 NAEYC.

Reflective Early Childhood Educators' Social Seminar

RECESS

Chicago, Illinois

Jeff Daitsman

T he term *research-based practices* often refers to the practice of teaching based on theories and philosophies rooted in a scientific understanding of children's early development. But as theories become more abstract, so too do the researchers developing them. Educational research thus moves farther away from the practical classroom applications of the theory. In order for there to be research-based practices, there needs to be practical research.

One form of practical research comes from practicing teachers. Teachers who reflect on their practices and consider the implications not only for their own classroom, but for others as well, can make unique contributions to the field of education. By collaborating with other reflective teachers, teacher researchers gain insights about the minds of the children they teach and about methods of improving classroom practices.

It is in this vein that the Reflective Early Childhood Educators' Social Seminar (RECESS) was created. A collective of reflective teachers of young children in the Chicago area, we dedicated ourselves to improving the quality of education in our classrooms. Through visiting each other's sites and conducting regular meetings, RECESS members shared teaching experiences to gain a greater understanding of children and how they learn.

Each member of the group investigated a particular focusing question in his or her classroom. When we met, we focused on one of these questions. We shared stories of our classroom experiences as they related to the topic of inquiry and raised questions based on these stories. As we discussed the questions, group members gained insight not only into the investigation presented at the meeting, but also into their own question as it related to the topic.

After each meeting we wrote up the stories we shared and the summaries of our discussions and posted them to our website at http://sites.google.com/site/aeraarsig/Home/action-research-world/recess, where they can be accessed for review.

Here are some examples:

- Allison Ashley of Covenant Nursery School investigated how teachers can create an atmosphere where children's questions and exploration are encouraged and welcome.

- Jeff Daitsman of McGaw YMCA Children's Center investigated children's understanding of the concept of death.

- Pearl Frantz of North Park Preschool investigated how aggressive play can be positively implemented in a preschool classroom.

- Roxanne Junge of Glenview New Church Preschool investigated the impact of nature on children's aggressive behavior.

Updated from "Teacher research initiatives: Inquiry work by early childhood teachers" in *Voices of Practitioners: Teacher Research in Early Childhood Education*, 9–10. Copyright © 2011 NAEYC.

Some Thoughts on Teacher Research in Early Childhood Education

Susan L. Lytle

Connecting teacher research and early childhood education, from some perspectives, seems like a foregone conclusion. After all, we know that children are natural inquirers, and the educators who work with them aim to foster their natural curiosity and support their multimodal and unique efforts to make sense of their worlds. So trying to figure out what is happening in a group of children as they learn together feels like a natural extension, a kind of marriage of what some might call teacher inquiry and inquiry-based pedagogy. Additionally, over the last 15–20 years, there have been some landmark studies of children's learning written by teachers, whether or not they call them themselves teacher researchers (and most do). One of the first books published in the *Practitioner Inquiry Series* (which I edit with my colleague and frequent co-author Marilyn Cochran-Smith) was a study of 6- and 7-year-olds in a first grade classroom written by Daniel Meier, one of the prime movers in making teacher research a way of knowing about many different facets of early childhood education. Names like Karen Gallas, Cindy Ballenger, and of course Vivian Paley come immediately to mind. Their work is not only seminal in the early childhood literature but also well known in the broader teacher research movement as well.

This book, nevertheless, is a milestone in the field, especially as it is designed to be useful and provocative to multiple audiences. It offers a range of approaches to conducting teacher research that are especially sensitive to the cultures of early childhood education. Chapter authors provide rich examples of ways for teacher educators and others to support this significant work in the lives of teachers, both new and experienced. And across the volume, there are numerous demonstrations that teacher researchers, teacher educators, and others invested in improving early childhood education have much to learn from teachers' questions and from the diverse ways individual and groups of teachers engage in systematic and intentional inquiry into their practices in many different settings and institutions.

As J. Amos Hatch opines in his introduction, this is important work, "now more than ever." As I have written elsewhere (Lytle 2008), one would think—given the devastating public representation of teachers and teaching, the steady proliferation of top-down policies and mandates, and the dismal views of public education—that teacher research would be in the process of disappearing. The fact that the field is actually alive and well surprises even (or maybe especially) those who have been closest to the work over time. It is important to remember that teacher researchers aim not primarily to "do research" but rather to *teach better.* The large and rapidly growing literature written by and with practitioners attests in many ways to the possibilities for positive change in education. Much practitioner inquiry remains radical and passionate, deeply personal and profoundly political—richly embedded in situations where teachers have agency around their own practice and where their commitments to educational access and equity remain clear in spite of these "trying times."

The persistence of the practitioner inquiry movement broadly, however, is nevertheless confounded by the fact that the practice of teaching is widely misunderstood and misinterpreted. Disturbingly absent from the public representations of teachers and teaching is knowledge of how the practice of teaching involves complex struggles on behalf of what my colleague Judy Buchanan refers to as improving the life chances of students. Particularly distressing to me has been the rapidly disappearing notion in the public discourse of teaching as a professional practice *with the capacity for and the commitment to improving itself.*

As the agency of teachers and other educators has eroded, equally problematic has been the erosion of images for what a truly engaging and meaningful education looks like for children and youth, often, ironically, in the name of higher standards and teacher quality. The professional knowledge and understandings teachers derive from their daily experiences and relationships with children are disturbingly missing in the mainstream reform discourse. The radical decontextualization of policy mandates combined with a pervasive aura of certainty have little resonance with teachers who know firsthand the day-to-day complexities of working with diverse groups of children in varying cultures and communities.

Back-mapping the curriculum from high stakes tests and using frequent benchmark assessments to maintain control and surveillance over teachers' instruction dramatically narrows the purposes of education and forwards an impoverished view of teaching, learning, curriculum, and schooling. As Marilyn Cochran-Smith and I have argued elsewhere (Cochran-Smith & Lytle 2007), the overall effect is both seductive and confusing. While current policies seem to be motivated by unassailable assumptions about equity and equality of educational opportunity, at the same time these moves towards standardization undermine in implicit and explicit ways the broader democratic mission of education. I am referring here to the increasingly commonplace view of teachers as technicians, children's learning as performance on tests, and teacher's learning as frontal training and retraining on "what works."

Narrowing of the curriculum may be especially damaging in the field of early childhood education. In a recent study of teacher resistance to mandated policies, Achinstein and Ogawa (2006) analyze the experiences of two new teachers working within "prescriptive instructional programs and control-oriented educational policies" (30). They argue that their two case studies illustrate resistance driven by teachers' adherence to professional principles, not, as is usually assumed in the literature, by psychological deficiency related to refusal to change. Referencing those who advocate for teaching as a profession, Achinstein and Ogawa define teachers' professional principles in the following way:

> Professional principles are conceptions about teaching and professionalism in which teachers view themselves as professionals with specialized expertise, who have discretion to employ repertoires of instructional strategies to meet the individual needs of diverse students, hold high expectations for themselves and students, foster learning communities among students, and participate in self-critical communities of practice. (32)

The authors show how the system exercises both technical and moralistic control over teachers and teaching by exploring the ways current policies limit dissent and debate, harness and constrain professional discourse, and ultimately contribute to teacher attrition. Along similar lines, in a case study of urban teachers' learning and leadership (Lytle 2006), I have argued that teachers in our study did not oppose standards, the need for highly qualified teachers, the assessment of outcomes, or policies that seek to rectify long-standing inequities in the system. What they resisted was the gross oversimplification of the complexity of the task at hand, and the proliferation of policies and high stakes tests that fail to take into account that teaching is not fundamentally technical work, but rather what many have regarded as a highly complex, deliberative, and adaptive process. In the public sector, when teachers of young children are not afforded opportunities to make decisions about the curriculum related to early literacy, for example, or when they are required to conduct excessive evaluations, the effects on the learning environment can be extremely detrimental. Teachers' perspectives—generated from close observation and documentation—can play an essential role in the struggle to maintain developmentally appropriate practices.

Much of the scripted curricula and high stakes testing routines being cemented into place through No Child Left Behind, Race to the Top, and related policies have the intent of dramatically altering the face of teaching as a profession. *In these times*, it is critically important that we have counter-narratives, especially in the words of teachers; we need images of a much richer notion of teaching, one that holds promise as a framework for discussion by teachers, teacher educators, school administrators, and policy makers. These images embrace (rather than deny) the myriad complexities and uncertainties of practice that when acknowledged and acted on, improve the likelihood of actually doing the job better. One of the compelling arguments for teacher research, as Andrew J. Stremmel notes in this volume, is to provide a framework for teachers to deliberately document and make sense of children's experiences in their classrooms. As he makes exquisitely clear, teachers are in the best position to write from insider standpoints about their experiences with children, drawing on their own questions and "those things that perplex and astonish them" (p. 109, this volume).

This book about teacher research in early childhood education, which brings together various perspectives offered by its diverse set of authors, provides a vision of teaching that is congruent with a *transformed and expanded* view of *practice* (Cochran-Smith & Lytle 1999; 2007). From this perspective, teaching goes way beyond what teachers do when they stand in front of children, just as children's learning is not limited to the four walls of a program, center or classroom. Rather than a process of using strategies certified by so-called scientifically-based research, teaching requires the intentional forming and re-forming of frameworks for understanding practice. It is about how children and their teachers construct the curriculum, co-mingling their experiences, their cultural and linguistic resources, and their interpretive frameworks. Teaching also encompasses how teachers' actions are infused with complex and multilayered understandings of learners, culture, class, gender, literacies, social issues, institutions, herstories and histories, communities, materials, texts, and curricula.

Teachers thus act in accordance with their "theories of practice"; teaching itself is a form of inquiry wherein teachers constantly question their own assumptions and collect and examine artifacts of learning. A critical dimension of teaching is how professionals work together to develop and alter their questions and interpretive frameworks. Teachers are informed not only by thoughtful consideration of the immediate situation and the particular children they teach and have taught, but also by their sense of the multiple social, economic, political, and cultural contexts within which they work. Furthermore, this expanded view of practice encompasses expanded responsibilities to children and their families, transformed relationships to teacher colleagues and other professionals in the educational setting, and deeper and altered connections to communities, community organizations, and school-university partnerships. All of these aspects of an expanded notion of practice appear in one or more of the chapters in this book.

In the chapters in Part I that offer detailed and compelling examples of teacher research, there is a fascinating range of topics, including children's play and peer culture, co-constructing curriculum around social justice in children's everyday lives, preschoolers' explorations of and relationships to the natural world, children's experiences of and self-perceptions of their connections to the environment, and toddlers' peer interactions and relationships with each other. The settings range from preschools to university-affiliated centers to public school classrooms. As a set, they provide valuable insights into the reciprocal relationships between adults' and children's learning and the ways teachers' prior knowledge and experience (e.g., as a teacher of theater or science) deeply inform the particulars of their practice and the lenses they use to make sense of children's learning. When teachers actively bring their prior experience and knowledge to their teaching through teacher research, they often come in turn to understand more deeply the contribution of children's own frameworks and cultural and linguistic resources to the life of the classroom.

In the accounts of their inquiries, these teacher researchers explore the conceptual or theoretical lenses they bring to bear on their practice, and discuss the prior research conducted by academics that has taken up similar topics. To these readings of academic research, they bring a kind of criticality that is one of the hallmarks of becoming an inquiring practitioner. Here they make visible that the knowledge teachers need to teach well can be generated when teachers treat their own sites of practice as spaces for intentional investigation, at the same time that they treat the knowledge and theory produced by others as generative material for interrogation and interpretation. Throughout these accounts, children's sense of place—variously interpreted—also reinforces the salience of context in teacher research, a key point in Stremmel's argument in this volume about the value of teacher research in this profession. In addition, this volume sheds light on the exquisite power of close and systematic observation, of reflecting critically on one's own frameworks and practices, and on the use of different genres to represent the research, including some new visual and interactive formats.

The chapters in Part II focus on supporting teacher research by looking at the work of programs, university-based centers and university-affiliated projects, as well as school-based inquiry communities. Here the authors reinforce how deeply collaborative this work is, and the crucial role these organizations play in building and sustaining ongoing learning and critical professional relationships over time. Teachers in these "communities of practice" are not trying to use their research to discover "best practices," but rather to bring informed and nuanced lenses to the everyday, with full recognition of the fact that many eyes are likely to complicate and deepen the stories about children in specific contexts, rather than to collapse them into a set of universal strategies.

The book also offers insider accounts of the many different structures for teacher research represented in the work of early childhood-focused programs of study and institutions. Some of these structures have been carefully developed over time in teacher education programs, while other modes of collaboration have sprung from the specific inquiry-oriented cultures of schools or school-university partnerships. Still others bring together early childhood educators from different settings in a region to build a sustainable network over time.

As a whole, this book represents an example of a collaborative process by a prominent professional organization for early childhood education that exists as a face-to-face organization, a multifaceted intellectual network, and an online community—all venues that can enable sharing of teacher research with and by differently positioned colleagues and practitioners. The examples here of university-based teacher education programs where teacher research is central to the mission show how support for taking an inquiry stance (Cochran-Smith & Lytle 2009) can potentially inform the nature of early childhood educators' work across the professional lifespan.

In all different kinds of inquiry communities, both knowledge generation and knowledge use may be regarded as inherently problematic (Cochran-Smith & Lytle 1999):

> [B]asic questions about knowledge and teaching—what it means to generate knowledge, who generates it, what counts as knowledge and to whom, and how knowledge is used and evaluated in particular contexts—are always open to question. Knowledge-making is understood as a pedagogic act—constructed in the context of use, intimately connected to the knower, and although relevant to immediate situations, also inevitably a process of theorizing. From this perspective, knowledge is not bound by the instrumental imperative that it be used or applied to an immediate situation but rather that it may also shape the conceptual and interpretive frameworks teachers develop to make judgments, theorize practice, and connect their efforts to larger intellectual, social, and political issues as well as to the work of other teachers, researchers, and communities. The basis of this knowledge-practice conception is that teachers across the professional lifespan play a central and critical role in generating knowledge of practice by making their classrooms and schools sites for inquiry, connecting their work in schools to larger issues, and taking a critical perspective on the theory and research of others (272–73).

Teacher networks, inquiry communities, and other program- and school-based collectives in which teachers and others conjoin their efforts to construct knowledge are, as several of the authors in Part II vividly explain, especially rich contexts for knowledge generation and professional development in the field of early children education.

I believe that this volume promises to go a long way in inspiring individuals and groups of early childhood educators at all levels to take up and strengthen their efforts to make teacher research a centerpiece of teacher education and professional development. Given the deeply social and contextual nature of teacher research, it by definition foregrounds analysis and interpretation of insights gained in a local context. As several authors in this volume have articulated, teacher research is not only a form of professional development but also, importantly, a form of local knowledge generation. What may be needed in this field (and K–12 education more widely) is a better understanding of the ways that so-called "local knowledge" can be extremely relevant and useful in other more diversified contexts.

Early childhood teacher researchers can contribute to the dialogue about what's best for children by studying the effects of current policies in particular settings. For the wider field to know more about the questions that early childhood educators regard as important to their practice would in itself be a major contribution to the teaching profession. Seeking more venues for presentation and publication (e.g., further exploiting the possibilities of digital networking) is a salient piece of this, as is making the work of other participants in the teacher research movement more visible by lateral citation to the work of other teacher researchers.

Teacher educators can include teacher research in their course syllabi and conference programs. Traditional approaches to professional development can be investigated and reinvented as contexts for ongoing inquiry-based teacher learning. Many early childhood educators are extremely knowledgeable about linking with families and other professionals concerned with children's health and social services, as well as with community activists. These connections contain "lessons" for teachers in other settings; these linkages could become intergenerational, participatory, and cross-field communities of inquiry that invite very differently positioned people to both conduct and support research that can profoundly affect the quality of education for young children.

Teacher research has evolved into an enduring social movement functioning over time and in very diverse settings to re-ground our educational efforts in the real lives and learning potential of children and their teachers. Built over decades, this movement is fundamentally about valuing teachers' access to textured and layered understandings of the daily complexities of the teaching life. The agency of teachers who have taken leadership in conducting research makes visible what is most important in their day-to-day practice and in their understandings of what it means to be professional educators.

To take an inquiry stance is in part "to reposition the collective intellectual capacity of practitioners"—a phrase from *Inquiry as Stance: Practitioner Research for the Next Generation* (Cochran-Smith & Lytle 2009, 124). In this book we describe four ways forward for the concept of inquiry as a stance and for the teacher research movement, including

1. deepening the local work of practitioner inquiry communities (with a focus on teachers but including other educators and those affiliated with educational projects)

2. reinventing the notion of professionalism and reconsidering what it means to call for the professionalization of practice, in these times

3. renegotiating the relationships of research, practice, and policy and, concurrently, rethinking the relationships of researchers, practitioners, and policymakers

4. connecting the practitioner inquiry movement to other transformative agendas and larger movements for educational and social change

Undertaken with the leadership of NAEYC, *Our Inquiry, Our Practice: Undertaking, Supporting, and Learning from Early Childhood Teacher Research(ers)* promises to inform and inspire many teachers and teacher educators in the field of early childhood education to find their own "ways forward." In doing so, they will contribute to the improvement of education for all children, as well as lend strength to the broader movement for teacher research as it evolves in the years to come.

References

Achinstein, B., & R. Ogawa. 2006. (In)fidelity: What the resistance of new teachers reveals about professional principles and prescriptive educational policies. *Harvard Educational Review* 76 (1): 30–63.

Cochran-Smith, M., & S.L. Lytle. 1999. Relationships of knowledge and practice: Teacher learning in communities. *Review of Research in Education 1999* 24: 249–306.

Cochran-Smith, M., & S.L. Lytle. 2001. Beyond certainty: Taking an inquiry stance on practice. In *Teachers caught in the action: Professional development that matters*, eds. A. Lieberman & L. Miller, 45–60. New York: Teachers College Press.

Cochran-Smith, M., & S.L. Lytle. 2007. Troubling images of teachers and teaching in No Child Left Behind. *Harvard Educational Review* 76 (4): 668–97.

Cochran-Smith, M., & S.L. Lytle. 2009. *Inquiry as stance: Practitioner research for the next generation.* New York: Teachers College Press.

Lytle, S.L. 2006. The literacies of teaching adolescents in these times. In *Reconceptualizing the literacies in adolescents' lives*, 2d ed., eds. D.E. Alvermann, K.A. Hinchman, D.W. Moore, S.F. Phelps & D.R. Waff, 257–78. Mahweh, NJ: Lawrence Erlbaum.

Lytle, S.L. 2008. At last: Practitioner inquiry and the practice of teaching: Some thoughts on 'better.' *Research in the Teaching of English* 42 (3): 373–79.

Lytle, S.L., D. Portnoy, D. Waff & M. Buckley. 2009. Teacher research in Philadelphia: 20 years working within, against, and beyond the system. *Educational Action Research* 17 (1): 23–42.

Stremmel, A.J. 2012. Reshaping the landscape of early childhood teaching through teacher research. In *Our inquiry, our practice: Undertaking, supporting, and learning from early childhood teacher research(ers)*, eds. G. Perry, B. Henderson & D.R. Meier. Washington, DC: NAEYC.

For Further Reading

Ballenger, C. 2009. *Puzzling Moments, Teachable Moments: Practicing Teacher Research in Urban Classrooms*. New York: Teachers College Press.
Offers a detailed portrait of how teacher research results are used to modify day-to-day practice and meet the needs of diverse groups of children. Also describes important principles and strategies for engaging in teacher research.

Brookline Teacher Research Seminar & C. Ballenger. 2003. *Regarding Children's Words: Teacher Research on Language and Literacy*. New York: Teachers College Press.
Written by members of the Brookline Teacher Research Seminar, a long-standing teacher research study group, this collection includes the history and functioning of the inquiry community and teacher research studies at the preschool and K–3 levels.

Castle, K. 2012. *Early Childhood Teacher Research: From Questions to Results*. New York: Routledge.
Written for early childhood professionals, this book explores all phases of the teacher research process.

Cochran-Smith, M., & S. Lytle. 1993. *Inside/Outside: Teacher Research and Knowledge*. New York: Teachers College Press.
Discusses the concern that knowledge about teaching is usually generated by those outside the classroom for teachers to apply in their classrooms. In contrast, the text suggests that teaching should relate to teachers' practical knowledge of their actual classrooms. Argues that teacher research can transform, not simply add to, the present knowledge base in the field, linking research with practice and inquiry with reform.

Cochran-Smith, M., & S. Lytle. 2009. *Inquiry as Stance: Practitioner Research for the Next Generation*. New York: Teachers College Press.
This comprehensive volume on practitioner research, by the most prominent U.S. leaders in the field, highlights the importance and meaning of assuming an inquiry perspective. Discusses the implications for schools, universities, and policymakers regarding the way knowledge about competent teaching is created and positioned in the larger educational and social contexts.

Compton-Lilly, C. 2003. *Reading Families: The Literate Lives of Urban Children*. New York: Teachers College Press.
Based on teacher research with first-grade students, their parents, and grandparents, this book challenges the stereotypical view that urban families don't care about their children's education. Shows how listening closely to the voices of children and families can move us beyond negative assumptions, revealing previously undocumented complexities.

Dana, N.F., & D. Yendol-Hoppey. 2009. *The Reflective Educator's Guide to Classroom Research: Learning to Teach and Teaching to Learn Through Practitioner Inquiry*. 2d ed. Thousand Oaks, CA: Corwin Press.
Takes readers step-by-step through the process of teacher inquiry: formulating a research question, collaborating with others, collecting data, analyzing data, writing, presenting, and assessing the quality of the classroom research projects.

Dewey, J. [1916] 1997. *Democracy and Education*. New York: The Free Press.
Addressing the challenge of providing quality public education in a democratic society, this seminal work on public education introduces theories about teaching and learning, emphasizing bringing the practical work of the community into the classroom curriculum.

Fu, V.R., A.J. Stremmel & L.T. Hill. 2002. *Teaching and Learning: Collaborative Exploration of the Reggio Emilia Approach*. Upper Saddle River, NJ: Merrill/Prentice Hall.
Reintroduces the Reggio Emilia approach through rich stories and examples of children's projects that invite readers to examine their personal learning processes. Offers innovative ways to meld theory with teaching and action research while considering the professional development of each reader.

Gallas, K. 1995. *Talking Their Way into Science: Hearing Children's Questions and Theories, Responding with Curricula*. New York: Teachers College Press.
Explores 'science talks' in primary classrooms to gain insights into how children and teachers think and talk about science. Offers details of the author's work as a teacher researcher and member of the Brookline (MA) Teacher Research Seminar.

Hall, I., C.H. Campbell & E.J. Miech. 1997. *Class Acts: Teachers Reflect on Their Own Classroom Practice*. Cambridge, MA: Harvard University Press.
Kindergarten and early elementary teachers write about teacher research projects, providing compelling reflections on practice as they find new ways of learning from children and making sense of their own teaching.

Hatch, J.A., ed. 2007. *Early Childhood Qualitative Research*. New York: Routledge.
This collection represents the best work being done in early childhood qualitative studies, offering descriptions of research methods and discussions of important issues related to current early childhood qualitative research.

Hill, L.T., A. Stremmel & V. Fu. 2005. *Teaching as Inquiry: Rethinking Curriculum in Early Childhood Education*. New York: Pearson Education.
This text encourages wonder, curiosity, asking questions, looking for answers, and making sense of the world in different ways. Promotes teaching as an art that supports the learner in multiple ways, using various tools responsive to individual orientations and multiple intelligences.

Hubbard, R.S., & B.M. Power. 1999. *Living the Questions: A Guide for Teacher Researchers*. York, ME: Stenhouse.
A good resource for teacher research methods, this guide for novice and veteran teacher researchers will challenge and inspire educators at all levels to see the potential for inquiry in their lives.

Meier, D.R., & B. Henderson. 2007. *Learning from Young Children in the Classroom: The Art and Science of Teacher Research*. New York: Teachers College Press.
Provides a comprehensive introduction to high-quality teacher research in early childhood settings. Features many excerpts and summaries of original research projects by teachers working with all early-childhood age groups.

Mohr, M., C. Rogers, B. Sanford, M. Nocerino, M.S. MacLean & S. Clawson. 2004. *Teacher Research for Better Schools*. New York: Teachers College Press.
Documenting the work of a network of experienced K–12 teacher researchers, this text describes teachers working together to improve teaching and how their research impacted and influenced their school system.

Paley, V.G. 1991. *The Boy Who Would Be a Helicopter: The Uses of Storytelling in the Classroom*. Cambridge, MA: Harvard University Press.
Paley, V.G. 1993. *You Can't Say You Can't Play*. Cambridge, MA: Harvard University Press.
These two books recount Paley's work of learning from children, examining and reflecting on her own practice. See Cooper's chapter of this volume for particular descriptions.

Project Zero. 2003. *Making Teaching Visible: Documenting Individual and Group Learning as Professional Development*. Cambridge, MA: Project Zero.
Researchers from Project Zero and schools in Reggio Emilia, Italy, collaborated with preK–8 teachers to reflect on how documentation of individual and group learning can serve as professional development.

Wells, G. 2001. *Action, Talk, and Text: Learning and Teaching Through Inquiry*. New York: Teachers College Press.
Drawing on work by the Developing Inquiring Communities in Education Project, this text provides a range of practical, replicable methods for building collaborative communities. Also offers strategies for facilitating inquiry-based learning and teaching.

Online Resources

American Educational Research Association (AERA)

AERA encourages scholarly inquiry and promotes the dissemination and application of research results. It includes special interest groups (SIGs) devoted to early childhood and teacher research. Potential members can join AERA and then choose the Action Research or Teachers as Researchers SIGs (See "**AR SIG, AERA**" and "**TR SIG, AERA**" below.) AERA holds an annual conference with presentations of early childhood teacher research among many other sessions.

> **www.aera.net**
> **Online search terms: AERA**

Action Research Special Interest Group, American Educational Research Association (AR SIG, AERA)

This group builds community among those engaged in action research and those teaching others to do action research. In addition to information on joining and activity, it also offers a blog, links to action research communities, and lists of action research books, journals, and conferences.

> **http://sites.google.com/site/aeraarsig/**
> **Online search terms: AERA AR SIG**

Teacher as Researcher Special Interest Group, American Educational Research Association (TAR SIG, AERA)

This group consists of AERA members who are teacher educators and preK–12th grade educators, and aims to present teacher research work and projects at the AERA conference and elsewhere nationally. Early childhood teacher research is an important part of the group.

> **www.aera.net/Default.aspx?menu_id=220&id=1178_**
> **Online search terms: Teachers as Researchers AERA**

The Center for Practitioner Research (CFPR) of the National College of Education at National-Louis University

Aims to affect education through collaborative scholarship contributing to knowledge, practice, advocacy, and policy in education. The website includes selected action research resources, including links to websites, book lists, conference information, and their online journal ***Inquiry in Education***. The journal publishes articles that contribute to scholarship and the knowledge base of practitioner research, including articles by early childhood teachers and teacher educators.

> **http://nlu.nl.edu/cfpr**
> **Online search terms: Center for Practitioner Research**

Classroom Action Research from the Metropolitan School District in Madison, Wisconsin

Supports public school teachers doing teacher research. Includes useful guides and information for all phases of a teacher research project. Links to a large database of abstracts and some full papers searchable by grade level or subject of the teacher research projects conducted by preK–12 teachers from 1990–2010.

> **http://oldweb.madison.k12.wi.us/sod/car/carhomepage.html**
> **Online search terms: Classroom action research**

Educational Action Research

An international journal concerned with exploring the dialogue between research and practice in educational settings.

> **www.tandf.co.uk/journals/reac**
> **Online search terms: Educational Action Research**

ERIC—Education Resources Information Center
The world's largest digital library of education literature, and invaluable for researching early childhood topics. Through using the search terms "early childhood teacher research" or various subtopics, resources such as books, articles, and related documents can be identified.

> www.eric.ed.gov
> Online search terms: ERIC ed

Harvard Educational Review
This scholarly journal of opinion and research in education provides an interdisciplinary forum for discussion and debate about the field's most vital issues.

> www.hepg.org/main/her/Index.html
> Online search terms: Harvard Educational Review

Let's Collaborate, Teacher Research from Access Excellence @ the National Health Museum
Includes useful supports for engaging in teacher research, including examples of K–12 research focused on science education. Offers information on starting a project, examples of teacher research projects, and links to online resources.

> www.accessexcellence.org/LC/TL/AR/
> Online search terms: Access Excellence Teacher Research

National Association of Early Childhood Teacher Educators (NAECTE)
Promotes the professional growth of early childhood teacher educators and advocates for improvements to the field. NAECTE's *Journal of Early Childhood Teacher Education* occasionally publishes teacher research articles, including a special issue focused on teacher research (Volume 31, Issue 3). NAECTE also provides **ResearchNets**, a forum to foster educational research with teacher research presentations.

> www.naecte.org
> Online search terms: NAECTE

Networks: An On-line Journal for Teacher Research at the University of Wisconsin
A venue for sharing reports of action research and discussion on inquiry for teachers at all levels. Provides space for discussion of inquiry as a tool to learn about practice and improve its effectiveness. Offers searchable articles.

> http://journals.library.wisc.edu/index.php/networks
> Online search terms: Networks teacher research

The Ontario Action Researcher
A journal intended for elementary, secondary, and university teachers concerned with both educational research and practice. It features teacher research, including research conducted in early elementary classrooms, methodological pieces, and reviews of teacher research books. Also contains a list of relevant links.

> http://oar.nipissingu.ca
> Online search terms: Ontario Action Researcher

Self-Study Teacher Research: Improving your Practice through Collaborative Inquiry, Student Study Guide from Sage Publications
This web-based student study site accompanies a book of the same name, but provides a wealth of information on its own for teachers or teacher educators who conduct studies of their own teaching practice.

> www.sagepub.com/samaras/default.htm
> Online search terms: self study teacher research student study guide

Studying Teacher Education: A Journal of Self-Study of Teacher Education Practices
Welcomes papers from authors who have an interest in research and practice in teaching and teacher education.
> www.tandf.co.uk/journals/titles/17425964.asp
> **Google search terms: Studying Teacher Education**

Teacher Action Research from George Mason University
Offers information about the teacher research process, resources for carrying out teacher research studies, and web/print resources. Also contains discussion of current teacher research issues and a comparison of teacher research to other forms of educational research and professional development.
> http://gse.gmu.edu/research/tr
> **Online search terms: Teacher action research**

Teacher Inquiry Communities Network from the National Writing Project (NWP)
Offers information on a mini-grant program supporting an inquiry stance toward teaching and learning. Includes information about the grant program, program reports, and examples of projects (including early elementary projects). Also features resources related to teacher research.
> www.nwp.org/cs/public/print/programs/tic
> **Online search terms: Teacher inquiry communities**

Teachers Network Leadership Institute, Action Research: Teacher Research
Features useful examples of teacher research projects completed by Teacher Network Leadership Institute MetLife Fellows. Project summaries are divided by topics and by K–12 grade levels. Also includes resources to help teachers engage in and share teacher research.
> http://teachersnetwork.org/TNLI/research/
> **Online search terms: Teachers Network action research**

Teaching and Teacher Education
This journal aims to enhance theory, research, and practice in teaching and teacher education through the publication of primary research and review papers.
> www.journals.elsevier.com/teaching-and-teacher-education/#description
> **Online search terms: Teaching and Teacher Education**

***Voices of Practitioners,* a publication of NAEYC**
A peer-reviewed professional online journal from NAEYC featuring the research of early childhood education teachers. Also includes practical information for early childhood teacher educators on incorporating teacher research into programs and supporting teacher research in early education communities.
> www.naeyc.org/publications/vop
> **Online Search Terms: Voices of Practitioners or NAEYC (then select "Publications")**

Editors

Gail Perry, PhD, has a more than 50-year career in early childhood education. She has taught at the graduate and undergraduate level, consulted, and researched a range of topics, including classroom discourse, the Reggio Emilia approach, and teacher research. At NAEYC, she is New Books editor for *Young Children* and Editor of *Voices of Practitioners*.

*   *   *

Barbara Henderson, PhD, is a professor of education at San Francisco State University. She co-coordinates the MA program in Education, Early Childhood Education Concentration, and teacher graduate and credential classes. Her interests are teacher research and children's development in cultural contexts. She is also co-editor of the online teacher research journal *Voices of Practitioners*.

Daniel R. Meier, PhD, is professor of elementary education at San Francisco State University. He holds degrees from Wesleyan University, Harvard University, and the University of California, Berkeley, and has worked with preschool and elementary school teachers on inquiry-based projects. He is the author of several books on education published by Teachers College Press, and co-editor of *Voices of Practitioners*.

Contributing Authors

Teacher Researchers

Jeff Daitsman is a student at National-Louis University, completing his BA in Early Childhood Education and Developmental Psychology. He has taught preschool for five years and is researching children's non-verbal expression of gender. He is chapter author of "'Once upon a time there was a . . .' Forms and functions of story dictation in preschool" in *Here's the Story: Using Narrative to Promote Children's Language and Literacy Learning*.

Isauro Michael Escamilla, MA, is the first in his family to graduate from college. His MA in education is from San Francisco State University, where he was recognized for outstanding academic achievement. He teaches at the Las Americas Early Education School in San Francisco, where he leads a teacher research group and parent workshops on child development and violence prevention. He presents at local and national conferences.

Anna Golden, MAE, is the *atelierista* at Sabot at Stony Point School, a progressive school for children age 2 through grade 8, in Richmond, VA. She is an artist and teaches in the education department at Mary Baldwin College. She blogs about her work at atelierista-anna@blogspot.com.

Elizabeth Goss, MA, NBCT, is the primary academic leader at Legacy Charter School in Chicago. She taught kindergarten through second grade on Chicago's West Side for 10 years. A founding teacher at Legacy Charter School, she is committed to the school's mission of social justice and has presented locally and nationally on the topic.

Ben Mardell, PhD, was the kindergarten head teacher and research coordinator at Eliot-Pearson Children's School, Tufts University, in Medford, MA. He is now an associate professor at Lesley University and supports teachers and graduate students in communities of practice.

Aaron Neimark, MA, teaches kindergarten at Dianne Feinstein Elementary School in San Francisco, CA. For the past 15 years, he has taught preschool and kindergarten; he has recently begun conducting teacher research about children's peer cultures and about his own teaching. His chapter "Learning from Children's Humor: Peer Culture as a Teaching Tool" is published in *Educating Toddlers to Teachers: Learning to See and Influence the School and Peer Cultures of Classrooms.*

Diane M. Spahn is the Theater Arts Teacher/Researcher at Boulder Journey School in Boulder, CO. She has a background in professional film and theater, which informs her early childhood teaching practice daily. Her work has been presented to members of Hawkins Centers of Learning, at numerous conferences hosted by Boulder Journey School, and most recently at NAEYC's 2011 National Institute for Early Childhood Professional Development.

Christopher Taaffe, MA, a preschool teacher for 33 years, is lead teacher of the 2's class at Hearts Leap School in Berkeley, CA. He has mentored several practitioners, evaluated preschool programs, and researched and prepared child care needs assessments for the International Child Resource Institute.

Contributing Authors

Shareen Abramson, PhD, is Fansler Chair for Leadership in Early Childhood Education at California State University, Fresno. She is the director of the Huggins Early Education Center and a professor in the Department of Literacy and Early Education. Her work addresses leader development, curriculum innovation, and technology applications for improving teaching and learning.

Carol Bersani, MS, is the child development director at the Kent State University Child Development Center. She is also an emeritus professor in early childhood education. Her current research focus is on teacher research interwoven with children's inquiry.

Bethany Carpenter, M.Ed., is professional development and education coordinator at Ready to Learn Providence in Providence, RI. Her support for other educators' reflective practice draws on her own experiences as a preK classroom teacher and Early Literacy Mentor, and is inspired by the vision of Ready to Learn Providence that, "All young children will be healthy and ready to learn."

Patricia M. (Patsy) Cooper, PhD, is an associate professor of early childhood education at Queens College, City University of New York. She received her M.Ed. in child development from the Erikson Institute and her PhD from Emory University. Her research focuses on effective teaching of young children. She is the founder and former director of the School Literacy and Culture Project at Rice University's Center for Education.

J. Amos Hatch, PhD, is professor of theory and practice in teacher education at the University of Tennessee. He is a qualitative researcher who has written numerous books and articles about research in education settings. He has served as editor of *Qualitative Studies in Education,* co-editor of the *Journal of Early Childhood Teacher Education,* and is on the editorial board of *Voices of Practitioners.*

Lilian G. Katz, PhD, is professor emerita of early childhood education at the University of Illinois (Urbana-Champaign) where she is currently on the staff of the Clearinghouse on Early Education and Parenting (CEEP). She consults and speaks widely in the United States and abroad, is a past NAEYC president, and is editor of the first online trilingual (English, Spanish, and Chinese) early childhood journal, *Early Childhood Research & Practice*.

Susan L. Lytle, PhD, is professor of education in the Graduate School of Education, University of Pennsylvania. She is founding director of the Philadelphia Writing Project and has worked closely with urban K–12 teachers and other educators to design and document a variety of inquiry-based collaborative research projects. She has published widely on literacy, teacher education, teacher learning and leadership, and practitioner inquiry.

Frances O'Connell Rust, PhD, is visiting professor and interim director of teacher education programs at the University of Pennsylvania. She is a professor emeritus at New York University, where she taught for 17 years at the Steinhardt School of Culture, Education, and Human Development. She has also directed and taught in teacher education programs at Hofstra University, Manhattanville College, and Teachers College, Columbia University, and is on the editorial board of *Voices of Practitioners*.

Andrew J. Stremmel, PhD, is professor and department head of teaching, learning, and leadership at South Dakota State University, Brookings. His writing and research focus on inquiry-based early childhood teacher education and Reggio Emilia-inspired practice. He is also on the editorial board of *Voices of Practitioners*.

More Resources from NAEYC

Growing Minds: Building Strong Cognitive Foundations in Early Childhood

Carol Copple, ed.

This collection of readings from books and *Young Children* articles outlines important dimensions of their early cognitive development and describes approaches for promoting it.

Item #: 362 • **List: $25** • **Member: $20**

Informing Our Practice: Useful Research on Young Children's Development

Eva L. Essa & Melissa M. Burnham, eds.

This volume contains 20 overviews of research on aspects of young children's social, emotional, cognitive, or physical development, as well as how the findings can be applied in the classroom.

Item #: 255 • **List: $29** • **Member: $23.20**

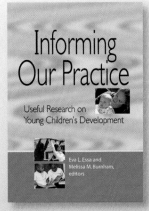

Teaching Adults, *Revisited*: Active Learning for Early Childhood Educators

Elizabeth Jones

This book follows master teacher Betty Jones in a hypothetical Intro to ECE course. Her approach emphasizes actively engaging students, because "adults who have practiced decision making for themselves in a college classroom may have the courage to share decision making with young children."

Item #: 205 • **List: $19** • **Member: $15.20**

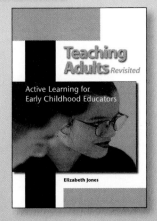

**For a complete listing of resources,
please visit www.naeyc.org/store or call 800-424-2460.**

Prices are subject to change.